Fruits
of
Hawaii

Fruits
of
Hawaii

Carey D. Miller
Katherine Bazore
Mary Bartow

Description, Nutritive Value, and Recipes

THE UNIVERSITY PRESS OF HAWAII
HONOLULU

Some Fruits of Hawaii

First Printing, 1936
Second Printing, 1937
Third Printing, 1939

Fruits of Hawaii

First edition, 1945
Second edition, 1955
Third edition, 1957
Fourth edition, 1965, 1971; paperback 1976

Library of Congress Catalog Card Number 54-11869

ISBN 0-8248-0448-1

Manufactured in the United States of America

FOREWORD

Much of the material in this book has appeared in previous Hawaii Agricultural Experiment Station publications, namely, Bulletin 77, *Some Fruits of Hawaii,* issued in 1936 and reissued in 1937, and Bulletin 96, *Fruits of Hawaii,* issued in 1945.

This enlarged and revised edition is published by the University of Hawaii Press, with the approval of the Director of the Hawaii Agricultural Experiment Station.

Most of the recipes were contributed by Katherine Bazore and Mary Bartow, who have tested, in the Home Economics Department, those collected from various sources as well as new ones which they devised. The rest were contributed by the senior author and others. For this new edition, five new sections have been added on fruits not previously included in this book: acerola, grapefruit, loquat, ohelo berry, and tangerine. Many refinements have been incorporated in recipes throughout the book, and several minor points have been brought up to date.

A number of people contributed to the preparation of the two bulletins and hence have contributed to this book. Some of the historical, descriptive, and chemical data for thirteen of the fruits in Bulletin 77 were taken from a thesis submitted by Ruth C. Robbins, in partial fulfillment of the requirements for the degree of Master of Science in Nutrition at the University of Hawaii in 1934. Miss Robbins was also coauthor of Bulletin 77.

Acknowledgment is made to the late Dr. W. T. Pope, former horticulturist at the Hawaii Agricultural Experiment Station, for information concerning the history, description, variety, and season of many of the fruits, and for some of the photographs. Other photographs were made by Masao Miyamoto and R. J. Baker from specimens collected and arranged by me.

Thanks are due Dr. Harold St. John, Professor in the Botany Department, University of Hawaii, for checking all scientific names, and to members of the Agricultural Economics Department, College of Agriculture, for providing data on the supply of certain fruits.

The authors are greatly indebted to Dr. William B. Storey, horticulturist, who made photographs of avocados and bananas, checked all data on description and history, and furnished information regarding many of the fruits. Other members of the Horticulture Department have also given us information and counsel.

A number of Experiment Station staff members have contributed in various ways. Barbara Branthoover and Kathryn Orr, former members of the Foods and Nutrition Department, prepared the table on vitamin content of fruits and the section on methods of freezing Hawaii fruits, respectively.

CAREY D. MILLER

Honolulu, Hawaii
1965

CONTENTS

APPENDIX

ILLUSTRATIONS

PHOTOGRAPHS

SUPPLIES AND EQUIPMENT

A few pieces of special equipment and certain supplies are recommended for convenience and efficiency in fruit preparation and preservation. Many of these will be found in any well-equipped kitchen. A list of such articles is given below and some of the less familiar ones are shown in the illustration on page 2.

Bottle brush—one with a long wire handle for thorough cleaning of bottles.

Bottle capper—desirable if large amounts of juice are to be preserved. Always use new caps.

Colander or strainer—for washing and draining small fruits.

Cooling rack—a wire cake rack (or a thick board).

Double boiler—for melting paraffin. Heating paraffin directly over the fire is dangerous as paraffin is very inflammable.

Food mill*—for puréeing fruits, removing seeds and skins. If small seeds go through the mill, they may be removed by pressing purée through poi cloth or fine sieve.

Funnels*—wide mouth for jars and glasses, narrow spout for bottles. They should be metal or glass, as plastic materials usually are not sufficiently heat resistant.

Jars—a variety of sizes, half-pint, pint, and quart, with well-fitting covers, depending on size of family and products.

Jelly bags—made of flour or sugar sacks, or several thicknesses of cheesecloth. For very clear jelly a wool flannel or an outing flannel bag is recommended. Bags made in the shape of a cornucopia with a pointed end are especially good for draining juice from the pulp.

Jelly glasses—with metal covers to prevent contamination from insects, dust, and dirt. They should be used in addition to covering the jelly or jam with paraffin.

Jelmeter*—a reliable device (when used as directed) for indicating the amount of sugar to be used for jelly making.†

---

* See illustration on p. 2.

† May be obtained from Jelmeter Co., P.O. Box 300, Milford, Delaware 19963.

Some recommended articles for fruit preparation and preservation: a) rotary pureer; b) food mill; c and d) aluminum funnels, small and wide mouth; e) candy or jelly thermometer; f) Jelmeter; g) stainless steel ladle; h) tongs.

Knives—sharp paring knives and a larger, heavy knife. Keeping knives sharp with manual or electric sharpener, or a hone, improves efficiency in preparation of fruits.

Labels—gummed labels, in two sizes, $1\frac{1}{4}$ by $1\frac{3}{4}$ inches and $2\frac{3}{4}$ by $1\frac{1}{2}$ inches, give your jars and glasses a neat appearance and should identify the product, giving the date when prepared.

Ladle*—a stainless steel ladle with wooden handle for transferring boiling hot products to jars, glasses, and bottles.

Measuring cups—several one-cup measures (standard half-pint), and

* See illustration on p. 2.

a set of measuring cups $\frac{1}{4}$, $\frac{1}{3}$, $\frac{1}{2}$, and 1 cup; a quart measure or a saucepan that holds exactly 4 cups.

Pans—a shallow pan is recommended for cooking jelly, and a flat shallow pan for holding glasses and jars while they are being filled.

Pot holders—large and thick enough to protect hands.

Preserving kettle—a 3- or 4-gallon aluminum kettle, with strong handles and cover, reserved for fruit preservation. Aluminum is more desirable than enamel ware, which is likely to be affected by acid fruits such as guavas.

Pressure cooker or saucepan—can be used for quick sterilization of containers as well as to process canned products.

Rotary puréer*—made of aluminum with a wooden pestle is excellent for making purée, and removing skins and seeds.

Scale—a household scale that will weigh up to 25 pounds.

Spoons—a long-handled wooden spoon is essential for stirring as it does not get hot as does a metal spoon.   Metal spoons, stainless or silver, are needed for making the jelly test.

Thermometer*—one that registers to a temperature of 300° F. assures greater uniformity and better quality products.

Tongs*—for handling hot equipment.

Common household measures and equivalents used in this book are:

1 cup $=$ $\frac{1}{2}$ pint
2 cups $=$ 1 pint
4 cups $=$ 2 pints $=$ 1 quart
4 quarts $=$ 1 gallon
3 teaspoons $=$ 1 tablespoon
16 tablespoons $=$ 1 cup

"pinch" of salt $=$ the amount   that will stay   on the   end of a pointed paring knife (equivalent to about one two-hundred-and-fiftieth of a teaspoonful of salt)

---

* See illustration on p. 2.

Fruit, foliage, and cross section of the acerola *(Malpighia glabra* L.*)*.

ACEROLA

Description. Acerola is the most common name, of Spanish origin, for *Malpighia glabra* L. (formerly called *Malpighia punicifolia* L.), a native of tropical and subtropical America. It is a small cherry-like fruit and is often referred to as the Barbados, the West Indian, or the Puerto Rican cherry.

The fruit is borne on short stems on a shrublike tree which grows to approximately 12 feet in height. The fruit varies in size from about ½ to 1 inch in diameter and weighs from 2 to 10 grams (approximately 0.1 to 0.4 ounce). The thin skin ranges in color from light reddish-yellow to deep red when ripe. The flesh is usually of a reddish-yellow hue, although some types with dark red skins have dark red flesh. Regardless of the size of the fruit, the three winged seeds (botanically, pyrenous carpels) are large in comparison to the flesh, but because of their light and pithy nature they constitute only about 20 percent of the weight. The fruit is sweet to acid in taste, depending upon the genetic type, with no distinct or pronounced flavor. Some think the flavor of thoroughly ripe acerola and its fresh raw juice resemble that of tart strawberries.

Although commonly called a cherry, acerola when cooked has an odor and flavor more like that of tart apples or crab apples than cherries. Malic acid, the only organic acid (other than ascorbic acid) which acerola contains, is also the principal acid in apples.

History. This plant was probably first introduced into Hawaii in 1946 by the Hawaiian Sugar Planters' Experiment Station. The Department of Horticulture at the Hawaii Agricultural Experiment Station, University of Hawaii, has a large testing program in progress to select well-shaped trees with fruit of good size and high nutritive value.

Nutritive value. Analyses of the edible portion of the acerola show that it contains less of each of the nutrients than the true cherry and somewhat less of the minerals calcium, phosphorus, and iron.

Like most other fruits, the acerola is a poor source of the three B vitamins—thiamine, riboflavin, and niacin—but a fair source of provitamin A, containing about as much as the tomato. It is an exceptionally rich source of vitamin C. The ascorbic acid (vitamin-C) content of acerola is approximately 30 to 50 times that of good oranges, so that one to two cherries, depending on the size and on the concentration of ascorbic acid, will furnish the recommended daily amount (75 mg.) of vitamin C.

The unusually large amount of ascorbic acid in this fruit was first pointed out in 1946 by Asenjo and De Guzman of Puerto Rico. By isolating the substance they demonstrated that it was pure l-ascorbic acid.

Since vitamin C is water soluble, a large proportion of the ascorbic acid can be extracted by cooking the acerola with water. Stainless steel, aluminum, or glass utensils should be used in the preparation and storage of acerola products. Do not allow the fruit or preparations to come in contact with copper, brass, or rusty utensils (such as sieves or jar lids), because these catalyze the oxidation and destruction of vitamin C.

The juice and purée should be stored in the refrigerator for no longer than one week, as slow destruction of the ascorbic acid occurs, even though there is no change in color or flavor. Preliminary experiments indicate that juice stored for 18 days at 45° F. in a good electric refrigerator will lose about 20 percent of the ascorbic acid.

It has been established that unripe cherries have a somewhat greater vitamin-C content than those fully ripe, but since the color and flavor improve upon ripening, ripe or almost ripe cherries are recommended for general use in the home.

Juice prepared as directed contains from 600 to 1500 mg. per 100 ml., or per 100 gm., depending upon the fruit from which it is made, the degree of ripeness, and the quantity of water used. (See recipes for further discussion on the quantity of ascorbic acid obtainable from various amounts of juice in household measures.)

Supply. At the time of writing (1963), acerola is not to be found on the markets. It is grown mostly in home gardens. Its potential in the production of juice of high vitamin-C potency for use in the food industry, however, is considerable.

As the quantity of fruit obtainable at any one time from one or two shrubs in the home garden is likely to be limited, the recipes that follow call for the use of relatively small portions of the fruit or juice. (However, Dr. Nakasone of the Hawaii Agricultural Experiment Station reports that one well-cultivated shrub approximately three years old can be expected to yield as much as 50 pounds in one season.) The best bearing period in Hawaii is from about May through November, varying somewhat from year to year.

Use. Because the fruit is small and the seeds are relatively large, use of acerola in the raw state is limited, except to eat out of hand. Small pieces cut from the cherries (seeds removed) may be added to fruit cup or fruit salad for piquancy and vitamin C.

Fruits generally are our best sources of vitamin C, but they vary greatly in their content of this nutrient. Using acerola in combination with apples, bananas, passion fruit, pears, and other fruits poor in ascorbic acid is highly recommended.

Acerola juice, prepared as directed, may be used for jelly, for punch, for the fortification of juices low in ascorbic acid, and in prepared dishes such as gelatin desserts and salads. Sweetened or unsweetened acerola juice may be used to prevent darkening (oxidation) of fruit (such as bananas) in fruit salad or fruit cup and will at the same time enhance the vitamin-C content of the product.

The prepared juices from ripe and half-ripe cherries with which we have worked had a pH of 3.2 to 3.5. That is, acerola is more acid than oranges but not so acid as lemons. Lemon juice, with a pH of 2.05, has a more distinct flavor and combines well with acerola.

Juices used for our experiments were taken from mixed lots of acerola from test plots of the Hawaii Agricultural Experiment Station. These juices contained sufficient acid but not enough pectin for good jelly.

The fruit makes an acceptable sauce or purée which may be used alone or in combination with other fruits. Purée may be made from the whole fruit, including some juice, or from the residue remaining after the preparation of juice.

Note. In the recipes that follow, when the kind of acerola juice called for is not specified, juice prepared according to any of the recipes may be used, depending on what the user has available.

FROZEN ACEROLA

If the fruit cannot be utilized soon after picking, it may be frozen for future use. The frozen fruit is not suitable to use raw for fruit cup or fruit salad because it becomes flaccid and soft in texture, but it is good for juice, sauce, or purée, either raw or cooked.

Pick over the acerola and use only those with unbroken skins. (Cherries with broken skins or slight bruises should be used at once as fresh fruit or for juice or sauce.)

Wash the fruit lightly (do *not* remove stems or blossom ends), drain thoroughly, measure, and place in plastic bags. Label the package with the date and the quantity so it is ready for use and need not be measured again. Store in freezer at 0° F.

HOT-PRESSED ACEROLA JUICE NO. 1 YIELD: 2 cups

1 quart (4 cups) whole acerola   2 cups water

$\frac{1}{2}$ cup juice contains 1000 to 1500 mg. vitamin C
1 tablespoon contains 125 to 180 mg. vitamin C

HOT-PRESSED ACEROLA JUICE NO. 2 YIELD: about 4 cups

1 quart (4 cups) whole acerola   1 quart water

$\frac{1}{2}$ cup juice contains 700 to 800 mg. vitamin C
1 tablespoon contains 80 to 100 mg. vitamin C

Pick over cherries and remove spoiled or decayed fruit. (Either fresh or frozen fruit may be used.) Stem and blossom ends need not be removed. Measure fruit, then wash. Place the fruit in a saucepan and crush with a potato masher or with the hand. According to our experiments, 20 to 25 percent more vitamin C may be extracted from crushed fruit than from whole fruit.

For Juice No. 1, use half as much water as fruit. For Juice No. 2, use an equal volume of water. Add water, bring to the boiling point, and cook until fruit is thoroughly soft (10 to 20 minutes). Strain in a jelly bag or two thicknesses of cheesecloth. If a clear juice is desired, do not squeeze the bag. The juice will be amber colored, pink, or red, according to the color and ripeness of the original cherries.

The residue is high in vitamin C, so do not discard but put it through a food mill to make a purée and use for sauce or jam.

COLD-PRESSED ACEROLA JUICE NO. 1 YIELD: 1 cup

3 cups ripe acerola

Pick over acerola and remove spoiled or decayed fruit. Stem and blossom ends need not be removed. Wash and drain acerola. Crush the cherries with a potato masher, or a stainless steel or silver fork. (See section on Nutritive Value regarding destruction of vitamin C.) Squeeze the crushed fruit in two thicknesses of cheesecloth. Use for fruit drinks or pour over fruit cocktail.

$\frac{1}{2}$ cup juice contains about 2000 mg. vitamin C
1 tablespoon juice contains about 250 mg. vitamin C

COLD-PRESSED ACEROLA JUICE NO. 2 YIELD: 2 cups

3 cups ripe acerola
¾ cup water

Pick over acerola and remove spoiled or decayed fruit. Stem and blossom ends need not be removed. Wash and drain acerola. Crush fruit with stainless steel or wooden potato masher or fork. (See section on Nutritive Value regarding destruction of vitamin C.) Add the water and allow to stand for 15 minutes, stirring occasionally. Squeeze the crushed fruit in two thicknesses of cheesecloth. Use as desired.

½ cup juice contains about 1500 mg. vitamin C
1 tablespoon juice contains about 190 mg. vitamin C

FROZEN ACEROLA JUICE YIELD: 16 cubes

3½ cups hot-pressed acerola   **¼ to ¾ cup sugar**
Juice No. 2

Use hot-pressed juice while still warm. Add sugar and stir thoroughly until it is completely dissolved. (The amount of sugar needed will depend on the acidity of the juice.) Pour into ice cube trays and freeze until solid.

Remove cubes from tray and store in two thicknesses of plastic freezer bags, or place in waxed cartons with polyethylene wrap between the layers. Store in freezer at 0° F. Use as desired.

Cold-pressed juice may be frozen in the same manner.

Each cube of frozen acerola juice will contain from 200 to 400 mg. of ascorbic acid.

Suggested uses: Use with ice cubes in a bowl of fruit punch. Add 1 cube of frozen juice to each glass of canned pineapple juice, passion fruit juice, or other juice.

Note. Both hot-pressed and cold-pressed frozen acerola juice retained about 85 percent of the original vitamin C after 8 months of freezer storage (0° F.).

BOTTLED ACEROLA JUICE

4 cups hot-pressed acerola juice   **1 cup sugar**

Use only hot-pressed acerola juice and add sugar while juice is still warm. Bring the mixture to the boiling point, pour into hot sterilized bottles and cap with metal, cork-lined bottle caps, or seal in sterilized jars. Store in a cool dark place.

Note. Bottled hot-pressed acerola juice retained about 60 percent of the original vitamin C after 8 months' storage at room temperature (70°–85° F.).

To Enhance or Fortify Other Fruit Juices with Acerola Juice

Passion fruit juice, pineapple juice, apple juice, grape juice, pear and apricot nectar, and some other fruit juices and nectars are relatively low in ascorbic acid.

Add 1 part of acerola Juice No. 1 to 10 parts of other fruit juice. The resulting product should contain from 80 to 100 mg. ascorbic acid per 100 cc. (Good orange juice contains about 50 mg. ascorbic acid per 100 cc.)

Guava juice may be an excellent source of vitamin C if made from guavas originally high in this vitamin. Common wild guavas vary greatly in their vitamin-C content and the juice product is often greatly diluted with water. Add 1 part of acerola Juice No. 1 to 15 to 20 parts of guava juice to produce a product with approximately 100 mg. ascorbic acid per 100 cc.

Note. Pinepaple juice, passion fruit juice, and guava juice fortified with acerola juice retained approximately 85 percent of the original ascorbic acid after 8 months of freezer storage (0° F.). The acerola juice had little or no effect upon the color or flavor of the other juices, when freshly prepared or after freezer storage.

These same juices fortified with acerola juice, when bottled and stored at room temperature (70°–85° F.) for 8 months, retained 65 to 75 percent of the ascorbic acid, 10 to 20 percent less than when frozen.

FROZEN ACEROLA AND PASSION FRUIT JUICE   YIELD: 16 cubes

1½ cups hot-pressed acerola Juice No. 2	1½ cups passion fruit juice
	½ cup sugar

These proportions are for unsweetened juices. Mix all ingredients well and pour into freezer tray. Freeze until solid. Remove cubes from tray, place in two thicknesses of plastic bags, or put each cube in polyethylene wrap. Store in freezer at 0° F.

Each cube will contain about 150 mg. of ascorbic acid.

ACEROLA SIRUP   YIELD: 2½ cups

2 cups hot-pressed acerola Juice No. 2	2 tablespoons lemon juice, if desired
2 cups sugar	

Mix ingredients and cook to a temperature of 216° to 218° F., or until thick. Use on pancakes or waffles.

ACEROLA JELLY NO. 1

3 cups hot-pressed acerola Juice No. 2
3 cups sugar

½ bottle liquid pectin (⅛ cup)

Put the measured juice in a large flat saucepan (to allow for expansion during boiling and to permit rapid evaporation). Bring to the boiling point and boil for 2 to 3 minutes, then add sugar and pectin, stirring constantly. Return rapidly to the boiling point and cook to a temperature of 219° or 220° F., or until a good jelly test is obtained (see Appendix III). Skim, pour into hot sterilized glasses, and cover with hot paraffin.

Note. 1 level tablespoon or 1 heaping teaspoon of Acerola Jelly No. 1 made as directed will provide 90 to 120 mg. of ascorbic acid.

ACEROLA JELLY NO. 2

1½ cups hot-pressed acerola Juice No. 2
3½ cups sugar

½ bottle liquid pectin (⅛ cup)

Mix hot-pressed juice and sugar thoroughly. Place over high heat and bring to a boil, stirring constantly. At once stir in ½ bottle of liquid pectin. Bring to a *full rolling boil* and boil hard for 1 minute,* stirring constantly. Remove from heat, skim, and pour into sterilized glasses. Cover with hot paraffin.

Note. 1 level tablespoon or 1 heaping teaspoon of Acerola Jelly No. 2 made as directed will provide 50 to 60 mg. of ascorbic acid.

If made with the more concentrated hot-pressed Juice No. 1, 1 level tablespoon or 1 heaping teaspoon of the jelly will contain from 90 to 100 mg. of ascorbic acid.

ACEROLA JELLY NO. 3

3 cups hot-pressed acerola Juice No. 2
4 cups sugar

1 box powdered fruit pectin (1¾ ounces)

Thoroughly mix dry powdered pectin with juice. Place saucepan over high heat and stir until mixture comes to a hard boil. At once stir in sugar. Bring to a *full rolling boil,** *then boil hard for exactly 1 minute,* stirring constantly. Remove jelly from heat, skim off foam, and pour at once into sterilized glasses. Cover with hot paraffin.

Note. 1 level tablespoon or 1 heaping teaspoon of Acerola Jelly No. 3 made as directed will provide 85 to 95 mg. of ascorbic acid.

If made with the more concentrated hot-pressed Juice No. 1, 1 level tablespoon or 1 heaping teaspoon of the jelly will provide from 140 to 160 mg. of ascorbic acid.

ACEROLA–GUAVA JELLY
YIELD: 2¼ cups

2 cups hot-pressed acerola
Juice No. 2
1 cup guava juice

2¼ cups sugar

Use a relatively strong extract of guava juice to provide the pectin lacking in the acerola. Slice guavas thinly, add half the measure of water, cook for 10 to 15 minutes until guavas are very soft, and drain.

Bring the mixed juices to the boiling point and boil for 5 full minutes; add the sugar. Cook to a temperature of 221° F. or until a good jelly test is obtained (see Appendix III). Pour into sterilized glasses and cover with hot paraffin.

ACEROLA–PASSION FRUIT JELLY
YIELD: 2 cups

1 cup hot-pressed acerola
Juice No. 2
1 cup passion fruit juice

2 cups sugar
½ bottle liquid pectin (⅓ cup)

Bring acerola and sugar to the boiling point. Add pectin and passion fruit juice. Cook to 220° F. Pour into sterilized glasses and cover with hot paraffin. Avoid long cooking of the passion fruit juice as it tends to spoil the flavor.

ACEROLA MINT JELLY
YIELD: 4½ cups

3 cups hot-pressed acerola
Juice No. 2
3 cups sugar

½ bottle liquid pectin (⅓ cup)
¼ teaspoon peppermint extract
few drops green coloring

---

* A full rolling boil is a steaming, tumbling boil that cannot be stirred down.

Bring acerola juice and sugar to the boiling point, add pectin, and cook to 220° F., or until it gives a good jelly test (see Appendix III). Remove from the heat, add peppermint extract and green coloring. Pour into sterilized glasses and cover with hot paraffin.

Use acerola juice that is light in color for the mint jelly, as the color of the resulting product will be a better looking green. If the juice is definitely red in color, omit the green coloring and use only the peppermint extract.

ACEROLA SAUCE NO. 1

YIELD: 2 cups

5 cups acerola
1¼ cups sugar

1 cup water

Put all ingredients into a saucepan. Boil gently, stirring occasionally until cherries become soft (10–15 minutes). Put product through a coarse sieve or food mill to remove seeds. Season with cinnamon or nutmeg if desired.

Serve as sauce or over ice cream, sliced bananas, or other fruit.

ACEROLA SAUCE NO. 2

YIELD: 1½ cups

1 cup acerola purée
1 cup sugar

2 teaspoons lemon juice

Use purée from juice. Mix purée and sugar in a saucepan and cook, stirring constantly, until the product changes color and becomes glossy. Pour into sterilized jars and seal. This product will not keep indefinitely if covered only with paraffin. It may be kept for a week or two if well covered in the refrigerator. For longer storage, it should be frozen or canned under sterile conditions. Use as a topping for ice cream, or sliced ripe bananas, or as a jam.

ACEROLA SPREAD

YIELD: 2 cups

1½ cups acerola purée
1½ cups sugar
1 tablespoon finely chopped
  candied ginger

1 teaspoon cinnamon
pinch of cloves
pinch of allspice

Mix the spices with ½ cup of the sugar. Mix the sugar and purée thoroughly and cook over low heat with constant stirring until the product is thick and glossy (10 to 12 minutes). Add ginger and cook 1 minute more. Remove from heat, pour into sterilized glasses, and cover immediately with hot paraffin.

Use as jam or as a topping for ice cream.

Note. To avoid burning the hands, use a long-handled wooden spoon to stir during cooking, because the product spatters badly.

If a spicier product is desired, increase the cloves and allspice to ¼ teaspoon each.

FROZEN ACEROLA AND PASSION FRUIT TOPPING

YIELD: 1½ cups

1 cup acerola purée	½ cup sugar
¼ cup passion fruit juice	

Mix all ingredients thoroughly. Chill and use on vanilla ice cream or sliced bananas. A dash of nutmeg may be added if desired.

This mixture may be frozen for future use.

ACEROLA GELATIN DESSERT

YIELD: 4 to 6 servings

1 package (3 ounces) sweetened, prepared gelatin (any flavor, preferably colored red or pink)	1 cup acerola juice 1 cup boiling water

Pour boiling water over contents of the package and stir over low heat until all gelatin is dissolved. Add acerola juice. Mix well and pour into 1 large or 4 to 6 small molds. Cool and place in refrigerator to set. Serve cold.

Note. For fruit gelatin, chill the product until it begins to gel, add 1 cup drained fruit, mix lightly, and pour into molds. Use as a salad or for dessert.

Note. If unsweetened acerola juice is used, add ¼ cup sugar to the above recipe.

GINGER ALE SALAD WITH ACEROLA

YIELD: 5 to 6 servings

1 tablespoon gelatin	¼ cup sugar
4 tablespoons acerola juice (or water)	1 tablespoon lemon juice
½ cup acerola juice	1 cup ginger ale

Soften gelatin in 4 tablespoons of juice or water. Heat the ½ cup of acerola juice, add softened gelatin, and stir until thoroughly dissolved.

Add sugar and lemon juice, and cool slightly. Add ginger ale, mix well, and cool in refrigerator.

When gelatin begins to set, stir in:

¼ cup chopped celery
2 tablespoons finely chopped
   candied ginger

½ cup drained, chopped
   pineapple (canned or
   frozen)

Pour into 5 or 6 molds and return to the refrigerator. When firm, turn out on lettuce leaves and serve with mayonnaise or other salad dressing.

BAKED BANANAS WITH ACEROLA JUICE   YIELD: 4 servings

4 cooking bananas
¼ cup acerola juice
1 tablespoon lemon juice

2 tablespoons sugar
pinch of salt

Parboil bananas or bake in skins in oven for 15 to 20 minutes. Remove bananas from skins and place in baking dish. Mix juices and sugar and pour over the bananas. Baste once or twice during the baking period. Bake at 350° F. for 20 to 30 minutes or until centers are soft.

Serve as a vegetable or a dessert.

BANOLA   YIELD: 6 servings

¼ cup sugar
1¼ cups unsweetened
   acerola juice

6 medium-size or 4 large, fully
   ripe bananas
¼ cup grated coconut, if desired

Mix sugar and acerola juice. Cut thin slices of bananas into juice. Chill. Serve garnished with coconut.

BAKED APPLE WITH ACEROLA JUICE   YIELD: 4 servings

4 apples
4 tablespoons brown sugar

¼ cup unsweetened acerola
juice

Peel the top fourth of the apple and remove core. Place apples in baking dish and put 1 tablespoon of sugar in the center of each apple. Pour juice over the apples and baste 2 or 3 times during the baking period. Bake at 350° F. about 40 minutes or until apples are tender.

APPLE CRISP WITH ACEROLA

Juice Mixture
½ cup acerola juice
3 tablespoons sugar

2 teaspoons quick-cooking
tapioca

Mix well and allow to stand 10 minutes or while preparing the other ingredients.

Topping
¼ cup flour
¼ cup brown sugar

1 teaspoon cinnamon
2 tablespoons margarine

Mix flour, sugar, and cinnamon; work in softened fat with fork or fingers.

Pare, core, and slice 3 apples. Place apples in a deep baking dish. Pour juice mixture over apples. Crumble topping over surface. Bake at 350°–375° F. until apples are tender and top is delicately browned (30–40 minutes).

BANANA–ACEROLA NECTAR

YIELD: 6 servings (¾ cup each)

4 medium-size ripe bananas
1 cup chilled unsweetened
acerola juice
1 cup ice water

⅔ cup sugar OR
6 tablespoons sugar and
¼ cup honey

Peel bananas and slice. Put all ingredients in an electric food blendor and mix for about 1 minute. Serve at once.

ACEROLA MILK SHAKE

YIELD: 2 cups

1 cup cold milk
1 cup acerola sauce or juice
1 tablespoon sugar

¼ teaspoon vanilla
pinch of salt

Put all ingredients into a blendor and blend for about half a minute. Serve cold.

ACEROLA SHERBET

YIELD: 1 quart

1 tablespoon gelatin
2 tablespoons cold water
1½ cups boiling water
3 tablespoons sugar
2 tablespoons lemon juice

1½ cups acerola sauce OR
1½ cups sweetened hot-pressed
acerola juice
1 egg white stiffly beaten

Soften gelatin in cold water. Stir gelatin into boiling water; add remaining ingredients, except egg white, and mix thoroughly. Pour into freezing tray and freeze to a mush. Fold into stiffly beaten egg white. Return to freezer, stirring occasionally.

Note. Other juices, such as passion fruit, may be used to replace $\frac{1}{2}$ to $\frac{1}{3}$ of the acerola juice.

AVOCADO

Description. There are three races of avocados (*Persea americana*), two of which, the West Indian and the Guatemalan, are common in Hawaii. The following key used by horticulturists shows the main differences:

(a) West Indian race. Summer and fall ripening; fruit large; rind leathery and not more than $\frac{1}{16}$ inch in thickness.

(b) Guatemalan race. Winter and spring maturing; fruit large; rind $\frac{1}{16}$ to $\frac{1}{4}$ inch in thickness, woody in texture.

(c) Mexican race. Leaves small and anise-scented; fruit small and thin-skinned.

The fruit is pear-shaped, round, or obovoid and sometimes weighs more than three pounds. The brilliant green skin, which changes in some varieties to red, purple, or purplish black as the fruit matures, varies from smooth to warty in texture. The yellow or light green flesh which surrounds the single large seed is smooth in texture and has a characteristic nutty flavor. The best varieties have very little fiber imbedded in the flesh.

For home gardens the Beardslee is highly recommended as a late-fall and winter variety of superior quality. Avocados should be grafted rather than produced from seed because they do not run true—the fruit from a seedling may or may not be like the parent.

Examples of avocado varieties showing types, sizes, seed cavities, and thickness of flesh and rind are shown on the next page.

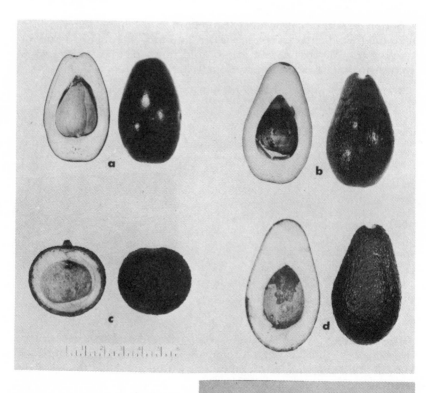

a. Seyde (summer)
b. Seedling (summer)
c. Macdonald
d. Kaguah
e. Beardslee
"a" and "b" have purple skins.
"c," "d," and "e" have green skins.

Varieties of avocados showing types, sizes, seed cavities, and thickness
of flesh and rind.

History. All races of the avocado are natives of tropical America, where they have been under cultivation for centuries. Don Francisco de Paula Marin, the Spanish horticulturist who introduced many valuable plants into Hawaii, is credited with having started the first avocado trees in the Islands sometime before 1825. As the fruit was of poor quality, the avocado did not become popular until better varieties were grown.

In 1895 Rear Admiral L. A. Beardslee brought to Hawaii three Guatemalan seedlings from which many of the present varieties have been developed. In 1919 the Hawaii Agricultural Experiment Station received through the Office of Foreign Seed and Plant Introduction of the United States Department of Agriculture a part of a fine collection of Guatemalan avocados made by Wilson Popenoe in the highlands of Guatemala.

Since that time the Experiment Station has introduced a number of varieties, which have become established in Hawaii and are now found in the markets. Selection of superior seedlings growing in Hawaii, introduction of promising varieties, and testing in Experiment Station orchards are being continued by the Horticulture Department.

The word "avocado" is derived from the Spanish *ahuacate* or *agucate,* which in turn was derived from the Aztec word *ahuacatl.* Many other spellings, such as "albecata," "arragato," "avocato," have been used by the various historians. The form "avocado" was first used in 1669 by Sir Henry Sloane, who spoke of the "avocado or alligator-pear." Both names have persisted and are common in English-speaking countries today. As the term "alligator pear" seems objectionable, efforts are now being made to replace it by the more euphonious "avocado."

Nutritive Value. With the exception of the olive, no other fruit contains as large a percentage of fat as the avocado. The fat content varies widely from 7 to 26 percent according to variety and race. The variation of water content is equally wide. The calorie value of any one sample of avocado, though always great in comparison with that of other fruits, will vary according to the fat and water content, one-fourth to one-half of a medium-size avocado yielding 100 calories.

In experiments on human digestion (done in other laboratories), the digestibility of the oils in fresh avocados was first found to be 93.7 percent, a value comparable to that for butter; but later experiments gave a value of 82.5 percent.

Avocados are a poor source of calcium, a fair to poor source of iron, and a fair source of phosphorus. They are a fair source of provitamin A and thiamine, a good source of riboflavin and niacin, and a poor source of ascorbic acid.*

---

* See Appendix VI for criteria for rating fruits as sources of minerals and vitamins.

Supply. Some varieties of avocado are on the market in Hawaii the year round. The peak of the season varies somewhat from year to year, but the fruit are found in greatest abundance from July to December. The hard-shell "winter" avocados (Guatemalan race) are marketed from November through June. The price and quality vary greatly.

Use. The avocado is a favorite salad fruit. The most common ways of serving it are "on the half shell" and in salads and fruit cocktails. Because of the high fat content of many varieties, the avocado combines best with acid fruits and vegetables such as pineapple, oranges, grapefruit, lemons, and tomatoes, or with an acid dressing such as vinegar. Some Orientals, however, prefer sugar instead.

The avocado contains a tannin which causes it to become very bitter if cooked; consequently no successful method of canning has been found. It may, however, be satisfactorily used in hot foods, such as vegetable soup, consommé, or omelette, if it is diced and added just before serving.

For salads or as a garnish, the avocado may be sliced, or diced, or scooped from the half shell with a teaspoon. The spoonfuls may be inverted to show the green portion next to the skin and arranged as desired on salad greens.

Avocados, with their mild flavor and large amount of fat, especially certain varieties, may be used to supply the fat content of frozen desserts such as ice creams and sherbets, with other ingredients supplying the flavor.

Only avocados of very high quality, without brown fibers, should be used for desserts and molded salads.

To date, avocados have not been frozen successfully except as a purée combined with sugar and acid. For directions on freezing, see Appendix I.

AVOCADO AND FRUIT JUICE MILK SHAKE*   YIELD: 1½ to 2 cups

¼ to ⅓ cup avocado purée	Few grains of salt
1 teaspoon lemon juice	¼ to ⅓ cup ice milk
½ tablespoon sugar	¾ cup milk

Blend avocado purée, lemon juice, sugar, and salt to a smooth paste. Add ice milk and fresh milk. Blend all ingredients in electric blendor for 1 minute or until thoroughly mixed. Pour into glasses and, if desired, sprinkle with nutmeg.

Variation. Substitute for lemon juice, 1 teaspoon lime juice or 1 tablespoon of pineapple or grapefruit juice (fresh, frozen, or canned).

---

* Contributed by Kathryn Orr, Cooperative Extension Service, University of Hawaii.

AVOCADO COCKTAIL

4¼ cups diced avocado
   (2 medium)
1 cup tomato catsup
1 teaspoon finely chopped
   onion

½ teaspoon salt
1½ tablespoons lemon OR
   1 tablespoon lime juice
½ teaspoon Worcestershire
   sauce

Sprinkle salt over avocado and chill. Combine other ingredients and chill. Place diced avocado in individual serving dishes and add dressing.

AVOCADO-GRAPEFRUIT COCKTAIL

2¼ cups avocado cubes
   (1 medium)

¼ teaspoon salt
2 cups grapefruit pieces

Sprinkle avocado cubes with salt. Remove membrane from grapefruit sections and cut into pieces about the same size as avocado cubes. Add to avocado, chill, and serve in cocktail glasses with Fruit Cocktail Dressing (see Index).

AVOCADO APPETIZER (Guacamole)

1 medium-size avocado
   (1 pound)
1 medium-size ripe tomato
1 tablespoon lemon juice
1 teaspoon Worcestershire
   sauce
1 small onion, minced

¼ teaspoon monosodium
   glutamate, if desired
½ teaspoon salt or garlic salt
Dash of pepper
Dash of Tabasco sauce,
   if desired

Peel avocado and tomato and mash together or force through a sieve. Add seasonings; taste and reseason, if necessary. Chill. Serve as a relish or dip, in a bowl set on the center of a large plate and surrounded by crackers, potato chips, or carrot, cucumber, or celery strips.

Note. Mixture may be used as sandwich filling.

AVOCADO WITH CREAMED FISH

2 tablespoons fat
2 tablespoons flour
1 cup milk
¼ teaspoon salt

¼ to ½ cup canned
   salmon or tuna (or
   other cooked fish)
2 medium-size avocados

Melt fat in upper part of double boiler; add flour, and stir until blended. Add milk slowly, stirring until thick and smooth. Add salt, fish, and additional seasoning if desired. Cook in covered double boiler for 10 to 15 minutes to heat fish thoroughly. Cut avocados into halves lengthwise and remove seeds. Fill each half with creamed fish and heat in a moderate oven (350° F.) about 10 minutes, or place under broiler for a few minutes to brown on top. The avocado should be warmed but not cooked.

Variation 1. Two to 3 teaspoons curry powder added with flour to above sauce. Serve with cooked rice and mango chutney.

Variation 2. Place slices of avocado on crisp toast and cover with creamed fish.

AVOCADO, CRAB, AND GRAPEFRUIT SALAD

YIELD: 4 to 5 servings

1 can crab (7 ounces)
⅔ cup coarsely chopped celery
1 cup grapefruit sections
Lettuce, cress, or endive

1 medium-size avocado (1 pound)
⅓ to ½ cup Favorite French Dressing (see Index)

Flake crab meat coarsely, removing celluloid-like pieces. Combine with celery and grapefruit sections, and toss with salad dressing. On each plate place ⅓ cup of mixture on bed of greens.

Cut avocado into halves crosswise, remove seed, and cut each half into 3 one-inch slices. Peel, cut circles into halves, sprinkle with salt, and arrange around crab and grapefruit mixture. Garnish top of salad with small extra pieces.

Note. For a salad bowl, cut avocado into cubes, break lettuce into small pieces, and toss with rest of mixture.

AVOCADO-PINEAPPLE SALAD

YIELD: 6 servings

6 slices fresh pineapple
2 cups avocado slices
⅓ cup mashed avocado pulp

½ to ¾ cup mayonnaise
2 tablespoons lemon OR
1¼ tablespoons lime juice

Place pineapple and avocado slices on lettuce leaves. Make dressing of other ingredients, chill, and pour 1 to 2 tablespoons over each salad.

AVOCADO-FRUIT SALAD

YIELD: 6 servings

1½ cups grapefruit sections
1¼ cups orange sections
12 slices ripe mango

12 slices avocado
Lettuce, cress, or endive
⅓ to ½ cup dressing

Remove membrane from orange and grapefruit sections. Chill all ingredients. Arrange on greens, and serve with Favorite French Dressing or variations (see Index).

AVOCADO SALAD PLATE
YIELD: 6 servings

Cut 3 medium-size avocados into halves lengthwise, twist to separate halves, and remove seed. Strip off peeling; sprinkle with salt and lemon or pineapple juice. If larger cavity is desired, hollow out center or slit each end of the halves and push open. Cut slice off bottom to make flat surface. Fill each cavity with $\frac{1}{2}$ to $\frac{2}{3}$ cup of one of following salads (see Index):

> Banana Waldorf Salad
> Lychee, Papaya, and Pineapple Salad
> Pineapple-Crab Salad
> Pineapple and Chicken Salad

Arrange halves on salad plates, tuck lettuce leaves or water cress sprigs around them. Serve with egg or ham sandwiches. Pass the desired dressing.

AVOCADO SALAD MOLD
YIELD: 8 to 10 servings

1 tablespoon unflavored gelatin

$\frac{1}{4}$ cup pineapple juice OR cold water

1 large ripe avocado (1$\frac{1}{2}$ pounds)

2 tablespoons lemon juice

1$\frac{1}{2}$ teaspoons onion juice, if desired

$\frac{1}{4}$ to $\frac{1}{2}$ teaspoon sugar, if desired

$\frac{3}{4}$ teaspoon salt

$\frac{3}{4}$ cup mayonnaise

Select high quality soft, ripe avocado. Sprinkle gelatin over pineapple juice or cold water and let stand 5 minutes. Heat over hot water until dissolved. Peel and remove pit from avocado; mash through fine sieve or food mill. Add lemon and onion juices, sugar and salt, and dissolved gelatin, stirring constantly until well blended. Stir in mayonnaise. Pour into 1$\frac{1}{2}$-quart mold or into individual molds. Chill until firm (about 6 to 8 hours).

Unmold on chilled platter; garnish with water cress sprigs and grapefruit and orange sections.

AVOCADO-GRAPEFRUIT SALAD DRESSING
See Index.

AVOCADO MILK SHERBET

1 medium-size avocado
(1 pound)
¾ cup milk
1 cup sugar
½ teaspoon salt

1 cup pineapple juice
¼ cup lemon juice
2 egg whites
¼ cup sugar

Press avocado through a fine sieve. To this pulp add milk, sugar, and salt. Stir until sugar is dissolved; add fruit juices. Pour into two freezing trays and freeze to a mush (1½ hours).

Beat egg whites until stiff but not dry; gradually add ¼ cup sugar, beating until glossy. Fold into avocado mixture and beat quickly until well blended. Return to freezing trays; moisten bottoms of trays and place in freezing compartment. Freeze to serving consistency.

Note. When using refrigerator that does not have a quick-freezing compartment, set refrigerator control to coldest temperature. Freeze to serving consistency and turn control back to a little colder than normal until ready to use.

A smoother mixture may be obtained by using an ice-cream freezer and 1 part salt to 8 parts ice.

AVOCADO-PINEAPPLE SHERBET

Follow Avocado Milk Sherbet recipe, substituting 1 cup crushed pineapple for pineapple juice and adding 1 tablespoon more lemon juice. If fresh pineapple is used, add sugar to taste.

BANANA

Description. The banana (*Musa paradisiaca*), which is now one of the best-known fruits throughout the world, was classed as a luxury and known to comparatively few people in the United States until late in the nineteenth century. Because it is so well known, a detailed description of the fruit seems unnecessary. The yellow cylindrical fruit, with the tough outer peel that acts as a prophylactic cover for the enclosed pulp, is a common sight in most parts of the world. Bananas grow in a bunch consisting of a number of clusters called "hands," each of which contains from five to twenty bananas,

History. The early history of the banana is closely interwoven with Eastern mythology. The legend that the serpent which tempted Eve in the garden of Eden (Paradise) hid in a bunch of bananas influenced the classifiers to name the fruit *Musa paradisiaca* (fruit of paradise) and *Musa sapientum* (fruit of knowledge). The fact that the fruit was called "apple of paradise" or "Adam's fig" before the word "banana" was adopted from an African Congo tribe also illustrates its connections with ancient mythology. The word "banana" seems to have been used originally for only those varieties which were eaten raw and the term "plantain" for those which were eaten only after cooking. At present there is no clear differentiation.

When the early Polynesians migrated to Hawaii from the islands to the south, they undoubtedly brought with them banana plants in the form of bulblike rhizomes and planted them in the mountain valleys, where they now grow wild. Until the introduction during the nineteenth century of varieties such as the Brazilian and Chinese or Cavendish, the fruit of these plants brought by the Polynesians was the only kind to be had in Hawaii. The Gros Michel variety (locally called Bluefields) was not introduced into Hawaii until 1903. Most of the Hawaii bananas (those varieties growing in the Islands when they were discovered by Captain James Cook in 1778) are more palatable after being cooked. Favorites among the Hawaii varieties are the *Maia-maoli*, the *Popoulu*, and the *Iholena*—which represent the three groups of Hawaii bananas.

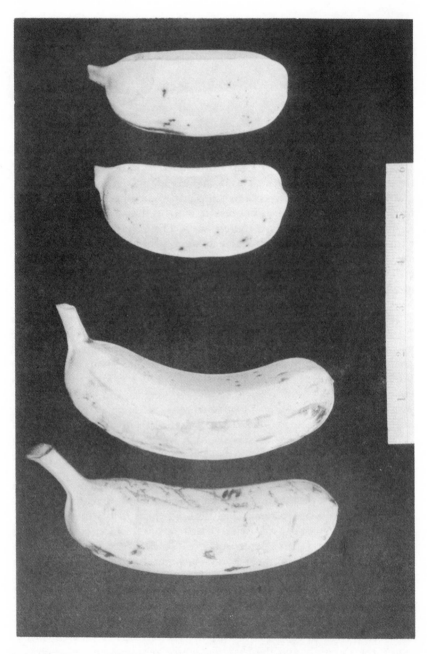

Some of the more important varieties of bananas grown in Hawaii– cooking bananas or plantains. Above, Popoulu; below, Maiamaoli.

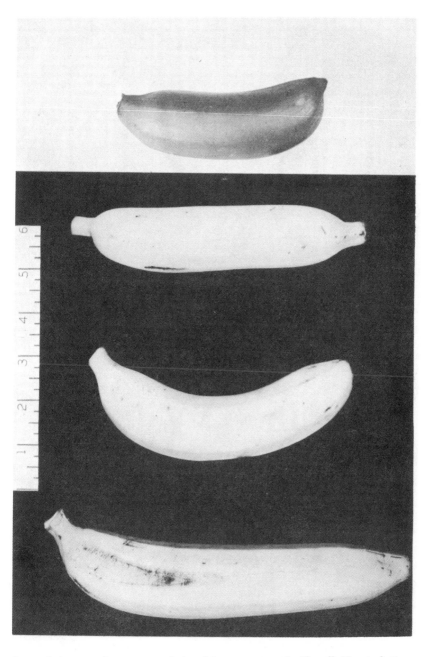

Some of the more important varieties of bananas grown in Hawaii. Top to bottom: Red Cuban, Brazilian, Chinese, Bluefields.

BANANA VARIETIES IN HAWAII AND THEIR USE

LOCAL AND VARIETY NAME	DESCRIPTION	RECOMMENDED USE
	BANANAS USUALLY EATEN RAW	
BLUEFIELDS (Gros Michel)	Size: largest of eating varieties Skin: smooth and yellow Flesh: creamy white and tender Flavor: mild and good	Best when eaten raw, but may be cooked if not fully ripe
BRAZILIAN (often wrongly called Apple banana)	Size: small to medium Shape: sides squarish between ridges, blossom end tip prominent Flesh: firm Flavor: tart	Raw or cooked
CHINESE (Cavendish)	Size: small to medium Skin: deep yellow Flesh: yellow and tender	Raw; not recommended for cooking
ICE CREAM	Size: small Shape: stubby Skin: light yellow with silvery bloom, tender, cracks easily Flesh: white and very tender Flavor: bland and sweet	Raw; excellent for ice cream and sherbet, but not recommended for cooking
RED*	Size: medium to large Skin: red over yellow-orange Flesh: creamy white to pink, slightly slippery but tender Flavor and odor: pungent	Raw; not recommended for cooking
LACATAN† (may be same as Hamakua)	Size: medium to large Skin: light green to light yellow, even when fully ripe Flesh: creamy white and very tender	Raw; not recommended for cooking

* Also called **Red Cuban** and **Red Spanish**.
† Recently introduced; resistant to Panama disease.

BANANA VARIETIES IN HAWAII AND THEIR USE

LOCAL AND VARIETY NAME	DESCRIPTION	RECOMMENDED USE
	BANANAS USUALLY COOKED	
MAIAMAOLI‡	Size: large Shape: long, round, and well filled at both ends Skin: deep yellow Flesh: tender, creamy pink when raw, yellow and translucent when cooked Flavor: tart	May be eaten raw, but not very palatable; best when cooked; excellent either baked or boiled
POPOULU	Shape: very thick, short, blunt with rounded ends Skin: deep yellow Flesh: light salmon pink and firm when raw; yellow and translucent when cooked Flavor: tart	May be eaten raw, but not very palatable; best when cooked; better texture and flavor when boiled than when baked

‡ A large number of "Hawaiian" bananas grow in the Islands, but only the two which are commonly found on the market are described here.

In 1951, when the Bluefields orchards in some areas were being severely devastated by Panama disease, the Horticulture Department of the University of Hawaii Experiment Station brought from tropical America several bananas resistant to this disease. (One of the varieties introduced was the Lacatan.)

Nutritive Value. Because bananas are an economical and nutritious food and are plentiful and available everywhere in Hawaii, greater use should be made of them.

In the half-ripe stage, one-half to one-third of the total carbohydrate may be in the form of starch. But when fully ripe and, in the case of many varieties, if the yellow skin is flecked with brown spots or is entirely brown, almost no starch remains and practically all the carbohydrate is in the form of sugars.

Unripe bananas may cause digestive disturbances, but in the fully ripe stage they are readily digested and have been used successfully combined with milk in infant feeding. There is no reason why bananas, if they are cooked or if they are used only in the fully ripe stage, cannot be used generously in children's diets. Like most fruits and vegetables, bananas yield an alkaline ash in the body.

All varieties of bananas are poor sources of calcium. The eating varieties are also poor sources of phosphorus and iron. The only cooking variety analyzed was found to be a fair source of phosphorus and a good source of iron.

Both eating and cooking varieties are fair sources of provitamin A, poor sources of thiamine, and fair sources of riboflavin and niacin. The two widely grown and generally available varieties, Bluefields and Chinese, are poor sources of ascorbic acid, but some of the other varieties such as the Brazilian, Ice Cream, and all the cooking varieties are fair sources.

Supply. Bananas are to be found on the market in Hawaii at any time during the year, the supply usually exceeding the demand, though certain varieties are not always available. The chief varieties of bananas grown and used in Hawaii and some of their culinary characteristics are summarized in the table of banana varieties in Hawaii.

Use. Bananas may be divided into two general classes: the cooking banana, more palatable after cooking, and the eating banana, which is usually used raw but may be cooked. Cooked ripe or green bananas may be served as a vegetable, taking the place of white or sweetpotatoes. In the uncooked state, they are a favorite breakfast or dessert fruit and may be used in fruit cocktails, salads, pies, cake fillings, and ice creams.

The banana is one of the few fruits which may be picked full-size but green and stored for a considerable length of time without injury to its flavor.

For directions on how to ripen bananas, see below. Fully ripe bananas are superior in flavor to half-ripe ones.

After peeling bananas, be sure to remove the fibrous strings which sometimes cling to the fruit, since they tend to have an astringent quality, probably due to their content of tannin, and often spoil the flavor of the fruit. The strings also darken upon cooking.

Eating bananas need special treatment for freezing. Cooking bananas make an excellent frozen product when fully or partially precooked. See Appendix I for directions on freezing.

HOW TO RIPEN BANANAS

a. Keep bananas at room temperature (70° to 80° F.). Keeping them in the refrigerator prevents proper ripening.
b. Bananas to be used for salad or fruit cup should be placed in the refrigerator to chill for several hours before peeling.

PROPER USE OF BANANAS ACCORDING TO STAGE OF RIPENESS

a. All yellow (some varieties usually eaten raw may have slight green tips).
   1. Excellent for cooking.
b. Fully ripe bananas with yellow peel flecked with brown.
   1. For immediate eating.
   2. For use in fruit cups, salads, desserts, and drinks.
   3. For use in baking.

BANANA MILK SHAKE
YIELD: 1 serving

1 very ripe banana	¼ teaspoon vanilla
1 cup milk	⅛ teaspoon salt

Choose a banana with skin flecked with brown spots or with skin entirely brown. Peel and press through medium sieve or mash with fork. Add other ingredients, gradually stirring with fork until well mixed. Chill thoroughly; beat with rotary beater or shake in fruit jar. If electric blendor is used, banana need not be mashed. Serve in tall glass.

Variation. Add 3 tablespoons guava juice and 1 tablespoon sugar.

BANANA-GUAVA NECTAR
YIELD: 6 servings (¾ cup each)

4 medium-size ripe bananas	⅔ cup sugar OR
1 cup unsweetened guava juice	6 tablespoons sugar and
1 cup water	¼ cup honey

Peel banana, slice, and force through coarse sieve. Combine with other ingredients, pour over cracked ice, and serve.

If electric food blendor is used, banana need not be mashed.

PAPAYA-BANANA NECTAR
See Index.

POHA FRUIT CUP
See Index.

BAKED BANANAS IN SKINS
YIELD: 6 servings

**6 large ripe cooking
or Bluefields bananas**

Wash bananas and place in baking pan with just enough water to cover bottom of pan. Bake at 350° F. until easily pierced with fork or until skins begin to burst (20 to 30 minutes). Slit skin lengthwise, season with margarine, salt, and pepper, and serve hot as vegetable.

BOILED BANANAS
YIELD: 6 servings

**6 large firm-ripe cooking
bananas**

3 cups boiling water

Wash thoroughly. Cook in boiling water until skin is easily pierced with fork (15 to 20 minutes). Drain. Slit skin lengthwise and serve in the skin, or peel and season with margarine and salt.

BROILED BANANAS
YIELD: 6 servings

**6 firm-ripe Bluefields bananas
Juice of ½ lemon**

6 strips bacon

Peel bananas, roll in lemon juice, and wrap each banana with a strip of bacon. Fasten at each end with a toothpick. Place on pan about 3 inches from broiler unit. Broil, turning several times, until bacon is cooked and bananas are soft (about 30 minutes). Serve hot as a vegetable.

FRIED BANANAS
YIELD: 6 servings

**3 or 4 large ripe cooking or
eating bananas
2 to 4 tablespoons margarine
2 tablespoons brown or
granulated sugar**

**Pinch of salt
2 tablespoons lemon juice OR
1½ tablespoons lime juice
2 tablespoons orange juice,
if desired**

Peel and cut bananas into halves lengthwise. Fry in fat until lightly browned. Add sugar and fruit juice; cover and simmer until bananas are soft. Serve hot as a vegetable.

BANANA CASSEROLE

6 cooking or eating bananas	**2 tablespoons orange juice**
¼ cup orange sections	**2 tablespoons lemon juice**
⅓ cup sugar	**Pinch of salt**

Peel bananas, cut lengthwise, and place in oiled baking dish. Remove membrane from sections of oranges. Arrange slices of oranges on top of bananas. Sift sugar over bananas and oranges, and add fruit juice. Bake at 300° to 350° F. for 30 to 45 minutes. Serve as a vegetable or a dessert.

MIXED GRILL

3 large or 6 small bananas	**8 ounces canned pork sausages**
3 or 4 medium-size tomatoes	**3 slices bacon, if desired**

Peel Brazilian or Bluefields bananas; scrape to remove strings, which darken in cooking. Place in a large flat baking dish and spread each with some fat from sausages. Cut unpeeled tomatoes into halves crosswise; arrange, cut side up, at one end of baking dish and dot with fat. Bake 20 minutes at 400° F.

Scrape excess fat from sausages and lay them on bananas. Bake 10 minutes longer, or until bananas are tender and sausages are well heated and slightly browned.

Garnish with well-drained bacon, fried or broiled. Serve in baking dish, with Spoon Corn Bread (see any standard cookbook for recipe).

Variations. Parboiled cooking bananas may be used instead of raw Brazilians or Bluefields. If raw sausages are used instead of canned, they should be cooked separately and longer, to make sure they are thoroughly done.

Bananas and tomatoes may be cooked separately, then arranged on a large heated platter, with bananas at one end and sausages, bacon, and tomatoes at the other.

GLAZED BANANAS

6 eating or small cooking bananas	**1 tablespoon water**
	Juice of ½ lemon, if desired
3 tablespoons margarine	**Pinch of salt**
¼ cup guava jelly	

Peel bananas and cut into halves lengthwise. Lay in oiled, shallow baking dish or pan. Spread with softened margarine and salt. Beat guava jelly, water, and lemon juice together and pour over bananas. Bake in moderate oven (350° F.) until soft (20 to 30 minutes).

Note. Bananas may be glazed in frying pan. Melt fat, brown pieces on one side, add jelly mixture and salt. Cover and cook very slowly 10 to 20 minutes, turning once or twice during cooking. Serve hot with meat course, or as dessert.

BANANA AND PEANUT BUTTER SPREAD   YIELD: 1¼ cups

¼ cup peanut butter	¾ cup mashed ripe banana

¼ cup hot water OR
    evaporated milk
	2 to 3 tablespoons lemon
	    or lime juice

Cream peanut butter, add hot water or evaporated milk, and blend thoroughly. Add banana pulp, and season with lemon juice.

BANANA WALDORF SALAD   YIELD: 6 servings

1 cup diced celery	1 tablespoon lemon juice or
¼ cup coarsely chopped peanuts or walnuts	pineapple juice, if desired
2 apples, diced (1¼ cups)	¼ to ½ cup mayonnaise or Hawaiian Dressing (see Index)
2 to 3 bananas, diced (2 cups)	Pinch of salt

Chill ingredients before preparing. Add fruit juice or salad dressing to diced apple and banana to prevent color change. Combine all ingredients and serve on lettuce leaves garnished with pimiento strips or guava jelly. Serve immediately; salad will darken if allowed to stand.

Variation. 1½ cups diced pineapple may be substituted for apple.

BANANA AND NUT SALAD   YIELD: 6 servings

3 large or 6 small ripe
    bananas
	¼ cup chopped nuts OR
	    grated coconut

Juice of 1 lemon,
    if desired
	¼ to ½ cup mayonnaise or
	    Hawaiian Dressing (see Index)

Peel and cut bananas into halves lengthwise. Roll in lemon juice or mayonnaise, then in nuts or coconut, and place on lettuce leaves garnished with mayonnaise or Hawaiian Dressing.

BANANA BREAD

YIELD: 1 large or 2 small loaves

1 cup mashed bananas	⅔ cup sugar
(2 to 3 medium)	⅓ cup shortening
1¾ cups flour	2 eggs
2 teaspoons baking powder	½ cup coarsely chopped
¼ teaspoon soda	nuts, if desired
½ teaspoon salt	

Sift flour, baking powder, soda, and salt together. Combine sugar and shortening in medium-size mixing bowl and beat until creamy. Add eggs one at a time, beating well between each addition. Add flour mixture alternately with bananas, a small amount at a time, ending with flour. Beat after each addition until smooth. Add nuts. Place in one loaf pan 8 by 4 by 3 inches deep or in two smaller pans 5 by 3 by 2 inches deep. Bake at 350° F. until done (1 hour).

BANANA BRAN MUFFINS

YIELD: 6 to 8 large or 18 small

¼ to ⅓ cup shortening	½ teaspoon soda
¼ to ½ cup sugar	½ cup chopped nuts, if desired
1 egg	1½ cups mashed bananas
1 cup "All Bran" cereal	(3 to 4 medium)
1½ cups flour	2 tablespoons water
2 teaspoons baking powder	1 teaspoon vanilla, if desired
½ teaspoon salt	

Cream shortening and sugar. Add egg and beat well. Add bran and mix thoroughly. Sift flour with baking powder, salt, and soda. Add nuts to flour mixture and add alternately with mashed bananas to which the water has been added. Stir in vanilla. Pour into oiled muffin pans and bake at 400° F. for 20 to 25 minutes.

BANANA CAKE

YIELD: 2 round 8-inch layers or 15 to 18 cupcakes

1½ cups mashed banana	½ teaspoon salt
(3 to 4 medium)	1¼ cups sugar
2¼ cups sifted cake flour	½ cup shortening
2½ teaspoons double-acting	2 eggs
baking powder	1 teaspoon vanilla
¼ teaspoon soda	

Preheat oven to 375° F. Line bottom of 2 round 8-inch layer-cake pans with wax paper to fit. Mash bananas through fine sieve.

3 5

Sift all dry ingredients into large electric mixer bowl, add shortening, unbeaten eggs, and ½ cup of mashed banana. Beat 2 minutes at medium speed, scraping bowl and beaters as necessary. Add vanilla and remaining banana and beat 1 minute longer. Pour into prepared cake pans.

Bake until cake shrinks from sides of the pans, or until an inserted toothpick comes out clean (about 25 minutes). Cool in pans on cake racks about 5 minutes. Invert on cake rack, remove pan and peel off paper. When cool, frost with Seven Minute Icing (see standard cookbook for recipe), if desired. Bake cupcakes 15 to 20 minutes.

If electric mixer is not available, beat briskly for the same amount of time, using 150 round-the-bowl strokes per minute.

SHORTCAKE

YIELD: 6 servings

- 2 cups flour
- 2 tablespoons sugar
- 2 teaspoons double-acting OR
  4 teaspoons quick-acting baking powder
- ¾ teaspoon salt

- ⅓ cup shortening
- ½ to ¾ cup milk OR
  ½ cup milk and 1 egg well beaten
- 1 to 2 tablespoons margarine

Sift dry ingredients, cut in shortening with pastry blender or with two knives held scissor-fashion until mixture resembles coarse meal. Add liquid, and mix only until all flour is dampened. Turn out on floured board; divide into halves. Pat or roll each half out to 8 inches in diameter. Place one half in 8-inch pie tin, spread with softened margarine, and place other half on top. Bake at 450° F., 12 to 15 minutes.

Cool slightly and place on serving plate. Remove top layer. Cover bottom layer with crushed, sweetened fruit or berries (about 1 quart per 6 servings). Replace other layer, then top with more fruit. Serve with thin or whipped cream.

BANANA ROLL

YIELD: 12 to 14 rolls

- 1 recipe shortcake dough (p. 22)
- 2 tablespoons margarine
- 1 large fully ripe banana

- 3 tablespoons sugar
- 1 to 2 teaspoons lemon juice
- Dash of nutmeg

Roll or pat dough into 2 strips about 7 by 14 inches. Spread with softened margarine. Cover with thinly sliced banana to within 1 inch of outside edge of dough. Sprinkle with lemon juice, sugar, and nutmeg. Moisten edge of dough with water. Roll up as for jelly roll and seal by pinching edge of dough into roll. Cut into 1-inch slices and place cut side up on greased pie tin or in muffin pan. Bake at 450° F., 15 to 20 minutes.

Variation. Brown sugar may be used in place of granulated, and tops of rolls may be sprinkled with chopped nuts.

BANANA FILLING FOR CAKE

YIELD: 1½ cups

1 cup ripe banana pulp (2 to 3 medium)
2 tablespoons margarine
1 cup sugar
¼ cup lemon juice
1 egg

Add margarine, sugar, lemon juice, and slightly beaten egg to banana pulp. Cook over hot water until as thick as custard (about 5 minutes). Use as filling for 2-layer or 3-layer cake.

BANANA PEANUT BUTTER CRISPIES

YIELD: 4 to 5 dozen

½ cup fat
½ cup plain or "chunk-style" peanut butter
½ cup brown sugar
½ cup granulated sugar
¼ cup mashed ripe banana (1 small)
1¼ cups flour
½ teaspoon baking powder
¾ teaspoon baking soda
½ teaspoon salt

Cream fat, peanut butter, and brown and granulated sugar together until well blended. Stir in banana. Sift flour, baking powder, soda, and salt together. Gradually add to other mixture. On wax paper or floured board, shape dough into a roll 1½ to 2 inches in diameter. Wrap in wax paper and chill in refrigerator overnight.

Slice ⅛ to ¼ inch thick and bake on ungreased cookie sheet about 12 minutes at 375° F., or until golden brown. Remove from oven, cool 2 to 3 minutes, then remove from cookie sheet to cake rack. When cool, store in airtight can.

Note. For drop cookies, do not chill dough. Drop by teaspoonfuls onto cookie sheet. Decorate with shelled peanut halves before baking, if desired.

BANANA OATMEAL COOKIES

YIELD: 3½ dozen

¾ cup shortening
1 cup sugar
1 egg
1 cup mashed bananas
(2 or 3 medium)
¼ teaspoon salt

1 cup quick-cooking rolled oats
1½ cups flour
½ teaspoon soda
¼ teaspoon nutmeg
¾ teaspoon cinnamon
½ teaspoon baking powder

Cream shortening and sugar. Add egg and beat thoroughly. Add banana and rolled oats; mix well. Sift other dry ingredients and stir into mixture. Drop by teaspoonfuls onto oiled baking sheet about 1½ inches apart. Bake at 400° F. for 13 to 15 minutes. Remove immediately, cool, and store in airtight container.

PLAIN PASTRY

YIELD: 9-inch 2-crust pie
or 2 9-inch pie shells

2 cups flour
¾ teaspoon salt
⅔ cup shortening

Cold water (about ¼ to
½ cup)

Sift flour and salt into mixing bowl. Cut in about half of shortening, either with pastry blender or with two knives held scissor-fashion, until mixture resembles coarse meal. Cut in remaining shortening until the particles are about the size of a pea. Stirring with a fork, add ⅓ cup cold water gradually. Stir until a ball is formed on the fork and the bowl is clean. Divide dough into two equal parts, flour board and rolling pin, and roll dough in circular form to about ⅛-inch thickness and about 1 inch larger than the pan.

Roll pastry on rolling pin, then unroll over pie pan. Push pastry down into pan being careful not to stretch it. Trim off surplus. Put in filling and moisten edges of pastry with water. Prick top crust or make design. Place over filling and cut so that about 1 inch overlaps the edge. Tuck top pastry under bottom pastry and flute edges or press with tines of fork. Bake according to directions for pie you are making.

PIE SHELL

Prepare one half of plain pastry recipe. Roll out dough 2 inches wider than diameter of pie pan. Place in pan as suggested for 2-crust pie. Turn edges under so that about 1 inch overlaps edge of pan. Flute rim and prick bottom and slides with fork. Just before baking put a second pie pan the same size as first inside shell. Bake at 475° F., 15 to 20 minutes. Remove second pan while pastry is hot.

If second pan is not used, bake about 8 minutes at 475° F., and if pastry puffs up during baking, prick several times to release hot air and steam.

BANANA CREAM PIE

Yield: 9-inch pie (5 to 6 servings)

1 baked pie shell (see above)
3 tablespoons cornstarch
¼ cup sugar
¼ teaspoon salt
2 cups milk
3 egg yolks, slightly beaten
1 tablespoon margarine

½ teaspoon vanilla
1¼ cups sliced bananas
   (3 to 4 medium)
3 egg whites
6 tablespoons sugar
Pinch of salt
¼ teaspoon vanilla

Combine sugar, cornstarch, and salt in saucepan; gradually stir in milk. Cook over moderate heat, stirring constantly until well thickened (15 to 20 minutes). Remove from heat. Stir small amount of hot mixture into egg yolks; pour back into remaining mixture, beating vigorously. Add margarine and cook for 2 minutes. Remove from heat; cool, stirring occasionally, and add vanilla.

Arrange layer of sliced bananas in pie shell and add filling. Top with meringue made of stiffly beaten egg whites, sugar, salt, and vanilla. Bake at 300° to 325° F., until delicately browned (15 to 20 minutes).

BANANAS WITH CUSTARD SAUCE

YIELD: 6 servings

¼ cup graham cracker crumbs
1 tablespoon sugar
¼ teaspoon nutmeg, scant

6 medium bananas
1¼ cups top milk or
   soft custard

Crush crackers, add sugar and nutmeg, and mix well. Cut bananas into ½-inch slices and roll in crumb mixture. Pile in serving dish or sherbet dishes and serve with chilled milk or soft custard.

GUABANAS

YIELD: 6 servings

4 tablespoons sugar
1¼ cups unsweetened guava
   juice

6 medium-size or 4 large
   fully ripe bananas
¼ cup grated coconut,
   if desired

Mix sugar and guava juice. Cut thin slices of bananas into juice. Chill. Serve garnished with coconut.

GUAVA DELICIOUS
See Index.

HAWAIIAN AMBROSIA
See Index.

PINEAPPLE FRUIT MOLD
See Index.

ROSELLE FRUIT MOLD
See Index.

BANANAS WITH COCONUT SAUCE
YIELD: 6 servings

6 small, firm-ripe bananas
¾ cup grated fresh coconut
1 cup milk

2 tablespoons sugar
2 teaspoons cornstarch
Pinch of salt

Do not peel bananas. Place in enough boiling water to cover, and cook until soft (10 to 20 minutes). Drain, remove skins, and cut into halves lengthwise. Mix cornstarch with sugar, and make smooth paste by adding gradually ¼ cup cold milk. Combine with remaining milk and with coconut, place over low heat, stirring until thick. Pour over bananas and serve as a dessert. May be garnished with grated coconut.

BANANA ICEBOX CAKE
YIELD: 6 servings

1 tablespoon unflavored
    gelatin
¼ cup cold water
1¼ cups mashed ripe bananas
    (3 to 4 medium)
¼ to ½ teaspoon vanilla
¼ teaspoon salt

3 tablespoons lemon juice
½ cup sugar
1½ cups whipping cream
2 dozen ladyfingers OR
    sponge cake sliced
    ½ inch thick

Sprinkle gelatin on cold water, let stand for 5 minutes and melt it by placing over boiling water. Combine it with mashed bananas, vanilla, salt, lemon juice, and sugar. Cool until mixture begins to thicken; whip cream and fold into mixture.

Line bottom and sides of pan with ladyfingers and cover with a layer of the banana-cream mixture. Alternate layers of ladyfingers and banana-cream mixture. Chill thoroughly. Serve with whipped cream; garnish with guava jelly.

BANANA MOUSSE
YIELD: 6 to 8 servings

¾ cup evaporated milk
½ tablespoon unflavored
    gelatin
2 tablespoons water
¼ cup sugar
½ cup boiling water

¾ cup mashed banana
    (2 medium)
Speck of salt
¼ cup lemon or lime juice
3 tablespoons orange juice

Pour evaporated milk into refrigerator freezing tray and chill until crystals begin to form. Pour into chilled bowl and whip with rotary egg beater until stiff.

Sprinkle gelatin over cold water and let stand 5 minutes. Combine sugar and boiling water, bring to boiling point, and add gelatin. Stir until dissolved. Cool and pour over mashed bananas. Season with salt, lemon and orange juice.

Pour into freezing tray and chill until mixture begins to set. Fold in whipped evaporated milk and allow to freeze. Stir mixture once during freezing period.

Variations. 1 cup whipping cream and $\frac{1}{4}$ cup thin cream may be used instead of evaporated milk. The whipping cream should be chilled before whipping; the thin cream should be added after the fruit juice. Sweetened guava juice may be used instead of orange juice.

BANANA SHERBET

YIELD: 6 to 8 servings

1 teaspoon unflavored gelatin	$\frac{1}{2}$ cup orange juice
1 cup water	1 cup mashed ripe bananas
1 cup sugar	(2 to 3 medium)
2 to 3 tablespoons lemon	2 egg whites
juice	Pinch of salt

Sprinkle gelatin on $\frac{1}{4}$ cup water and let stand 5 minutes. Combine sugar with remaining $\frac{3}{4}$ cup water and heat to boiling. Add gelatin and stir until gelatin and sugar are dissolved. Cool and add fruit juice.

Mash bananas or press through fine sieve. Combine with sirup mixture. Pour into refrigerator tray and freeze to a mush (45 to 60 minutes). Add salt to egg whites and beat until stiff. Add frozen banana mixture and beat until blended.

Pour into 2 freezing trays; moisten bottoms of trays and place on coldest shelf in freezing compartment. Wash bowl and beater, and place in refrigerator to chill.

When mixture is frozen stiff (1 to $1\frac{1}{2}$ hours), turn into chilled bowl and break up with spoon. Beat until fluffy and well blended but not melted. Quickly pile sherbet back into two trays. Moisten bottoms of trays; return to freezing compartment. Freeze to serving consistency. See Note under Avocado Milk Sherbet.

BREADFRUIT

Description. The seedless variety of breadfruit *(Artocarpus incisus)* commonly found in Hawaii and known as the Hawaiian breadfruit is a large round or oblong fruit 4 to 8 inches in diameter. The rind, green in the unripe stage, acquires a greenish-brown or yellow tint as the fruit matures. The slightly fibrous pulp surrounds a tough central core. It is white, bland, and starchy in the green stage; light yellow and sweet in the ripe stage.

History. Breadfruit trees were brought to Hawaii from Tahiti before the coming of the white man. G. P. Wilder states in *The Fruits of the Hawaiian Islands* that the first suckers were brought by Hawaiians who landed at Ewa and carried them across the mountains to one of the chiefs of Oahu.

In Hawaii the breadfruit has never been as important an article of diet as in Tahiti and other South Pacific islands. Most ancient sites of civilization, especially those around Kona and Hilo, show large areas of cultivated breadfruit trees, and the trees now grow wild in hot, moist sections of all the Islands. Their Hawaiian name, *ulu*, corresponds to the Tahitian *uru*.

Nutritive Value. Breadfruit has about the same quantity of total carbohydrate (starch and sugar) as sweetpotato and taro, and more than the white potato. Like bananas, breadfruit when fully ripe give no test with iodine, indicating that all the starch has been changed to sugars.

The Hawaiians preferred their breadfruit ripe or at least half ripe, not in the unripe or starchy state as did the Tahitians and Samoans. The Polynesians used breadfruit as a supplement to or a substitute for taro and sweetpotato, and there seems to be no reason why it should not be so used today.

The calcium content of breadfruit is higher than that of white potatoes and about the same as that of sweetpotatoes and taro. Compared with the other fruits in this book, breadfruit is considered to be only a fair source of calcium, but when eaten in large quantities it

Fruit and foliage of the breadfruit *(Artocarpus incisus)*. ⅓ natural size.

can supply a good proportion of the day's needs. Different varieties have been found to be good to fair sources of phosphorus and poor sources of iron.

Breadfruit is a poor source of provitamin A. It is a good source of thiamine and niacin, and when eaten in quantities that meet much of the daily caloric needs, it constitutes an important source of these two vitamins. Breadfruit is a fair source of riboflavin and ascorbic acid.

Supply. Breadfruit may be purchased in the stores at intervals from July to February and occasionally at other times during the year. Although breadfruit seem to be plentiful, the quantity reaching the market does not exceed the demand.

Use. Breadfruit may be picked in the *tepau* stage, when the milky sap comes to the surface but the fruit is still firm, green, and starchy. If a riper and therefore sweeter stage is desired, it may be picked when the rind is yellow-green or just beginning to turn brown. It is always cooked before it is eaten. If boiled in the *tepau* stage, it is an excellent food resembling the potato in flavor. If it is to be used ripe, the fruit should be kept until it becomes soft and the outside rind partially brown in color.

The ancient Hawaiians cooked the whole breadfruit in the underground oven or *imu.* Today it is usually baked or steamed.

After cooking, it may be made into *poi* and used as a substitute for taro *poi,* or may be combined with it. However, breadfruit *poi* is not as commonly used by the Hawaiians as by other Polynesians.

Tests to date indicate that breadfruit does not yield a good frozen product, cooked or uncooked.

BOILED GREEN BREADFRUIT

YIELD: 6 servings

4 cups diced green breadfruit	¾ teaspoon salt
3 cups boiling water	Pepper to taste
3 tablespoons margarine	

Choose a breadfruit which is mature but is firm and has a green rind. Peel and dice. Add water and cook until tender (about 1 hour). Uncover and evaporate excess water; season with margarine, salt, and pepper, or with salt and sugar. Serve as a starchy vegetable.

BAKED RIPE BREADFRUIT

Choose a ripe breadfruit which is soft, the small sections of rind flattened and partially brown in color. Wash, and place whole breadfruit in pan containing just enough water to keep pan from burning. Bake in moderate oven (350° F.) for 1 hour. Remove from oven, pull out core and stem, cut breadfruit into halves, and season with margarine, salt, and pepper, or margarine and sugar.

If preferred, remove core and stem before baking, place 1 tablespoon margarine and 1 tablespoon sugar in cavity, and replace stem during baking period.

STEAMED BREADFRUIT

Remove stem, core, and also the rind if desired, from a soft-ripe breadfruit. Cut into halves or quarters, place on pan, and steam in covered steamer until thoroughly cooked (1 to 2 hours). Season with margarine, salt, and pepper.

Note. Breadfruit may be steamed in a pressure-cooker saucepan, for 10 to 15 minutes at 15 pounds pressure for very soft fruit. Firm-ripe fruit should be cooked 20 to 30 minutes, depending upon the degree of ripeness.

FRIED BREADFRUIT

Slice steamed or baked breadfruit into pieces $\frac{1}{2}$ inch to $\frac{3}{4}$ inch thick and fry in hot fat until golden brown. The breadfruit may be rolled in flour before frying.

BREADFRUIT CHOWDER   YIELD: 6 servings

2 thin strips bacon	$\frac{1}{4}$ cup diced raw carrots
$\frac{1}{4}$ cup sliced onion	2 teaspoons salt
2 cups diced raw green breadfruit	3 cups boiling water
	1$\frac{1}{4}$ cups milk

Cut bacon into small pieces and fry until light brown. Add onion, and cook until light brown. Add vegetables, salt, and water. Boil until vegetables are tender. Add milk and serve hot.

BREADFRUIT AND COCONUT PUDDING   YIELD: 6 servings

1 coconut	3 cups soft-ripe breadfruit pulp
1 cup coconut water and boiling water	$\frac{1}{4}$ cup sugar
	$\frac{1}{4}$ teaspoon salt

Prepare coconut milk (see Index). If it does not yield 1$\frac{1}{2}$ cups extracted milk, add water to make that amount. Combine with breadfruit pulp, sugar, and salt. Place in oiled baking dish and bake 1 hour or more at 350° F. Serve warm with coconut cream (Thick Coconut Milk, see Index).

Fruit, foliage, and cross section of the carambola *(Averrhoa carambola)*.

CARAMBOLA

Description. The carambola *(Averrhoa carambola)* is a translucent yellow or yellow-green fruit 4 to 5 inches long and about 2 inches in diameter. It has five prominent ribs which make it distinctly star-shaped in cross section. The thin waxy rind encloses a very juicy pulp and several smooth brown seeds. There seem to be two varieties—the sweet carambola and the sour carambola. Both are quite mild in flavor.

History. Like many other fruits found in Hawaii, the carambola is believed to be native to the Malayan archipelago and to have been brought to America at an early date. The history of its introduction into Hawaii is not known, but the tree may have been brought from southern China by early Chinese immigrants or by sandalwood traders.

Nutritive Value. Carambola juice contains about 10 percent sugar. In comparison with other fruit juices it is a poor source of calcium, phosphorus, and iron. The carambola is a poor source of provitamin A, thiamine, and riboflavin, a fair source of niacin, and a good source of ascorbic acid.

Supply. The carambola is grown chiefly as an ornamental shrub and the fruit is rarely found in the stores. It ripens during November and December.

Use. The watery pulp of the fruit has a pleasant taste and is refreshing when eaten ripe or used in an iced drink. An unpleasant bitter flavor develops when the fruit or juice is cooked or canned. Although the fruit contains a small quantity of pectin, it is not recommended for making jelly.

Though it may be frozen successfully as a purée, it is not highly recommended.

CARAMBOLA JUICE

YIELD: 2 cups

15 to 20 carambolas

Wash carambolas and cut into small pieces. Press through sieve or squeeze in coarse cloth to obtain juice.

SWEET CARAMBOLADE

YIELD: 6 servings

2 cups sweet carambola juice   4 cups cold water

Mix juice with water and pour over cracked ice.

SOUR CARAMBOLADE

YIELD: 6 servings

2 cups sour carambola juice   4 cups cold water
¾ cup sugar

Add sugar and water to juice and pour over cracked ice.

SOUR CARAMBOLA SHERBET

YIELD: 1½ quarts

1 teaspoon unflavored gelatin   2 cups boiling water
¼ cup cold water   1½ cups sour carambola juice
⅞ cup sugar   1⅓ tablespoons lemon juice

Sprinkle gelatin on cold water and let stand 5 minutes. Add sugar to boiling water and boil for 5 minutes. Remove from heat and add gelatin, stirring until dissolved. Cool to lukewarm, add fruit juice, and freeze, using 8 parts of ice to 1 of salt.

CARISSA
(Natal Plum)

Description. The fruits of the carissa *(Carissa grandiflora)* are oval or round and vary in size and shape; a typical fruit is about an inch in diameter and an inch and a half long. The skin of the fully ripe fruit is bright crimson streaked with darker red; it is thin and bruises easily. The flesh is deep red, or crimson, with white mottling. In the center there are about twelve small brown flat seeds. The fresh fruit has a mild, slightly pungent flavor, is slightly granular in texture, and is somewhat astringent.

When bruised, broken, or cut, the fruit and branches exude a white latex that is harmless except that it may be irritating if it comes in contact with the eye.

History. The carissa, a native of Natal Province in the Union of South Africa, is often called the Natal plum. It was introduced into

Hawaii in 1905 by the Hawaii Agricultural Experiment Station a year after the Bureau of Plant Industry obtained it from Africa. During the following years, many carissa plants were distributed throughout the Islands. The thorny shrub with dark-green leaves, fragrant white blossoms, and bright-red fruit is used especially for hedge planting.

Nutritive Value. The carissa has relatively large quantities of sugar and sufficient acid and pectin to make a good jelly. It is an excellent source of ascorbic acid, containing somewhat more than the average orange. However, it is only a fair to poor source of all the other vitamins investigated. No analyses of the various minerals in carissa are available.

Supply. The fruit are not sold on the Honolulu market. The plant produces fruit the year round, usually yielding the best crop in the spring, but a rather large planting is necessary to obtain a quantity of fruit at one time.

Use. The carissa may be used fresh but it is more satisfactory when cooked. The cooked juice and pulp have an unpleasant milky-red appearance but become an attractive bright red when cooked with sugar. The jelly has an exquisite red color with a delicate, characteristic flavor suggestive of raspberry. The sauce, made by straining or sieving the stewed fruit and cooking it with sugar, is preferred by some to cranberry jelly.

The white latex in the fruit forms a rubbery, sticky ring around the pan in which the carissa are cooked. To remove, rub with a piece of dry paper towel or with a coarse bit of cloth soaked with salad oil. Do not use steel wool or an abrasive powder as these make the sticky substance more difficult to remove.

CARISSA JELLY

YIELD: 4 six-ounce glasses

4 cups crushed or sliced ripe carissa

2 cups water

Sugar (1 cup to each cup of strained juice or pulp)

Wash and drain fruit; slice, or crush if fruits are very soft. Add water, bring to boiling point and simmer until fruit is tender (15 to 20 minutes). Drain through jelly bag for clear jelly, or put through sieve or fine colander for jelly containing pulp.

Measure juice or juicy pulp; use equal amount of sugar. Bring juice to boiling point. Add sugar and boil until mixture sheets from the spoon (see Appendix III). Pour into sterilized jelly glasses and seal with paraffin.

Note. If tart jelly is desired, use $\frac{3}{4}$ cup sugar for each cup juice and pulp. Using some carissa that are not fully ripe also makes a more tart jelly.

Fruit, foliage, flower, and cross section of the carissa *(Carissa grandiflora)*.

JELLIED CARISSA SALAD

1 tablespoon unflavored gelatin
¼ cup cold water
1¼ cups boiling carissa juice or
    juice and pulp
    (see Carissa Jelly)

¼ cup sugar
¼ teaspoon salt
2 tablespoons lemon juice
1¼ cups chopped celery

Sprinkle gelatin on cold water and let stand 5 minutes. Dissolve sugar, salt, and softened gelatin in boiling carissa juice. Allow to cool and add lemon juice. When mixture begins to thicken, add chopped celery. Turn into mold and chill. When firm, unmold on bed of shredded lettuce and garnish with mayonnaise.

CARISSA CREAM

YIELD: 6 servings

1 tablespoon unflavored gelatin
½ cup cold water
1 cup carissa juice
    (see Carissa Jelly)

¼ cup sugar
Pinch of salt
1 cup whipping cream

Sprinkle gelatin on cold water and let stand 5 minutes. Bring carissa juice to boiling point, add softened gelatin, sugar, and salt. Stir until gelatin and sugar dissolve, then chill until slightly thickened. Fold in whipped cream, turn into mold, and chill until firm. Unmold and serve as a dessert.

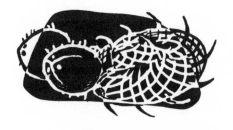

COCONUT

Description. The coconut is the large, one-seeded fruit of the coco palm *(Cocos nucifera)*. The endosperm within the nut is the edible portion. A fibrous husk encloses the brown, hard-shelled nut which is usually 4 to 5 inches in diameter.

G. P. Wilder states in *The Fruits of the Hawaiian Islands:* "After being fertilized by the adjacent staminate flowers, the hollow interior of the shell becomes filled with sweet water. The spherical fruits gradually increase to from 4 to 8 inches in diameter. The endosperm, at first an opaque, jelly-like substance, forms in the inner walls of the shell, and gradually absorbs the water; it attains a firm thickness of from 0.25 to 0.5 inch. This is known as the coconut meat and forms an important article of diet for the Polynesian people."

In the early stages the meat is soft and jelly-like and is known as "spoon coconut" because nowadays it usually is eaten with a spoon. Later the meat becomes crisp and firm. In this book the watery liquid within the coconut is called water and the juice obtained by squeezing the grated coconut meat is called milk.

History. Most varieties of coconuts growing in Hawaii at the present time were introduced within the last century. Those growing in the Islands when the first missionaries arrived were small and of inferior quality and are often called Hawaiian coconuts to distinguish them from later introductions. This original strain or variety was probably brought to Hawaii by early Polynesians when they migrated from islands to the south.

Botanists have classified all kinds of coconuts as one species, *Cocos nucifera*. The Hawaiians and South Sea Islanders distinguish the varieties by differences in the color and texture of the husk, the thickness and flavor of the meat, and the amount of oil present.

Although the Hawaiian Islands are near the northern limit for growing coconuts, many excellent varieties thrive, but they do not bear as abundantly here as farther south.

Nutritive Value. The chemical composition of the edible portion of the coconut varies with the stage of development.

The water from immature coconuts has been shown to contain as much calcium as some fruits and vegetables, if not more. The phosphorus content is variable, and the iron content is negligible. Immature coconuts contain from 300 to 700 cubic centimeters of water.

Coconut water has an acid reaction. Samples of water from very young coconuts having little or no meat were found to have an average pH of 4.7. The water from within fresh young coconuts contains ascorbic acid in small amounts, but, compared with fruits generally, it is a very poor source of this vitamin.

The southern Polynesians and other peoples inhabiting tropical islands where coconuts grow make great use of coconut water, and early voyagers in the Pacific area relate that they drank the coconut water offered them by the natives. Water taken directly from an uncontaminated nut is normally sterile.

The meat begins to form when the nut is about six months old, that is, six months after the spathe has opened. As the meat develops, its water content gradually decreases, the fat and total ash increase, and the protein and sugar content show less marked changes. The meat of mature coconuts contains a relatively large amount (5.4 percent, fresh basis) of crude fiber.

Analyses of expressed coconut milk show it to be high in fat (27 percent) and low in protein (4 percent), and it has been pointed out that neither coconut water nor coconut milk are comparable to cow's milk in organic nutrients or calcium and phosphorus content.

The mature coconut is a poor source of calcium and a good source of phosphorus and iron. Coconut has no yellow pigment, or provitamin A, and in the mature state it is a poor source of thiamine and riboflavin and a fair source of niacin. It has little or no ascorbic acid.

Supply. Though the retail demand is small, coconuts are available the year round and may be purchased in most of the larger stores and at many roadside stands.

Use. At present many coconuts are used commercially for preparing coconut chips, coconut sirup, and coconut candy, but no significant amount of copra is made in Hawaii.

Though a plentiful supply of coconuts is normally available, they are not generally used in the home, undoubtedly because of the labor and time required to prepare them.

Considerable time and effort may be saved by using a grater such as the Hawaiians and Samoans use. Figure 1 shows a grater made from a piece of steel about 9 inches long, 2 inches wide, and $\frac{1}{4}$ inch thick, having one end flattened and slightly curved upward with teeth a little less than $\frac{1}{8}$ inch wide and $\frac{1}{8}$ inch long. This metal piece may be nickel

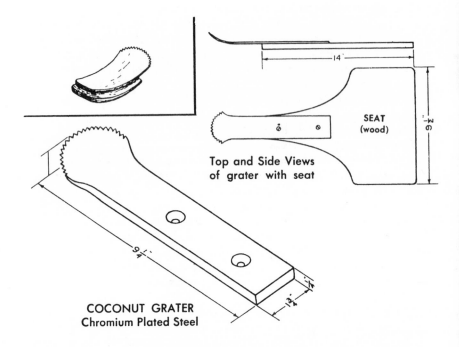

Fig. 1. —Diagram of coconut grater. Insert shows grater made from coconut shell.

or chromium plated in order to prevent rusting. The metal grater may be screwed to a straight piece of wood or, better, to a wooden seat.

The coconuts should be broken into halves, but when using the type of grater just described the meat should not be removed from the shell. To use the coconut grater, place it on a chair or stool, sit on the wooden seat to hold it firmly in place, hold a piece of coconut in both hands, and scrape the meat over the metal grater so that the grated coconut drops into a pan placed underneath the grater.

Kenneth P. Emory of Bernice P. Bishop Museum, Honolulu, recommends making a grater from coconut shell as follows: "With a saw, cut a thick, rectangular section of coconut shell, $1\frac{3}{4}$ inches wide and about 3 inches long. The cutting edge should be curved, beveled on the under side, and toothed by a row of 10 to 15 notches, about $\frac{1}{8}$ inch deep (Fig. 2, above). The notches are most readily made with a file but it is possible to cut the bevel and notches with a knife. The grater should be reinforced by a second rectangular section of shell placed under it." The completed grater should be screwed, or lashed with rope or heavy twine, to a board and may be used in the same manner as the metal grater.

For some uses the coconut may be prepared by putting the meat through a vegetable grater or meat grinder. Fresh frozen grated coconut may be used in all recipes requiring grated fresh coconut, but it is usually a coarser product than that prepared at home when a fine grater is used.

For high-quality grated coconut, the brown skin must be removed and the pieces grated on a fine grater.

Coconuts are used in different stages of ripeness. Spoon coconuts may be chilled before serving—the liquid to be drunk through a straw and the meat to be eaten with a spoon. Halves of young coconuts with adhering soft meat may be used as individual containers for fruit cocktail.

The milk extracted from the grated coconut meat may be used in place of cow's milk in curries, coconut puddings, and frozen desserts. The Hawaiians add coconut milk to cooked chicken, fish, or taro leaves

Fig. 2.—Coconut and Fruit Cocktail.

near the end of the cooking process. Polynesians also combine the milk with bananas, breadfruit, sweetpotatoes, and taro in baked or steamed puddings. Commercially frozen coconut milk may be used in all recipes calling for coconut milk.

Fresh grated coconut may be used in candy, cake icings, and pies.

Grated coconut may be successfully frozen by packing firmly to press out the air and sealing in airtight containers (or packages). For convenient use, wrap the grated coconut in $\frac{1}{2}$-cup or 1-cup portions before placing them in a larger package. Freeze with or without added sugar. For directions on freezing, see Appendix I.

HOW TO CRACK AND GRATE A COCONUT

YIELD: 3 cups grated coconut from 1 medium-size nut

Choose a coconut which is mature but contains a good amount of liquid. Remove outer husk. Using a nail or ice pick, open the 2 soft eyes and drain the liquid into a cup for future use. Vigorously tap the nut with a hammer around its circumference until shell cracks open. Grate with Hawaiian-type grater (see Fig. 1) without removing meat from shell.

If a Hawaiian grater is not available, remove meat from shell, cut off the brown skin and grate or put through a food chopper using a medium-coarse blade.

Finely grated coconut for toppings, cakes, and confections may be prepared as follows: After draining water from the coconut as directed above, place whole coconut in an oven at a temperature between 250° F. and 275° F. for 1 hour This causes the meat to shrink slightly from the shell and facilitates removal of meat in large pieces. The coconut may crack in the oven.

Remove from oven and cool. Tap the shell over the entire surface with a hammer to help loosen the meat. Crack and break into 2 to 4 large pieces. Pry out the kernel with a screwdriver. (Do not use a sharp-pointed knife as it may break.)

Peel off the brown skin, wash, and drain. Grate on a medium grater and use at once or freeze for future use.

THICK COCONUT MILK

Add $\frac{1}{4}$ to $\frac{1}{2}$ cup coconut water or boiling water to 3 cups grated coconut. Let stand 15 minutes. Knead with hands and squeeze through 2 thicknesses of cheesecloth or a poi cloth, removing as much milk as possible.

Thick Coconut Milk is used in Hawaiian dishes or over puddings.

THIN COCONUT MILK

Add 1 to $1\frac{1}{2}$ cups coconut water or boiling water to 3 cups grated coconut.

Thin Coconut Milk is used in the Curry Sauce or Haupia.

TOASTED COCONUT CHIPS

Pierce the eyes of the coconut and drain off the liquid. Heat coconut in oven for 1 hour at 300° F. Remove from oven and let cool. Tap surface with a hammer until the shell breaks into pieces. Remove coconut meat in large pieces; it is not necessary to remove thin brown peeling. Slice very thin and spread on shallow baking pan.

Place in oven at 200° F. for 2 hours. Reduce the heat as low as possible to keep coconut from becoming too brown. Heat at lower temperature for another 2 hours or longer, stirring several times. Remove from oven, let cool, and store in airtight jars in a cool place. Serve as an appetizer or in place of salted nuts.

COCONUT SIRUP*   YIELD: $1\frac{1}{2}$ cups

1¼ cups water	¼ teaspoon cream of tartar
3 cups grated coconut (1 nut)	1½ cups sugar

* Trimble, Alice P., *Emergency Uses of Coconut*, Hawaii Univ. Agr. Ext. Serv. Home Econ. Cir. 137, 1942.

Prepare coconut and coconut milk as described above, saving water from coconut and adding sufficient boiling water to make a total of $1\frac{1}{4}$ cups. To 1 cup of extracted coconut milk, add sugar and cream of tartar. Stir until sugar is dissolved. Cook slowly without stirring until temperature reaches 224° F. Then stir in additional $\frac{1}{4}$ cup extracted coconut milk. Cook until the temperature again reaches 224° F. Stir in another $\frac{1}{4}$ cup and cook to same temperature. If darker sirup is desired, add another $\frac{1}{4}$ cup and again cook to 224° F. By adding milk several times the sirup is caramelized, which gives it a light-brown color and a more distinct coconut flavor.

Remove sirup from the range, pour into sterilized jars, and seal immediately. Sirup made for immediate use may be put in jars that are not airtight, if they are kept in the refrigerator. Use with waffles or as a topping for frozen desserts.

COCONUT AND FRUIT COCKTAIL   YIELD: 6 servings

3 coconuts with spoon meat	6 ginger or orchid
3 to 4 cups mixed fresh	blossoms
Hawaii fruits	

Remove husks from coconuts and rub shells with rough cloth or paper towel to clean and remove bits of husk. Saw each coconut into halves and chill. Support half shells with circles of twisted ti leaves (see Fig. 2).

Fill coconut halves with a combination of three of the following fruits chilled and sweetened to taste: banana, lychee, mango, guava, orange, papaya, passion fruit, pineapple, and sweet Surinam cherry. Decorate ti leaf with ginger or orchid blossom.

The soft meat of the coconut may be eaten with the fruit.

HAWAIIAN CURRY DINNER   YIELD: 6 to 8 servings

$\frac{1}{4}$ cup sliced onion (1 medium)	$\frac{3}{4}$ cup milk
6 tablespoons margarine	$\frac{3}{4}$ cup chicken broth
6 tablespoons flour	$1\frac{1}{2}$ cups Thin Coconut Milk
2 to 3 teaspoons curry powder	4 cups boned chicken or
$1\frac{1}{4}$ teaspoons salt	serving pieces (4 to 5
2 teaspoons grated ginger root	pounds stewing chicken)

Fry onions in margarine until slightly browned. Remove from range and add flour, curry powder, salt, and grated ginger root. Stir until well blended and smooth. Return to range. Gradually add milk and broth, stirring constantly until sauce is thickened (about 10 to 15 minutes); mixture should be very thick. Add coconut milk and boned chicken

5 7

Hawaiian Curry Dinner and Accompaniments.

and reheat. Taste and reseason with salt and other seasonings if needed. Thin with broth or milk if necessary. Serve with rice and any of the curry dinner accompaniments (see below).

SHRIMP CURRY

1½ to 2 pounds cooked shrimps may be used in place of chicken in the above recipe. Prepare sauce as directed, but use double amount of milk (1½ cups), omit chicken broth, and add 1 to 1½ tablespoons lemon juice.

CURRY DINNER ACCOMPANIMENTS   YIELD: 6 to 8 servings

Use as many as you wish of the following:

¾ to 1 cup mango chutney
1 cup shredded or grated
   fresh coconut
¼ pound chopped peanuts,
   almonds, or
   macadamia nuts
¼ pound crisp bacon, crumbled
2 hard-cooked eggs,
   finely chopped

¼ cup chopped preserved
   ginger
1 large green pepper, chopped
1 cup chopped green onion
1 cup raisins
1 cup sliced banana
¼ cup sweet pickle relish

Serve accompaniments in Oriental bowls or sauce dishes arranged down the center of the table. Place china soup spoon or small silver spoon beside each bowl.

MALIHINI DINNER   YIELD: 6 servings

6 coconuts
1¼ cups chicken broth
2 small onions
¼ bay leaf
1 teaspoon salt
4 sprigs parsley, minced
1 green pepper, chopped
¾ cup milk
¾ cup thin coconut milk (p. 42)
1 almond-size ginger root,
   grated

¼ to ½ teaspoon prepared
   mustard
¼ to 1 teaspoon Worcestershire
   sauce
6 tablespoons margarine
6 tablespoons flour
1 to 1½ cups grated coconut
1½ to 2 cups diced pineapple
3 cups boned chicken

Saw off ¼ of each coconut at the top (see Fig. 3). Grate out about half of the meat. Using 3 cups of grated meat, prepare Thin Coconut Milk. Simmer chicken broth with onion, bay leaf, salt, parsley, and green pepper for 10 to 15 minutes. Remove bay leaf and add milk, coconut milk, ginger, mustard, and Worcestershire sauce.

Melt margarine, add flour, and stir until well blended. Gradually stir in the liquid mixture and cook until thickened. Taste and reseason. Add large pieces of boned chicken, 1 to 1½ cups grated coconut, and pineapple. Fill prepared coconut shells with hot mixture. Place each shell on inverted Mason jar ring in shallow baking pan or roaster. Cover each with coconut lid, seal with flour-and-water paste. Add 1 inch depth of water in baking pan. (Keep water at about the same level throughout the baking period.) Bake at 375° F. until heated through (1½ to 2 hours).

Place each shell on ti leaf stand on individual plate and serve. Make ti leaf stand by twisting together 3 or 4 ti leaves, 18 to 20 inches long. Tie ends to make a ring (Fig. 4).

Serve with rice and tossed salad.

COCONUT TARTLETS

YIELD: 36 tarts

¼ cup margarine
1 cup sugar
¼ teaspoon salt
¾ teaspoon vanilla

3 cups grated fresh coconut (1 nut)
1 recipe Plain Pastry

Cream margarine, sugar, salt, and vanilla together. Add coconut and mix well. Form small balls, using 1 teaspoonful of the mixture for each, and chill.

Fig. 3.—Preparation of Malihini Dinner: a) Filled coconut sealed with paste of flour and water, standing on Mason jar ring, ready for oven. b) Coconut placed on a stand for serving, with paste removed. c) Malihini Dinner ready to be eaten.

Prepare Plain Pastry. Cut into rounds with a 2-inch cutter. Place chilled balls of coconut mixture on half of the rounds. Wet edges of remaining rounds, place on top of coconut balls and press edges together, using tines of a fork. Bake at 450° F. until delicately browned (15 minutes). Serve with frozen desserts or tea.

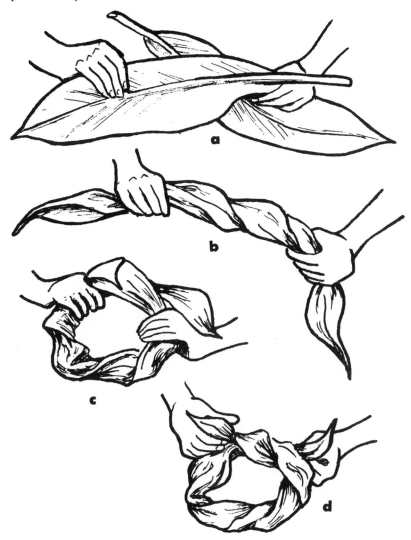

Fig. 4.—How to make a ti leaf stand: a) Grasp leaf in each hand and place together with pointed ends outward. **b)** Twist together, covering stem ends. **c)** Form circle of twisted leaves. **d)** Entwine ends to make ring.

WAIKIKI COCONUT CREAM PIE

YIELD: 8-inch pie
(5 to 6 servings)

1 baked pie shell (see Index)
¼ cup sugar
3 tablespoons cornstarch
   Pinch of salt
2 cups milk

3 egg yolks, slightly beaten
1 tablespoon margarine
¼ teaspoon vanilla
¾ cup whipped cream
¾ cup grated fresh coconut

Combine sugar, cornstarch, and salt in saucepan. Gradually stir in the milk, and cook over moderate heat, stirring constantly until well thickened (15 to 20 minutes). Remove from heat.

Stir small amount of hot mixture into egg yolks; slowly pour back into remaining hot mixture, beating vigorously. Add margarine and cook 2 minutes longer. Remove from heat; cool, stirring occasionally, and add ½ teaspoon vanilla. Pour cooled filling into pie shell and place in refrigerator. Just before serving, spread with whipped cream and sprinkle with coconut.

COCONUT SPANISH CREAM PIE

YIELD: 9-inch pie
(5 to 6 servings)

1 baked pie shell (see Index)
4 teaspoons unflavored gelatin
3 tablespoons cold water
2 cups scalded milk
3 egg yolks, beaten
¼ cup sugar

Pinch of salt
¼ teaspoon vanilla
2 to 3 cups grated fresh
   coconut (1 nut)
3 egg whites
2 tablespoons sugar

Sprinkle gelatin on cold water and let stand 5 minutes. Add sugar and salt to egg yolks and a small amount of the scalded milk. Stir gradually into rest of milk and cook until mixture coats the spoon. Do not allow mixture to boil. Remove from heat, add softened gelatin, and stir until dissolved. When cool, stir in the vanilla and half of the grated coconut. Chill until mixture begins to thicken.

Beat egg whites until stiff, gradually beat in 2 tablespoons of sugar, and fold into thickened gelatin mixture. Sprinkle top with remaining coconut. Chill until firm (3 to 4 hours). A thin layer of whipped cream may be spread over pie before topping with coconut.

COCONUT CANDY I

YIELD: 1½ pounds

3 cups sugar
1 cup water

3 cups grated fresh coconut
Pinch of salt

Combine sugar and water. Heat slowly to the boiling point, stirring until sugar is dissolved. Remove crystals from side of pan with a fork wrapped in a small piece of damp cloth, or cover pan for 2 to 3 minutes until crystals are dissolved. Continue boiling until mixture spins a thread (235° F.) and forms a soft ball in very cold water.

Stir in coconut; bring to boiling point and boil slowly for 10 minutes longer (244° F.). Remove from heat, cool slightly, and beat vigorously until creamy and of proper consistency to drop from a teaspoon onto waxed paper.

This candy is soft immediately after making but hardens slightly after standing.

COCONUT CANDY II

YIELD: 1½ pounds

3 cups grated fresh coconut	**Pinch of salt**
(1 nut)	**½ cup milk**
3 cups sugar	**¾ teaspoon vanilla**

Thoroughly mix coconut, sugar, salt, and milk. Place over low heat, bring to boil, and cook about 5 minutes or until mixture appears glassy around edge of pan. Stir frequently. Remove from heat and beat 5 minutes until partially cool. Add vanilla and drop from teaspoon onto waxed paper. This candy should be used the day it is prepared—it becomes sugary after standing.

COCONUT CONFECTION

YIELD: ¾ pound

4 cups grated fresh coconut	**¼ cup white corn sirup**
(p. 41)	**2 egg whites**
⅞ cup sugar	

Use only finely grated coconut meat. Place grated coconut, corn sirup, and sugar in top of double boiler. Cook over rapidly boiling water, stirring constantly until translucent (about 5 minutes). Add egg whites and cook until mixture feels sticky when tried between the fingers (10 minutes). Spread in a wet pan, cover with wet paper, and let cool. Then chill by placing in refrigerator.

Dip hands into cold water, then shape mixture into balls. Using about 1½ tablespoons for each, make 40 to 50 balls. Warm a baking sheet and rub lightly with paraffin or oil. Place balls on sheet, flatten slightly, and bake in slow oven (300° to 325° F.) until delicately browned (30 to 40 minutes). Loosen at once with spatula to prevent sticking to pan.

ROYAL HAWAIIAN DELIGHT
See Index.

HAWAIIAN AMBROSIA
See Index.

GUAVA DELICIOUS
See Index.

BANANAS WITH COCONUT SAUCE
See Index.

COCONUT CUSTARD

YIELD: 4 servings

2 eggs
4 tablespoons sugar
2 cups milk
¼ teaspoon vanilla

3 tablespoons Coconut Sirup
4 tablespoons finely grated
   fresh coconut

Beat eggs slightly, add sugar, milk, and vanilla; mix thoroughly. Place about 2 teaspoons of coconut sirup in bottom of each custard cup. Divide custard mixture evenly into 4 cups. Sprinkle each custard with a tablespoon of grated coconut.

Place custard cups in pan of hot water and bake at 350° F. until set (30 minutes). Test by inserting point of knife in center of custard: if it comes out clean, custard is done. Remove from hot water at once.

HAUPIA (COCONUT PUDDING)

YIELD: 16 2-inch squares

9 cups grated coconut (3 nuts)
3 cups coconut water and
   boiling water

¼ cup plus 1 tablespoon
   cornstarch
⅓ cup sugar

Prepare coconut and Thin Coconut Milk.

If 4½ cups of expressed coconut milk are not obtained, add water to make that amount. Mix cornstarch with sugar and add sufficient coconut milk to make smooth paste. Heat remaining milk to boiling and gradually add cornstarch paste, stirring constantly. Continue cooking until mixture thickens. Pour into greased 8-inch-square layer-cake pan and allow to cool. Cut into 2-inch squares and serve Hawaiian style (on pieces of ti leaf).

HAOLE HAUPIA

YIELD: 16 2-inch squares

6 cups grated coconut (2 nuts)
2 cups coconut water and
   boiling water OR 4 cups
   frozen coconut milk and
   ½ cup water

6 tablespoons cornstarch
6 tablespoons sugar
1½ cups milk
1½ cups grated fresh coconut
¾ teaspoon vanilla

Prepare coconut and Thin Coconut Milk.

If 3 cups of expressed coconut milk are not obtained, add milk to make that amount. Mix cornstarch with sugar and add ½ cup coconut milk, stirring to make a smooth paste. Combine remaining coconut milk with milk, heat to boiling and gradually add cornstarch paste, stirring constantly. Continue cooking until mixture thickens. Cool, add 1⅓ cups grated coconut and ¾ teaspoon vanilla. Pour into greased 8-inch-square layer-cake pan and cool. Cut into 2-inch squares and serve Hawaiian style (on pieces of ti leaf).

BREADFRUIT AND COCONUT PUDDING
See Index.

PAPAYA-COCONUT PUDDING
YIELD: 6 servings

3 cups grated coconut (1 nut)	7 tablespoons cornstarch
1 cup coconut water and	¾ cup sugar
boiling water	¾ teaspoon salt
1½ cups thick papaya pulp	

Prepare coconut and Coconut Milk. If 1½ cups expressed coconut milk are not obtained, add water to make that amount.

Press papaya pulp through medium sieve, then measure. Mix cornstarch, sugar, and salt together and gradually stir into papaya. Cook over low heat, stirring constantly, until mixture thickens. Add coconut milk and cook until it will barely hold its shape when cool (5 to 10 minutes). It should not be stiff enough to mold. Pour into deep dish or pan and chill. Thick Coconut Milk may be served over pudding if desired.

HAWAIIAN COCONUT SHERBET
YIELD: 6 to 8 servings

2½ cups Thick Coconut Milk	½ cup sugar
¼ cup white corn sirup	¼ teaspoon vanilla
2 egg whites	Pinch of salt
1 teaspoon unflavored gelatin	

Chill egg whites and corn sirup in medium-size bowl. Sprinkle gelatin over ½ cup of coconut milk (use small saucepan) and let stand 5 minutes. Add sugar; heat until sugar and gelatin are dissolved. Cool and add 2 cups coconut milk; pour into refrigerator tray and freeze to a mush. Beat egg whites and sirup mixture until very stiff (7 to 10 minutes). Add frozen coconut mixture, beating until just blended.

Pour into freezing tray; moisten bottom of tray and place on coldest shelf in freezing compartment. Wash bowl and beater and place in refrigerator to chill.

When mixture is frozen stiff (1 hour), turn into chilled bowl and break up with spoon. Beat until fluffy and blended, but not melted. Quickly pile sherbet back into two trays. Moisten bottoms of trays and return to freezing compartment. Freeze to serving consistency. See Note under Avocado Milk Sherbet.

DRESSINGS FOR FRUIT COCKTAILS AND FRUIT SALADS

AVOCADO-GRAPEFRUIT SALAD DRESSING   YIELD: 6 servings

½ cup mashed avocado pulp	¼ cup grapefruit juice OR
¼ teaspoon salt	⅓ cup lime juice

Press avocado through coarse sieve if pulp is fibrous. Add other ingredients and mix until smooth paste is obtained. Chill and serve over lettuce.

FAVORITE FRENCH DRESSING   YIELD: 1½ cups

¼ cup brown or granulated sugar	½ teaspoon Worcestershire sauce
½ teaspoon dry mustard	½ cup tomato catsup
⅛ teaspoon black pepper	¾ cup salad oil
¼ teaspoon celery salt, if desired	¼ cup vinegar
½ teaspoon salt	1 small onion, chopped (¼ cup)

Measure dry ingredients into small mixing bowl and blend well. Add remaining ingredients and beat with rotary beater. Store in screw-topped jar. Just before using, shake jar vigorously. Use 1 or 2 tablespoons per individual serving, or if used on tossed salad, only enough to make the leaves glisten.

HAWAIIAN DRESSING FOR FRUIT SALAD   YIELD: 1 cup

¼ cup sugar
2 tablespoons cornstarch
¼ tablespoon dry mustard
¼ teaspoon salt
¾ cup pineapple juice

1 egg
1 tablespoon lemon or
    lime juice
1 tablespoon margarine

Combine dry ingredients in top of double boiler. Add pineapple juice gradually and cook over direct heat until very thick. Place over hot water. Beat egg in custard cup, add 1 tablespoon of hot mixture, beat and add 2 tablespoons more, beat again. Pour this into mixture in double boiler and cook a few minutes longer, stirring constantly. Add lemon juice and margarine; stir and cool. Serve on any fruit salad.

Variation. Whip ½ cup cream and fold into an equal amount of dressing.

HONEY AND CELERY SEED DRESSING   YIELD: 1½ cups
FOR FRUIT SALAD

¾ cup sugar
1 teaspoon paprika
1 teaspoon dry mustard
¼ teaspoon salt
1 tablespoon celery seeds

1 teaspoon grated or
    chopped onion
¼ cup honey
1 tablespoon lemon juice
¼ cup cider vinegar
1 cup salad oil

Combine all ingredients in a pint jar in order given. Stir until well blended.

Variation. Substitute 2 to 4 tablespoons toasted sesame seeds in place of celery seeds. See Sesame Seed Dressing below for method of toasting seeds.

SESAME SEED DRESSING FOR FRUIT SALAD*   YIELD: 1½ cups

¾ cup sugar
1 teaspoon paprika
¼ teaspoon dry mustard
1 teaspoon salt
¼ cup cider vinegar
1 cup salad oil

¼ teaspoon Worcestershire
    sauce
1 drop Tabasco sauce, if desired
2 teaspoons grated onion,
    if desired
¼ cup sesame seeds, toasted

Combine all ingredients, except sesame seeds, in pint jar in order given. Stir until well blended. Toast sesame seeds in frying pan over low heat, stirring constantly until delicate brown. Store in airtight

* Contributed by Elsie M. Boatman, Professor of Home Economics, University of Hawaii.

container until ready to use. Pour amount of dressing to be used into bowl, allowing about 2 tablespoons per serving. Add 1 to 2 teaspoons sesame seeds per serving, stir well, and pour over fruit salad.

FRUIT COCKTAIL DRESSING

Juice of 2 lemons (about ¼ cup)   ½ cup sugar

Squeeze juice into glass measuring cup. Add sugar gradually, stirring constantly until it is sirupy. Amount of sugar depends upon amount of juice. Bottle and chill. Just before serving, pour 1 or 2 tablespoons of dressing over fruit cocktail.

Note. Lime juice, which requires more sugar, may be used in place of lemon juice.

FIG

Description. Different varieties of figs (*Ficus carica*) vary greatly as to size and color of flesh and skin. The leading variety grown in Hawaii is known as the Turkish Brown or Brown Turkey, commonly called Turkey. It is pear-shaped, 1½ to 3 inches in diameter, and mainly of a mahogany-red color if exposed to the sun. Others are green with cheeks or streaks of mahogany-red-brown.

The thin, easily bruised skin encloses a soft pinkish-white pulp and many tiny seeds. The fruit matures from a large number of small flowers which develop within a protecting shell. This accounts for the small hollow in the center of the pulp, around which can be seen a layer of seeds and tiny dried flowers. The flavor is sweet and pleasing.

History. The fig has been under cultivation for centuries and is mentioned in the oldest European literature. Some variety was probably introduced into Hawaii near the beginning of the nineteenth century; Don Marin records in his diary that figs were growing in his garden in 1809. This variety, which was probably the Mission fig of the Spanish missionaries in California, did not thrive at that time, but it was later reintroduced and is now reported to be growing satisfactorily. The University of Hawaii Agricultural Experiment Station has tested a number of other varieties, the most successful of which is probably the Kadota, a white fig. The Turkey is grown on all the Islands.

Nutritive Value. Compared with other fruits in this book, figs are a fair source of calcium and a poor source of phosphorus and iron. The Brown Turkey variety was found to be a poor source of all vitamins tested.

Supply. The supply of best quality figs does not equal the demand at any time. They ripen throughout the year, but the main season is from May through July.

Use. Practically all the figs produced here are used in the fresh state. Superior flavor and texture may be had only in thoroughly ripened figs, therefore they should not be used in the half-ripe stage. A favorite way of serving them is a breakfast or dessert fruit with cream and sugar. Excellent shortcakes, sherbets, puddings, preserves, and jams may be made from them.

PRESERVED FIGS
YIELD: 2 quarts

4 pounds firm-ripe figs	**5¼ to 6 cups sugar**
(20 to 25)	**4 cups water**

Wash figs and remove blemishes. (Figs may be peeled, if desired. Blanch 1 to 2 minutes in boiling water, cool quickly in cold water, and remove skins.) Boil sugar and water 5 minutes in broad, shallow kettle. Add figs; cover and simmer until fruit is transparent and glossy (1½ to 2 hours). Carefully turn figs several times during cooking. When tender, bring to brisk boil. Pack in hot sterilized jars. Cover with boiling sirup, and seal at once.

Variation. ¼ to ½ cup lemon, sliced paper-thin and cut in quarters, may be combined with sirup before figs are added.

FIG JAM
YIELD: 1½ quarts

5 pounds figs	**5¼ cups sugar**
(10 cups)	**¼ cup lemon juice**

Peel and chop figs. Add sugar, then divide quantity into two kettles. Cook slowly until fruit is thick (about ½ hour). Stir frequently to prevent scorching; add lemon juice just before removing from range. Pour into hot sterilized jars and seal with paraffin.

If desired, add 1½ tablespoons finely chopped fresh ginger root to the sugar.

PICKLED FIGS*

4 pounds ripe figs
(about 24 large)
Whole cloves
4 cups sugar
2 cups vinegar

2 cups water
4 2-inch sticks of cinnamon OR
¼ teaspoon ground
cinnamon

Wash figs. Stick one or two whole cloves in each fig. Cook sugar, vinegar, water, and cinnamon together until sirup is fairly thick (about 10 minutes). Add figs and cook slowly until tender (about 1 hour). Place figs in hot sterilized jars, cover with boiling sirup, and seal at once.

FIG COCKTAIL

YIELD: 6 servings

2¼ pounds ripe figs (4½ cups)
½ to 1 cup orange juice
2 tablespoons sugar

2 tablespoons lemon juice OR
1¼ tablespoons lime juice

Wash, peel, and cut figs into small pieces. Add sugar to fruit juice and pour over figs. Chill 1 hour before serving in cocktail glasses.

FIG-LYCHEE COCKTAIL

YIELD: 6 servings

3 cups peeled and cubed
fresh figs (1½ pounds)
1½ cups shelled lychees
(36 fruit)

2 tablespoons lemon juice
¼ cup lychee juice
Sugar to taste

Wash, peel, and dice figs. Cut lychees into quarters. Combine all ingredients and chill for 1 hour before serving in cocktail glasses.

FIG FILLING FOR CAKE

YIELD: ¾ cup

2 cups diced figs (8 medium)
¾ cup water

¾ cup sugar
2¼ tablespoons lemon juice

Cook figs and water together until figs are soft enough to mash against side of pan. Add sugar and lemon juice, and cook until mixture is thick enough to spread (about 10 minutes). Cool and spread between layers of yellow or white cake.

*Contributed by University of Hawaii Agricultural Extension Service.

ISABELLA GRAPE

Description. The Isabella grape (*Vitis labrusca*), the only variety of grape grown commercially in Hawaii, is an American seedling grape of the slipskin type. The bunches are from 4 to 6 inches long and are very firmly packed. When ripe, the individual grapes are a deep purple-black with a light-blue bloom, and are about a half inch in diameter.

History. Many different types of grapes are grown throughout the world. They were introduced into Hawaii at an early date—Captain Vancouver spoke of leaving grapevine plants and orange plants on March 4, 1792. Don Marin wrote of his vineyard in his diary in 1815, and recorded the making of wine. The grape Marin grew probably was the Mission grape from California, which has since disappeared.

The date of the introduction of the Isabella grape into Hawaii is not known, but must have been after 1816, the date of the discovery of the Isabella as a seedling in South Carolina. Because it is grown largely by the Portuguese in Hawaii, it is often erroneously called a Portuguese or European type of grape.

Nutritive Value. Grapes are of value in the diet largely because of their distinctive flavor and refreshing qualities. Their sugar content is similar to that of other fresh fruits of the same water content.

Isabella grapes were analyzed for minerals in two different conditions: with seeds and skins removed, and with only seeds removed. The product with only seeds removed was a better (although only poor) source of calcium, phosphorus, and iron, than the one with both seeds and skins removed.

The Isabella grape is a fair source of thiamine, and a poor source of provitamin A, riboflavin, niacin, and ascorbic acid.

The acids of Concord grapes (a related variety) consist of approximately 60 percent malic acid and 40 percent tartaric acid, a large portion of which exists in the form of alkali salts.

Supply. The supply available for the market is irregular and does not equal the demand. The main crop comes on the market in summer, but some fruit may be seen during other months of the year.

Use. This grape may be eaten fresh or used in making jelly, grape juice, or conserves.

GRAPE JUICE

YIELD: 2 quarts

5 pounds grapes   **Water to cover**

Choose underripe grapes for jelly or firm-ripe grapes for juice to drink. Wash, and place in a large kettle with enough water to cover fruit. Mash fruit with potato masher and cook slowly until fruit is very soft (about 20 minutes). Pour into jelly bag and hang to drip. For clear juice, do not squeeze bag.

Juice may be canned or bottled for future use (see Appendix II). If sweetened product is desired, measure juice, bring to boiling point and add $\frac{1}{3}$ to $\frac{1}{2}$ cup sugar for each quart of juice. Boil 3 minutes, pour into hot sterilized jars or bottles, and seal at once.

Grape Butter (below) may be made from pulp.

GRAPE JELLY

YIELD: 5 cups or
10 four-ounce glasses

3 cups juice   **2$\frac{1}{4}$ to 3 cups sugar**

Choose underripe grapes and prepare grape juice as described at top of page. Use Jelmeter to determine amount of sugar required (see Appendix III). Grape jelly should be made in small quantities, not over 3 cups at a time. Place juice in large shallow kettle (preferably of 4-quart capacity). Boil juice rapidly for 5 minutes. Add sugar and bring quickly to boiling point; remove scum and boil vigorously about 5 minutes. As mixture nears jelling stage, test frequently with metal spoon or thermometer. Pour jelly into hot sterilized glasses and seal with paraffin.

GRAPE CONSERVE

YIELD: 2$\frac{1}{2}$ quarts

4 pounds grapes (6$\frac{3}{4}$ cups   5 cups sugar
pulp and skins)   2$\frac{1}{4}$ cups chopped walnuts
2$\frac{1}{2}$ cups seedless raisins

Wash, and remove skins of ripe grapes. Soften pulp by heating slowly until seeds can be pressed out by rubbing pulp through sieve. After seeds are removed, combine pulp and skins. Look over raisins, remove stems, and wash. Combine grapes, raisins, and sugar. Boil for 5 minutes. Add nuts and cook 5 minutes longer. Pour into hot sterilized jars and seal with paraffin.

GRAPE BUTTER

YIELD: 1 quart

3 cups grape pulp from jelly   3 cups sugar
extraction, measured after $\frac{1}{4}$ cup grape juice
removal of seeds

To remove seeds and skins press grape pulp through a coarse sieve. Measure; add sugar and grape juice. Cook slowly until thick. Stir frequently to prevent burning. Pour into hot sterilized glasses and seal with paraffin.

SPICED GRAPES   YIELD: 6 cups

3 pounds grapes (2 quarts when removed from stems)	**1 teaspoon ground cinnamon**
	½ teaspoon ground allspice
¼ cup water	**¼ teaspoon ground cloves**
¼ cup vinegar	**4½ cups sugar**

Wash and drain grapes. Remove grapes from stems, then measure. Remove skins and place skins and pulp in separate saucepans. Add water to skins, cover saucepan, and boil gently until skins are tender (about 20 minutes). Cook pulp (without water) in another covered saucepan until seeds separate easily (about 20 minutes). Strain to remove seeds.

Combine tenderized skins and juice with strained pulp and remainder of ingredients. Cook 20 to 25 minutes, until mixture gives a good jelly test (see Appendix III). Pour into sterilized glasses or jars and seal with paraffin.

GRAPEFRUIT

Description. Grapefruit (*Citrus paradisi* Macf.) are globose, 3 to 4 inches in diameter, and their color is yellowish-green or sometimes yellow with a pink flush. A rind that varies in thickness from thin to very thick encloses the edible flesh containing a large amount of inner pulp made up of segments of juice sacs. The flesh may be light yellow, pink, or reddish in color and mildly acid to very acid in flavor, depending upon the variety, the environment, and sometimes the maturity. Some fruits are seedless; others have a large number of seeds.

The term pomelo is sometimes used instead of grapefruit, but the latter term has come to be the one most favored. It originated because the fruit grows in clusters somewhat like grapes, despite the great disparity in size between the two fruits.

The term shaddock is usually reserved for the extremely large, coarse, occasionally almost inedible, form of the species, also called pummelo (as distinct from pomelo).

History. The first description of grapefruit came from Barbados in 1750. The fruit was described as being originally a sport of the larger fruited shaddock (pummelo). The name grapefruit was used in Jamaica by 1814 or earlier and has come to be generally accepted. It is reported that grapefruit have never been found wild in eastern Asia, which is the home of the shaddock.

Grapefruit or pomelo were introduced into Florida by the Spanish and were first grown commercially about 1880.

Grapefruit were introduced into Hawaii at an early, unknown date. Hillebrand, whose observations in Hawaii were made before 1871, stated that *Citrus decumana* (the shaddock) "have been so long in cultivation as almost to claim a place in the flora of the Islands." In 1934 Pope listed ten varieties of grapefruit growing in the Hawaii Agricultural Experiment Station plots. Seven of these were brought from Florida or California by the Station in 1905 and 1906; the other three were later introductions.

Nutritive Value. Grapefruit is a fair source of calcium but a poor source of phosphorus and iron. The local fruit, like that grown elsewhere, proved to be an excellent source of ascorbic acid but a poor source of other vitamins studied.

Supply. Grapefruit of excellent quality can be grown in Hawaii. In addition to that grown in home gardens, small commercial supplies have been appearing on the Honolulu markets since about 1960. Most of the fruit grown commercially is the Ruby Red and comes from Kihei, Maui. A smaller amount of a light yellow (marsh) variety comes from Waianae, Oahu.

Use. The quality of these fruits is sometimes improved if they are stored at room temperature: the grapefruit for a few days, the pummelo for 10 to 15 days.

The grapefruit is especially desirable as a breakfast fruit but may be used in many ways when a fresh, tart citrus is desired.

THREE FRUIT MARMALADE
See Index.

AVOCADO-FRUIT SALAD
See Index.

GRAPEFRUIT SECTIONS

YIELD: 2 servings

1 grapefruit
1 tablespoon powdered
sugar, if desired

Mint leaves, papaya ball, or
guava jelly, if desired

Wash and dry fruit. Using a sharp paring knife remove rind and membrane, paring it as you would an apple. Loosen segments of grapefruit by slipping knife down on either side of the membrane. Remove seeds. For serving, arrange sections in a circle on a plate or in a sherbet glass. Chill. Just before serving add sugar and garnish as desired.

GRAPEFRUIT HALVES

YIELD: 2 servings

1 grapefruit
1 tablespoon sugar, if desired

Mint leaves, papaya ball, or
guava jelly, if desired

Wash and dry fruit. If necessary trim off a thin slice of rind to provide a flat base. Cut fruit crosswise halfway between stem and blossom ends. With grapefruit knife or sharp paring knife, cut around edge to separate pulp from skin. Loosen pulp by cutting on each side of membrane. With scissors or knife cut center core at base of fruit. Remove core and membranes. Replace any disarranged section. Chill. Just before serving, add sugar and garnish as desired.

CANDIED GRAPEFRUIT PEEL

YIELD: 75 to 100 pieces

2 grapefruit
2 cups sugar
1½ cups water

1 teaspoon grated fresh ginger,
if desired
⅛ teaspoon salt
½ tablespoon unflavored gelatin
2 tablespoons cold water

Cut grapefruit peel into ¼ inch strips. Cover with water and boil 15 to 20 minutes. Drain and repeat two more times. Measure drained peel and for each 2 cups of strips add the amounts of sugar, water, ginger and salt given above. Bring to a boil, lower heat to simmer and cook until peel is transparent. If sirup evaporates before peel is transparent, add more water. In the meantime, soften gelatin in 2 tablespoons cold water for 5 minutes. When peel is done, remove from heat and add the gelatin. Stir until dissolved. Let stand until cool. Drain and roll peel in granulated sugar.

75

CATTLEY GUAVA
(Strawberry Guava)

Description. In addition to the common lemon guava, there are two kinds of strawberry guava in Hawaii—the dark-red strawberry guava (*Psidium Cattleianum*) and another (*Psidium Cattleianum* var. *lucidum*), which is pale yellow when ripe.

Both are small round fruits ¾ to 1½ inches in diameter and are quite different from the common guava. The center of the fruit is filled with a very juicy pulp and numerous small hard seeds. The sweet and somewhat acid flavor has but faint resemblance to that of the strawberry.

Because the red guava produces a deep-brown stain difficult to remove, care should be used in handling the fruit.

History. Although the Cattley guava is a native of Brazil, it has been carried to all parts of the world. According to Otto Degener, the "Psidium Chinense" listed by Andrew Bloxam as "brought alive from England in the 'Blonde' to the Sandwich Islands and transplanted May 28, 1825" was probably the strawberry guava. Introduced into Europe by way of China, it is sometimes called the "Chinese guava." It is commonly called the Cattley guava after the English horticulturist, William Cattley, who fostered its cultivation in England in the early 1800's.

The fact that both Cattley guavas have Hawaiian names—the yellow variety being called *waiawi* and the red *waiawi ulaula*—also indicates they were early introductions which became widely distributed and well established.

Because of its beautiful glossy deep-green leaves, the strawberry guava is sometimes grown in private gardens as an ornamental shrub. The yellow variety grows to a greater height, sometimes 30 to 40 feet. Both kinds thrive best at elevations from several hundred feet to one or two thousand feet above sea level.

Nutritive Value. The Cattley guava is a poor source of calcium, phosphorus, and iron. Tests have shown that it is a poor source of

Fruit, foliage, and cross section of the Cattley guava *(Psidium Cattleianum).*

provitamin A, thiamine, and riboflavin, and a fair source of niacin. Both red and white varieties are excellent sources of ascorbic acid.

Supply. The fruit ripens at intervals from May to November. It is seldom found in stores.

Use. The strawberry guava is sweeter and has a more delicate flavor than the common guava. It is delightful eaten fresh. The juice of ripe or half-ripe fruit makes a pleasing acid drink or, combined with the juice of pineapple or citrus fruits, a delectable punch.

The strawberry guava makes a deep-red jelly. If a few are added to half-ripe common guava, a very attractive pink jelly is obtained. Strawberry guava marmalade and preserves are delicious but laborious to prepare because the fruit is small, and removing the seeds is tedious.

STRAWBERRY GUAVA JUICE
YIELD: 6 to 7 cups

5 pounds strawberry guavas   **Water to cover fruit**

Choose firm-ripe fruit. Wash, remove blossom ends and blemishes. Slice, and place in large kettle with enough water to barely cover fruit. Boil until very soft (15 to 20 minutes). Pour into jelly bag and hang to drip. For clear juice, do not squeeze bag.

Use juice for jelly or punch. It may be canned, bottled, or frozen (see Appendix II).

STRAWBERRY GUAVA JELLY
YIELD: 2½ to 3 cups

4 cups strawberry guava juice   **3 to 4 cups sugar**

Prepare juice as directed for making Strawberry Guava Juice. To determine the amount of sugar to be used test with Jelmeter or apply pectin test (see Appendix III). Place juice in a shallow kettle of a capacity at least four times the volume of the juice. Boil rapidly 5 to 10 minutes, add sugar, and bring to boiling point. Boil vigorously 15 to 20 minutes. Remove scum that forms as mixture boils. As it nears the jelling stage, test frequently with a metal spoon or thermometer (see Appendix III). Pour jelly into hot sterilized glasses and seal with paraffin.

STRAWBERRY GUAVA-ADE
YIELD: 6 servings

6 cups ripe strawberry guava   **1 to 1½ cups sugar**
juice

Prepare juice as directed for making Strawberry Guava Juice, using fully ripe fruit. Mix ingredients, pour over cracked ice, and serve.

STRAWBERRY GUAVA PUNCH

YIELD: 6 servings

3 cups strawberry guava juice   2 cups orange juice
¾ cup lemon juice   1 to 1½ cups sugar

Combine ingredients, stir until sugar is dissolved, pour over cracked ice, and serve.

COMMON GUAVA

Description. The guava (*Psidium guajava*) is a medium-size round, or oblong, yellow fruit 1½ to 3 inches in diameter, with a thick, coarse, edible rind surrounding a mass of seeds imbedded in a firm, soft pulp. The flesh varies from white to yellow to red. Though the fruit may be either sweet or sour, it always has a distinctive, characteristic flavor.

History. The guava is a native of tropical America and the name is derived from the Haitian name for the fruit, *guayaba*.

Although Thrum's *Hawaiian Annual* has stated that the common lemon guava was brought to the Islands from Australia by G. Montgomery in 1851, some variety was undoubtedly growing in the Islands before that, for Sereno E. Bishop, a clergyman born in 1824, at Kailua, Hawaii, says in *Reminiscences of Old Hawaii* that guavas were a choice fruit in the later 1830's and did not become wild until 20 years later.

At present the guava is the most common wild fruit in the Islands. It grows well under conditions unfavorable for many plants, and in some places has become a pest.

Since 1951 horticulturists of the Hawaii Agricultural Experiment Station have been planting and selecting guavas from among wild ones growing in the Islands and have also introduced a large number of plants and seeds from Africa, the Philippines, and other areas. If the guava is to be utilized extensively for commercial purposes, plantings of selected, fine-quality fruit with high ascorbic acid content should become available in place of the uncertain and variable product which grows wild.

Fruit and foliage of the common guava *(Psidium guajava)*.

Nutritive Value. Because of the high nutritive value of guavas, use should be made of those which grow wild at the lower altitudes on all the Islands.

Compared with other fruits described here, the guava is a poor source of calcium, phosphorus, and iron. The common lemon guava is a fair source of niacin, and a poor source of provitamin A, thiamine, and riboflavin. The wild guavas growing in Hawaii vary greatly in ascorbic acid content, some having two to five times as much as others. However, all may be considered excellent sources of this vitamin.

The thick rind portion of the common guava contains more ascorbic acid than the pulp and seeds, both because there is a greater proportion of the rind than pulp in each guava, and because per unit of weight the rind is richer in ascorbic acid.

A watery extract of guavas, called guava juice (see below), is an excellent source of ascorbic acid. Samples prepared in the laboratory have tested from 70 to 130 milligrams of ascorbic acid per 100 cubic centimeters.

Fifty samples of home-canned guava products—14 of guava pulp, 6 of pulpy juice, and 30 of strained juice*—were collected from different localities on four islands. The samples varied in their ascorbic acid content from 32 to 130 milligrams per 100 cubic centimeters with an average of 66 milligrams. This means that one may easily obtain a day's quota of ascorbic acid from $\frac{1}{3}$ to $\frac{2}{3}$ of a cup of home-prepared guava juice or pulp.

The mild, less acid guavas yield juices that are especially good for infant and child feeding.

A number of factors influence the vitamin content of prepared guava products, e.g.: (1) the original ascorbic acid content of the guavas; (2) the quantity of water used in preparation of the product; (3) contact or contamination with metals, especially copper which tends to destroy the vitamin; (4) exclusion or inclusion of air; (5) length of storage; and (6) contact with light.

To obtain guava juice and pulp of high vitamin content the following recommendations should be observed:

(1) Use guavas of good quality at the height of fall season and prepare as soon after picking as possible.

(2) Use aluminum, stainless steel, or enamel kettles that are not chipped.

(3) Cook sliced guava in only enough water to nearly cover them.

(4) For draining the pulp use a strainer free from copper or rust (an aluminum or enameled colander is satisfactory if followed by a poi cloth for pulp or a jelly bag for juice).

* Most of the samples were obtained by the home agents of the University of Hawaii Agricultural Extension Service in 1943, through the courtesy of Kathryn Shellhorn, Assistant Director.

(5) Fill bottle or container to be used for canning to very top with boiling hot product before putting on cover or cap (space at top is then a vacuum and not air containing oxygen).

(6) Put juice in dark bottles if you cannot store it away from light (juice in light-colored bottles seems to keep as well as in dark bottles if well protected from light).

(7) Use preserved products within a year. Even when juice is properly prepared, sealed, and stored, there seems to be a slow but definite loss of ascorbic acid (approximately 30 percent in one year according to experiments).

Cooked guava juice or pulp keeps well in the refrigerator. However, it is well not to store it for more than a week. Experiments have shown that bottled guava juice once opened, even though tightly covered, loses ascorbic acid rather rapidly. Flavor and color do not seem impaired after a month's storage but guava juice has been found to lose in two weeks one- to two-thirds of its original ascorbic acid content, and in four weeks to lose practically all.

The high nutritive value of the guava is due to its large amount of ascorbic acid. This fact merits the development of varieties having maximum values of ascorbic acid, and commercial freezing and canning of guava products on a large scale.

Supply. Guavas are most plentiful from June to October, but small quantities may be obtained at other seasons. They are not found in Honolulu stores at any time of the year, for no attempt is made to pick and offer them for sale. Some wild guavas are very tart, others mild.

As wild guavas disappear from areas near the city, and horticultural varieties of good quality are developed and cultivated, they may become available in markets, although careful handling will be required for this perishable fruit.

Use. For all recipes using guava shells or purée, only large juicy guavas yield satisfactory products. The small dry guavas often obtained during a dry season are suitable only for juice. The common guava, when of good quality, may be used as a fresh fruit, served with sugar for dessert and shortcake, or combined with citrus fruit and pineapple in cocktails and salads.

Guava juice makes an excellent substitute for orange or tomato juice in child feeding and is a pleasing addition to punch.

The guava is highly prized for jelly making because of its distinctive flavor and high pectin and acid contents. It also may be used for butters, jams, marmalades, and preserves. The confection called guava paste may be made by evaporating strained guava pulp until it is very thick. This paste is sold commercially in many parts of the world.

Guavas may be successfully frozen in several forms (see Appendix I).

GUAVA JUICE

YIELD: 6 to 7 cups

5 pounds guavas (40 to 45 lemon-size fruit or 60 to 75 small fruit)
Water to barely cover fruit

Choose half-ripe or firm-ripe guavas. Wash; remove blossom ends and blemishes. Slice, and place in large kettle with enough water to barely cover the fruit. Boil until fruit is very soft (15 to 20 minutes). Pour into jelly bag and hang to drip. For clear juice, do not squeeze the bag.

Use juice for jelly or punch. It may be canned or bottled for future use (see Appendix II).

GUAVA JELLY

YIELD: 3½ cups
(7 four-ounce glasses)

4 cups guava juice   4 to 4½ cups sugar

Choose half-ripe sour guavas, and prepare Guava Juice as described above. Use Jelmeter to determine amount of sugar required (see Appendix III). Place juice in large shallow kettle, preferably of 4-quart capacity. Heat juice 5 to 10 minutes. Add sugar and bring quickly to boiling point; remove scum. Boil vigorously about 15 minutes. As mixture nears jelling stage, test frequently with a metal spoon or thermometer (see Appendix III for jelly tests). Pour jelly into hot sterilized glasses and seal with paraffin.

GUAVA TOPPING

YIELD: 1½ cups

4 cups sliced guava shells   ¼ cup water
1 cup sugar

Only large, ripe, juicy guavas should be used; otherwise product is unsatisfactory.

Wash guavas. Cut into halves, pare thinly, and remove pulp and seeds with spoon. Cut shells in slices ⅓ inch wide. Mix sugar and water, bring to a boil, and add guava slices. Bring to a full boil and cook 2 minutes. Reduce heat and cook 3 minutes longer or until soft but not mushy. To retain shape of slices, amounts larger than this should not be cooked at one time. Pour into hot sterilized jars and seal or quick-freeze. This is excellent to serve over vanilla ice cream.

Seeds may be sieved from the fresh pulp and the pulp then combined with 1 part sugar to 4 or 5 parts purée, according to sweetness desired. Mix thoroughly and quick-freeze (see Appendix I).

GUAVA SAUCE

YIELD: 6 servings

12 to 15 soft ripe guavas   Pinch of salt
½ cup water   ½ to ¾ cup sugar

Wash and peel guavas. Cut into halves, remove pulp, and press through strainer, discarding seeds. Cook pulp and shells in water until tender. Add sugar and salt a few minutes before guavas are done. Serve hot or cold as a breakfast or dessert fruit. It may also be served with shortcake, or over ice cream, bread, or cereal puddings.

Sauce may be canned for future use (see Appendix II for canning instructions).

KETAMBILLA-GUAVA JELLY
See Index.

PURPLE-FLESHED JAVA PLUM AND GUAVA JELLY
See Index.

GUAVA SIRUP*
YIELD: 2 quarts

4 cups guava juice
4 cups water

6 cups sugar

Prepare juice as directed in recipe for Guava Juice. Combine juice, water, and sugar. Boil slowly until proper consistency for sirup (about 30 minutes). Pour into hot sterilized jars and seal. Use on griddle cakes, as sauce for ice cream and puddings, or in Guava Milk Shakes.

GUAVA PUREE
YIELD: 1 to 1¼ cups

2 pounds guavas

Purée made from pulp and seeds has a smoother texture and better color than that made from whole guavas or from shells. Shells may be used for marmalades, guava topping, and guava pickle.

Wash guavas, cut into halves, and remove pulp and seeds with a spoon. Remove seeds from pulp by using a food mill or by pressing through a fine sieve. Since very small seeds may go through food mill, it is advisable also to put the pulp through a poi cloth or fine sieve.

This purée may be used fresh, or may be frozen or canned for future use. (See Appendix I for directions on freezing and Appendix II for instructions on canning.)

GUAVA MARMALADE
YIELD: 1½ pints

4 cups guava strips
(15 to 20 medium guavas)
3 cups sugar
2 cups water

½ lemon, cut in small paper-thin slices (¼ cup)
1 teaspoon grated fresh ginger root, if desired

*Contributed by University of Hawaii Agricultural Extension Service.

Wash guavas; remove stems, blossom ends, and blemishes. Cut fruit into halves. Remove soft inner pulp and seeds with a spoon (see note below). Cut guava shells into strips $\frac{1}{4}$ inch wide, combine with sugar, ginger, and $1\frac{1}{2}$ cups water. (The amount of water needed depends upon the juiciness of the guavas.) Add $\frac{1}{2}$ cup water to lemon slices. Allow both mixtures to stand 2 to 3 hours to increase liquid and pectin.

Cook lemon over low heat until rind is transparent, adding more water if necessary. Add lemon to guava mixture and boil rapidly in large saucepan for 20 to 25 minutes until juice sheets from spoon and gives jelly test (see Appendix III). Pour into hot sterilized jars and seal immediately, or pour into jelly glasses and cover with paraffin.

Note. Put pulp through sieve to remove seeds. This purée may be frozen or canned for use in ice cream, mousse, pudding sauce, or cake icing (see Appendix I and Appendix II).

GUAVA BUTTER
YIELD: $1\frac{1}{4}$ quarts

8 cups cooked guava pulp (pulp left from jelly making may be used)

6 cups sugar

3 tablespoons grated fresh ginger root

6 tablespoons lemon juice (2 lemons) or

4 tablespoons lime juice

$\frac{3}{4}$ teaspoon ground allspice

$\frac{3}{4}$ teaspoon ground cinnamon

Press guava pulp through sieve before measuring quantity. Add remaining ingredients. Cook slowly until thick, stirring frequently to prevent burning. Pour into hot sterilized jars. Cool and cover with paraffin.

GUAVA-PAPAYA BUTTER
YIELD: $2\frac{3}{4}$ quarts

1 cup thin orange slices

1 cup water

4 cups raw or cooked guava purée

4 cups fresh papaya pulp

8 cups sugar

$\frac{1}{4}$ cup lemon juice

Cut orange in very thin slices as for Orange Marmalade. Add water and soak 4 hours or overnight. Boil orange slices and water gently in covered saucepan until rind is tender (about 15 minutes). See recipe for preparation of Guava Purée. Combine guava and papaya pulp and cook, stirring frequently, until some of the water has evaporated. Add cooked orange slices, sugar, and lemon juice, and cook until thick. Mixture must be stirred frequently during cooking to prevent scorching. Pour into hot sterilized jars, and seal with paraffin.

Note. If guavas are very sour, lemon juice may be omitted.

GUAVA-PINEAPPLE MARMALADE

YIELD: 2 pints

4 cups sliced guava shells
(about 15 to 20 guavas)
3¼ cups sugar
1 cup water
¾ teaspoon finely chopped
fresh ginger root

¼ cup thin lemon slices OR
3½ tablespoons lime or
lemon juice
2 cups shredded fresh
pineapple

Wash and prepare guava as for Guava Marmalade. Cut shells into strips ¼ inch wide; combine with sugar, ginger, and ½ cup water. Add ½ cup water to lemon slices. Allow both mixtures to stand 2 to 3 hours. Cook lemon over low heat until rind is transparent, adding more water if necessary. Add lemon and pineapple to guava mixture. Boil rapidly in large saucepan until juice sheets from spoon (about 25 minutes) and gives a jelly test (see Appendix III). Pour into hot sterilized jars and seal immediately, or pour into jelly glasses and cover with paraffin.

GUAVA CATSUP*

YIELD: 2½ quarts

5 medium-size onions, finely
sliced
¼ cup water
3 quarts guava pulp (pulp left
from jelly making may be
used)
2 large cloves garlic,
finely sliced

5 small peppers, finely chopped
(seeds removed) OR
¼ teaspoon ground pepper
1¼ to 2 cups vinegar
4 teaspoons ground allspice
3 teaspoons ground cinnamon
2 teaspoons ground cloves
6 cups sugar
1 tablespoon salt

Cook onion in water until soft. Combine all ingredients and cook for 30 to 40 minutes. Pour into hot sterilized jars and seal immediately. This is excellent to serve with meat or avocados.

GUAVA SHELL PICKLES

YIELD: 2 pints

30 large firm-ripe guavas
4½ cups sugar
1 cup water
¾ cup mild vinegar

2 dozen whole cloves
2 sticks cinnamon OR
¼ teaspoon ground
cinnamon

Wash guavas. Remove stems, blossom ends, and blemishes; cut into halves. Remove pulp and save for use in guava desserts. Tie spices in

*Contributed by University of Hawaii Agricultural Extension Service.

piece of cheesecloth. Combine guava shells and all other ingredients and let stand 3 to 4 hours, then simmer for 1 hour or longer until fruit is tender. Remove spice bag. Pour into hot sterilized jars and seal.

GUAVA JELLY MINT SAUCE
YIELD: 1 cup

1 6-ounce glass guava jelly (¾ cup)

3 tablespoons orange juice

1 tablespoon lemon juice

1 tablespoon finely chopped mint leaves

Cut guava jelly into ⅜-inch cubes. Add orange juice, lemon juice, and mint leaves, and stir lightly with a fork, breaking cubes as little as possible. Let stand an hour or longer and serve with roast lamb.

GUAVALETS*
YIELD: 1¼ pounds

2 cups strained cooked guava pulp

3½ cups sugar

1 teaspoon unflavored gelatin

2 tablespoons cold water

¼ cup chopped walnuts

Cook pulp and sugar together over very slow heat until mixture is very thick and seems to leave sides of pan. Stir frequently to prevent burning. Soak gelatin in cold water for 5 minutes, melt over hot water, and add to guava pulp. Remove from heat, cool, add nuts, and pour into buttered shallow pan. When cold, cut into 1-inch squares and wrap each piece in waxed paper.

FRESH GUAVA FRUIT PUNCH
YIELD: 6 servings (1 cup each)

¼ finger of fresh ginger root

1½ cups water

6 ripe guavas

3 cups medium-strength tea

¾ cup sugar

¾ cup orange juice

¼ cup pineapple juice

¼ cup lemon juice

Peel ginger root and chop fine. Boil with ½ cup water until strong ginger flavor is obtained. Cool and strain through cloth, squeezing ginger root. Wash guavas, cut, and press through fine sieve to remove seeds. Combine all ingredients, stir until sugar is dissolved, and pour over cracked ice before serving.

ALOHA PUNCH
YIELD: 12 servings (1 cup each)

2 cups sugar

4 cups water

2¾ cups unsweetened guava juice

2¾ cups orange juice

1½ cups lemon juice

1¼ cups shredded pineapple

Grated rinds of 1 orange and 1 lemon

A few drops of red coloring

*Contributed by University of Hawaii Agricultural Extension Service.

Boil sugar and water for 3 minutes. Cool and add fruit juice and pineapple. Pour over cracked ice before serving.

MANOA FRUIT PUNCH

YIELD: 100 servings (⅓ cup each)

3 tablespoons finely chopped ginger root (1 ounce)
7 cups water
7 cups sugar
6 cups guava juice
9 cups fresh pineapple juice

10 cups orange juice (4 dozen small oranges)
2 cups lemon juice (1 dozen lemons)
¼ cup finely chopped fresh mint leaves

Boil chopped ginger with 3 cups of water until a strong ginger flavor is obtained. Cool and strain through cloth, squeezing ginger root. Boil sugar and remaining 4 cups of water to make a sirup, then cool. Combine all ingredients and pour over cracked ice. If punch is too strong dilute with cold water.

GUAVA MILK SHAKE

YIELD: 1 large glass

1 cup milk
1¼ tablespoons guava sirup OR
4 tablespoons guava juice

1¼ teaspoons sugar, if juice is used

Combine ingredients, pour into glass jar, and cover with tight-fitting lid. Chill and then shake ingredients thoroughly. Serve in a tall glass. If juice is used and product curdles, beat vigorously with rotary beater.

BANANA-GUAVA NECTAR
See Index.

HOT SPICED GUAVA JUICE

YIELD: 3¼ cups

2 cups water
12 cloves
¼ teaspoon crushed cinnamon stick
¼ teaspoon grated fresh ginger root, if desired

8 circles lemon rind, size of a dime
2 cups guava juice
2 teaspoons lemon juice
Sugar to taste

Tie spices loosely in cloth. Add spices and lemon rind to water. Cover and boil for 10 minutes. Add fruit juices and sugar and heat to simmering point. Serve hot in small punch glasses, placing a piece of lemon rind in each glass.

GUAVA DUMPLINGS

9 thoroughly ripe sour
guavas
1 cup sugar
⅛ teaspoon salt
1 teaspoon cinnamon,
if desired
1 to 2 tablespoons margarine

2 cups flour
2 teaspoons double-acting
baking powder
1 tablespoon sugar
¾ teaspoon salt
⅓ to ⅔ cup fat
¼ to ½ cup water

Wash guavas, remove blemishes, and peel if desired. Cut into halves, scoop out pulp, and press through sieve. Add sugar and ⅛ teaspoon salt and let stand a few minutes.

Sift flour with baking powder, sugar, and ¾ teaspoon salt. Cut in half of fat until thoroughly blended. Cut in other half until pieces are about the size of small peas. Sprinkle with only enough water to make small balls which hold together.

Divide dough into 6 equal parts, place on slightly floured board and roll each one into a round piece about 5 inches in diameter and ⅛ inch thick. Place 3 half shells of guava, one inside the other, in the center of a piece of dough. Fill with pulp. Sprinkle with cinnamon and dot with margarine. Lift edges of dough, moisten, and press together at top. Place in greased muffin tins or baking dish. Bake at 425° F. for 10 minutes; reduce heat to 375° F.; bake 25 minutes. Serve hot with top milk, cream, Guava Sauce, or Guava Pudding Sauce.

Note. Sweet guavas may be used if 3 tablespoons lemon or 2 tablespoons lime juice are added to strained pulp.

PAPAYA ONO-ONO
See Index.

GUAVA MERINGUE SQUARES

1¾ cups sifted flour
¼ teaspoon salt
½ cup brown sugar,
firmly packed
¾ cup shortening
2 egg yolks
1 teaspoon vanilla

½ cup Guava Butter or
thick marmalade
2 egg whites
½ cup sugar
¼ teaspoon cinnamon
¼ cup coarsely chopped
walnuts

Combine flour, salt, and sugar. Cut in shortening until very fine. Beat egg yolks, add vanilla, and add to other mixture. Pat dough firmly into unoiled 8 x 12 pan; bake in moderate oven (375° F.) for

15 minutes. Cool slightly, spread with guava butter or marmalade and then with meringue topping made as follows:

Beat egg whites stiff; gradually add sugar and cinnamon. Continue beating until smooth meringue is formed. Spread over baked mixture and sprinkle with nuts. Brown in oven at 325° F., for 20 minutes. Cut into 2-inch squares and cool before serving.

FRESH GUAVA ICING

YIELD: enough for 2-layer 8-inch cake

1 cup guava purée
1 to 1½ cups sugar

1 egg white
⅛ teaspoon salt

Prepare purée according to directions for Guava Purée. Combine all ingredients in a mixing bowl. Beat until mixture is of proper consistency to spread on cake, or until peaks are formed when beater is lifted from bowl (15 to 20 minutes).

GUAVA JELLY ICING

YIELD: enough for 2-layer 8-inch cake

½ cup guava jelly
1 egg white
Pinch of salt

½ teaspoon lemon juice,
   if desired
1 to 2 drops of red coloring

Put all ingredients in top of double boiler; place over boiling water. Beat constantly with rotary beater until egg and jelly are well blended. Remove from heat and beat until mixture stands in peaks (7 to 10 minutes).

GUAVA CHIFFON PIE

YIELD: 9-inch pie
(6 to 8 servings)

1 baked pie shell (see Index)
1 tablespoon unflavored
   gelatin
¼ cup water
1 cup sugar
¾ cup strained guava pulp
   (unsweetened)
4 egg yolks

3 to 4 tablespoons lemon or
   lime juice
¼ cup guava juice
4 egg whites
⅛ teaspoon salt
½ cup sweetened whipped
   cream, if desired

Sprinkle gelatin over cold water and let stand 5 minutes. Combine ½ cup sugar, guava pulp, and egg yolks. Beat until well mixed. Cook over hot water, stirring constantly, until it thickens. Add gelatin, remove from heat, and stir until thoroughly combined. Cool and add fruit juice.

When guava mixture begins to congeal, beat egg whites and salt until stiff; add ½ cup sugar and beat until glossy. Gently fold guava mixture into beaten egg whites, pour into pie shell, and place in re-frigerator to chill. Before serving, filling may be spread with whipped cream sweetened to taste.

Variation. Guava Icebox Cake Filling may be used for an uncooked filling.

GUAVA PUDDING SAUCE
YIELD: 2 cups

¾ to 1½ cups sugar
2 tablespoons cornstarch
¼ teaspoon salt

1 cup guava purée
1¼ cups water
3 tablespoons margarine

Combine ⅔ cup sugar, cornstarch, and salt in saucepan; make a smooth paste by slowly adding ¼ cup water. Add guava purée, the re-maining water, and margarine, and cook, stirring constantly, until thickened (about 10 minutes). Taste, and add more sugar if needed, stirring until dissolved. Serve lukewarm over guava dumplings or cot-tage pudding or cold over Spanish Cream or ice cream.

GUAVA JUICE SAUCE
YIELD: 1 cup

¼ cup sugar
1 tablespoon cornstarch
Pinch of salt

½ cup unsweetened guava juice
½ cup boiling water
2 tablespoons margarine

Combine sugar, salt, and cornstarch; make a smooth paste by slowly adding the guava juice. Stir gradually into boiling water, add mar-garine and cook, stirring constantly, until sauce thickens. Serve hot or cold on griddle cakes, waffles, puddings, or ice cream.

GUAVA DELICIOUS
YIELD: 6 servings

8 or 9 large ripe guavas
¾ to ¾ cup sugar
3 large ripe bananas

1 cup grated coconut
½ cup whipping cream

Select only the best quality ripe guavas. Wash, pare thinly, and cut into halves. Scoop out pulp and press through a sieve to remove seeds. Add ⅔ cup sugar to strained pulp, mix thoroughly, taste, and add more sugar if desired. Slice guava shells and bananas not more than ¼ inch thick.

Place half of the guavas in a serving dish, cover with half of the bananas, pour half of the sweetened guava pulp over fruit, and sprin-kle with ½ cup coconut. Repeat. Cover dish and chill 2 to 3 hours. Garnish with whipped cream.

91

GUAVA BROWN BETTY

YIELD: 5 servings

1½ cups fresh guava strips
   (15 to 20 medium guavas)
1 cup sugar
¼ teaspoon ground cinnamon
¼ teaspoon ground nutmeg

3 tablespoons lemon juice
¼ cup water
¼ cup margarine
2 slices stale bread

Wash guavas; remove blossom ends and blemishes. Cut fruit into halves. Remove soft inner pulp and seeds with a spoon; save pulp for use in guava ice cream, mousse, pudding sauce, or cake icing. Cut guava shells into strips ¼ inch wide. Add sugar, spices, lemon juice, and water.

Cut bread into ¼-inch cubes or pull apart with the fingers. Melt margarine and blend with bread cubes. Cover bottom of greased baking dish with half the bread; add guava strips, cover with remaining bread, and pour juice from guavas over the mixture. Cover and bake for 30 to 35 minutes at 350° F. Remove cover after 20 minutes and allow crumbs to brown. Serve warm with cream or top milk.

GUABANAS
See Index.

GUAVA TAPIOCA

YIELD: 4 to 5 servings

¼ cup minute tapioca
1 cup sugar
¼ teaspoon salt
1 cup water
1 tablespoon lemon juice,
   if desired

1 teaspoon grated lemon rind
1 cup unsweetened
   fresh Guava Purée
¼ cup thinly sliced guava shells

Combine tapioca, sugar, salt, and water. Cook slowly over direct heat until tapioca is clear (about 5 minutes). Remove from range and stir in remaining ingredients. Pour into individual dishes or serving bowl, and chill. Serve with thin cream or whipped cream.

GUAVA ICEBOX CAKE*

YIELD: 6 servings

1 tablespoon unflavored gelatin
3 tablespoons cold water
¾ cup sugar
3 tablespoons boiling water
¾ cup fresh-frozen or
   cooked Guava Purée

¼ cup shredded pineapple
2 tablespoons lemon juice
2 beaten egg whites
8 ladyfingers
¼ cup whipping cream

---

* Isabella S. Thursby, Fla. Univ. Agr. Ext. Bul. 70.

Sprinkle gelatin over cold water and let stand for 5 minutes. Add gelatin and sugar to boiling water and stir until dissolved. Cool and add fruit pulp and juice. Mix thoroughly and place in refrigerator to congeal. When mixture is partially congealed, beat until foamy; fold in beaten egg whites. Line a mold with halves of ladyfingers. Pour in mixture and chill 4 to 6 hours. Turn out on large plate and garnish with whipped cream and guava jelly.

Variation. Use thin slices of sponge cake instead of ladyfingers.

GUAVA SHERBET

YIELD: 6 to 8 servings

¼ cup white corn sirup
2 egg whites
1 cup unsweetened Guava Juice
1 teaspoon unflavored gelatin
¼ cup sugar

1 to 1¼ cups
 uncooked Guava Purée
Pinch of salt
¼ scant teaspoon red coloring

Set refrigerator control to coldest point. Chill egg whites and corn sirup in medium-size bowl. Sprinkle gelatin over ¼ cup of the guava juice (use small saucepan) and let stand 5 minutes. Add sugar; heat until sugar is dissolved. Cool and add remaining guava juice and purée. Pour into refrigerator tray and freeze to a mush.

Beat egg whites and sirup mixture until very stiff. Add frozen guava mixture and red coloring. Beat until just blended. Pour into freezing tray; moisten bottom of tray and place on coldest shelf in freezing compartment. Wash bowl and beater, place in refrigerator to chill.

When mixture is frozen stiff (1 to 1½ hours), turn into chilled bowl and break up with spoon. Beat quickly until fluffy and blended but not melted. Quickly pile sherbet back into two trays. Moisten bottoms of trays; return to freezing compartment. Freeze to serving consistency. Turn control back to a little colder than normal until ready to serve. (See Note under Avocado Milk Sherbet.)

GUAVA ICE CREAM

YIELD: 1½ quarts

2¼ cups fresh Guava Purée
2 tablespoons lemon juice

1 cup thin cream
1 cup milk
2 cups sugar

Combine guava purée and lemon juice. Add milk, cream, and sugar. Stir until sugar is dissolved. Pour into freezer and freeze, using 8 parts ice to 1 part salt.

GUAVA MOUSSE YIELD: 6 to 8 servings

1 cup fresh Guava Purée	2¼ cups whipping cream OR
1 tablespoon lemon juice	1 cup evaporated milk and
¾ cup sugar	¼ cup whipping cream

Add sugar and lemon juice to purée. If evaporated milk is used, chill thoroughly by surrounding with ice or by placing in freezing pan in refrigerator until tiny crystals begin to appear around sides. Pour chilled evaporated milk or cream into chilled bowl and whip until it thickens. Fold in guava mixture and freeze 4 to 6 hours.

JAVA PLUM
(Jambolan)

Description. The Java plum or jambolan (*Eugenia cumini*) is a small dark-maroon or purple fruit about the size and shape of an olive. There are at least two varieties in Hawaii, one with small somewhat irregular-shaped fruit and one with slightly larger symmetrical olive-shaped fruit. The smaller variety has purple flesh and the larger type has whitish flesh. Some trees produce better quality fruit, both in size and flavor, than others. The white-fleshed Java plum is sweeter and less astringent than the purple-fleshed variety. The astringent quality is believed to be due to the presence of tannins.

The Java plum tree, with handsome green foliage the year round, grows to a height of 40 to 50 feet. It produces a large quantity of fruit which fall to the ground and stain everything with which they come in contact. It is often considered an undesirable tree in Hawaiian gardens and along roadways or streets because of the unsightly litter produced beneath the trees.

History. It is not known when or by whom the Java plum was introduced into Hawaii, but it has been a familiar tree for many years. Since it is mentioned by Dr. William Hillebrand, it must have been growing in the Islands before 1870 and may have been introduced by him.

Fruit, foliage, and cross section of the Java plum *(Eugenia cumini).*

Birds have scattered the fruit and seeds far and wide so that now the tree (especially the purple-fleshed variety) grows in a semiwild state in many valleys at lower elevations and up to 4,000 to 5,000 feet on all the islands.

Nutritive Value. The Java plum is a fruit high in sugars and organic acids. No data are available on mineral content. The plums are an excellent source of riboflavin and a good source of ascorbic acid, but a poor source of thiamine and niacin. They have little or no pro-vitamin A.

Supply. Java plums do not appear in Honolulu stores but ample supplies of the fruit can usually be obtained from trees in vacant lots and along roadways in late summer and fall.

Use. Because of their astringent qualities, fresh fruits of both the purple- and white-fleshed varieties pucker the mouth and are undesirable to eat out of the hand, though many Island children seem to enjoy them.

The purple-fleshed fruits produce a strong-flavored, deep-purplish-red juice that makes an excellent jelly when combined with guava juice.

Because the purple-fleshed fruits contain little or no pectin, it is necessary to combine the juice with that of a fruit of high pectin content or use commercial pectin in order to make jelly.

In contrast with the purple-fleshed fruit, the white-fleshed Java plum contains relatively large amounts of pectin. Jelly made from the white-fleshed plum gives the best texture when cooked only until a faint jelly test is obtained; otherwise it becomes too stiff on standing. Tough jelly is produced if the juice is cooked until it gives a good jelly test. Jelly made from the juice of the white-fleshed plum is mild flavored. In order to obtain a stronger plum flavor, as much juice as possible should be pressed from the cooked pulp. This does not detract from the appearance of the product, since the drained juice does not yield a clear or transparent jelly. One tablespoon lemon juice should be added to each cup of juice if a tart jelly is desired.

If both the white-fleshed and purple-fleshed varieties are available, jelly of good consistency and pronounced flavor can be made by combining the two in equal proportions and using $\frac{3}{4}$ cup sugar to each cup of juice.

Jam may be made from the pitted fruit of the white-fleshed variety, but it is not recommended because the astringent quality of the plum is retained in the pulp.

Juice or pulp of the ketambilla, which is high in acid, combines well with the juice of the white-fleshed plum, which is low in acid and high in pectin.

PURPLE-FLESHED JAVA PLUM JUICE

YIELD: 4 cups

8 cups firm-ripe plums   1¼ cups water

Wash plums and remove stems. Place in kettle with water and cook until fruit is soft (20 to 25 minutes). Pour into thick jelly bag and allow juice to drain. Do not squeeze bag. Allow sediment in juice to settle before pouring off clear liquid for jelly.

WHITE-FLESHED JAVA PLUM JUICE

YIELD: 4 cups

10 cups firm-ripe plums   2 cups water

Wash plums and remove stems. Half cover plums with water and cook rapidly until fruit is soft (about 20 minutes). Pour into jelly bag and allow juice to drain. Squeeze bag to obtain all juice; allow sediment to settle before pouring off clear liquid for jelly.

PURPLE-FLESHED JAVA PLUM AND GUAVA JELLY

YIELD: a) 2¾ cups; b) 3 cups

a) 1 cup Java plum juice   or   b) 1 cup Java plum juice
1¼ cups half-ripe guava   2 cups half-ripe guava
**   juice   juice**
2 cups sugar   2¼ cups sugar

Combine juices and boil in a broad shallow pan for 2 to 3 minutes. Add sugar, stir until dissolved, and boil rapidly until it gives the jelly test (see Appendix III). Skim, pour into hot sterilized glasses, and seal with paraffin.

PURPLE-FLESHED JAVA PLUM JELLY

YIELD: 7 cups

1¾ cups Java plum juice   7 cups sugar
1¼ cups water   4 ounces liquid commercial
½ cup lemon juice   pectin (½ cup)

Combine water and juice; bring to boiling. Add sugar and heat to boiling quickly; add pectin, stirring constantly. Allow to come to a brisk boil and boil vigorously for ½ minute. Remove from range, skim, pour quickly into hot sterilized glasses, and seal with paraffin.

WHITE-FLESHED JAVA PLUM JELLY

YIELD: 4 cups

4 cups plum juice   3 to 4 tablespoons lemon
3 cups sugar   juice, if desired

Boil juice in broad shallow pan for 2 to 3 minutes. Add sugar and boil rapidly until it gives a faint jelly test (see Appendix III). Skim, pour into hot sterilized glasses, and seal with paraffin.

Caution. A stiff, tough jelly results from cooking until a positive jelly test is obtained.

Variation. For a sweet jelly use 1 cup sugar to 1 cup juice and, if desired, omit lemon juice.

WHITE-FLESHED JAVA PLUM AND KETAMBILLA JELLY

YIELD: 3 cups

1¼ cups white-fleshed plum juice

¾ cup Ketambilla Juice and pulp (see below)

¼ cup water

2 teaspoons lemon juice

3 cups sugar

Combine juices and water. Boil in a broad shallow pan 2 to 3 minutes, add sugar, and boil rapidly until a good jelly test is obtained (see Appendix III). Skim, pour into hot sterilized glasses, and seal with paraffin.

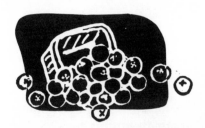

KETAMBILLA

Description. In size and shape the ketambilla (*Dovyalis hebecarpa*) resembles a small plum or cherry. It is globe-shaped and varies from about ½ to slightly more than 1 inch in diameter. The ketambilla has a thin, tough, deep-purple skin covered with short grey-green hairs which give it a velvety or frosted appearance. It has nine to twelve small seeds imbedded in the fibrous, deep-maroon or purple flesh. It has a strong acid flavor and stains a deep red or purple.

The fruit hang by short stems on the under side of the thorny branches of a shrub that grows to a height of 10 to 15 feet.

History. The ketambilla is a native of Ceylon and is sometimes called the Ceylon gooseberry. Seeds of the plant were brought to the Islands by the Hawaiian Sugar Planters' Experiment Station from the Harvard Botanical Garden in Cuba in 1920. Plants from these seeds have since been widely distributed throughout the Islands. The plant is hardy and grows in a variety of soils and locations.

Nutritive Value. No data are available on the mineral content of ketambilla. They have been found to be a fair source of provitamin A and riboflavin, a poor source of thiamine and niacin, and an excellent source of ascorbic acid.

Fruit, foliage, and cross section of the ketambilla *(Dovyalis hebecarpa).*

Supply. Ketambilla are not marketed commercially but may be found in many Hawaii gardens.

Use. The fruit contain enough acid and pectin to make a good jelly but have too strong a flavor to use without dilution or combination with other fruits. When diluted, it is necessary to add commercial pectin to make a satisfactory jelly or jam.

KETAMBILLA JUICE
YIELD: 4 cups

4 cups ketambilla (1¼ pounds)   1¼ cups water

Wash ketambilla and crush in bottom of kettle. Add 1¼ cups water, bring to boiling point, and simmer until tender (10 to 15 minutes). For a clear juice turn into jelly bag and allow juice to drain, shifting pulp occasionally to keep juice flowing. For a pulpy juice, ketambilla may be put through a sieve or fine colander.

SPICED KETAMBILLA JELLY
YIELD: 4 cups

2 cups ketambilla juice   **2 teaspoons ground cinnamon**
3¼ cups sugar   **1 teaspoon nutmeg**
1 teaspoon ground cloves   **¼ cup liquid commercial pectin**

Prepare juice as directed above. Bring juice to boiling. Mix spices with sugar and add to boiling juice. Bring to a rolling boil and boil vigorously 1 minute, stirring constantly. Remove from heat and stir in commercial pectin. Skim, pour into sterilized glasses, and seal with paraffin.

KETAMBILLA-PAPAYA JAM
YIELD: 3 cups

2 cups pulpy ketambilla juice   **3 tablespoons lemon juice**
2 cups ripe papaya pulp   **Grated rind of ¼ lemon**
4 cups sugar

Prepare pulpy juice as directed for Ketambilla Juice. Measure, combine with papaya pulp, and bring to boiling point. Add sugar and boil rapidly until mixture sheets from spoon (see Appendix III). Add lemon juice and rind, and pour into sterilized glasses. Seal with paraffin.

KETAMBILLA-GUAVA JELLY
YIELD: 4 cups

2 cups pulpy ketambilla juice   **4 cups sugar**
2 cups guava juice

Prepare pulpy juice as directed for Ketambilla Juice. Measure, add guava juice, and bring to boiling point. Boil rapidly 5 minutes, skim, then add sugar, stirring until dissolved. Boil rapidly until jelly sheets from spoon (see Appendix III). Pour into sterilized glasses and seal with paraffin.

KETAMBILLA AND APPLE BUTTER

YIELD: 4 to 5 cups

2 cups chopped apples
2 cups crushed ketambilla
1 cup water

¾ cup sugar for each cup
cooked fruit pulp

Combine ketambilla, apples, and water and bring to the boiling point. Simmer until ketambilla and apples are tender. Force through a coarse sieve or vegetable ricer. Measure and add ¾ cup sugar for each cup of fruit pulp. Bring to boiling point and cook rapidly until mixture sheets from spoon (see Appendix III). Pour into sterilized glasses and seal with paraffin.

WHITE-FLESHED JAVA PLUM AND KETAMBILLA JELLY
See Index.

KUMQUAT

Description. Kumquats are commonly referred to as citrus fruits although they have now been classified in a separate genus, *Fortunella.* The fruit are small, either oval or round, 1 to 1¾ inches long and about 1 inch in diameter, and are borne on a small tree whose height usually does not exceed 10 feet. The sweet, highly flavored peel may be eaten along with the juicy subacid pulp which contains a number of small seeds. Elsewhere, the fruit usually develops a deep orange color when ripe, but in Hawaii, it is likely to be pale orange with a greenish tinge. The Chinese name, *Chin kan,* mentioned in early Chinese writings means "gold orange."

History. Kumquats were brought to Hawaii in early days, as Dr. William Hillebrand (1888) mentions them along with other citrus fruits as being of such early introduction that they appear to be growing wild in some sections. Since kumquats are a native of China, where they have long been cultivated, it is possible that they were brought directly from the Orient. L. H. Bailey reports that they were not introduced into the United States until about 1850. Several varieties of kumquats are grown in Hawaii, but the Nagami (*Fortunella margarita*) is the most common.

Nutritive Value. No data are available on kumquats grown in Hawaii, but analyses made elsewhere indicate they have less ascorbic acid than good oranges.

Supply. The fruit are not sold in Honolulu stores but are found in many old Hawaii gardens.

Use. Kumquats, although palatable, are not very desirable in the raw state. They are best used in a preserved form and, combined with other fruits, add piquancy to salads, fruit cocktails, and desserts.

KUMQUAT PRESERVES   YIELD: 2 pints

4 cups kumquats	1 teaspoon grated fresh
(1½ to 2 pounds)	ginger root, if desired
1 tablespoon soda	3 cups sugar
4 paper-thin slices of lemon,	3 cups water
if desired	1 cup white corn sirup

Wash kumquats, sprinkle with soda, cover with water, let stand 10 minutes, and rinse twice. Place in a shallow kettle and cover with water. Bring to a boil, cook until tender (about 25 to 30 minutes), and drain.

Cut lemon slices into small pie-shaped pieces, cover with water, add grated ginger, and cook until tender.

Combine sugar, water, and corn sirup in a shallow kettle, bring to a boil, and boil 5 minutes. Add drained kumquats, cooked lemon slices and ginger, and simmer until glossy and transparent (35 to 45 minutes). Keep in sirup in a covered jar in refrigerator; or pack into hot sterilized jars, cover with boiling sirup, and seal.

LEMON

Description. Several kinds of lemons (*Citrus limon*), varying greatly in size and appearance, are grown in Hawaii. One of the larger varieties, 4 to 6 inches long, has a thick, warty, greenish-yellow rind. The flavor of the fruit is strongly acid but pleasant. Common commercial varieties are grown only to a limited extent.

History. The lemon, a native of southern Asia, is now grown in many warm sections of the world. Lemon plants are said to have been introduced into Hawaii early in the nineteenth century.

Nutritive Value. The small quantities of lemons and limes used in the average diet make their nutritive value of minor importance. Both yield an alkaline ash in the body because their high acidity is due to citric acid and its basic salts. Both fruits are good antiscorbutics, though the different varieties of lemons and limes may vary somewhat in their content of ascorbic acid.

Supply. The lemon season is the same as that of the orange— October, November, and December. Although lemons are produced in small quantities during most of the year, there is usually a period of one or two months in the spring when they are not obtainable.

Use. Lemon juice, used alone or in combination with other fruit juices, makes a refreshing iced drink. It is combined with a great many other foods in order to improve their flavor.

TART ORANGE MARMALADE
See Index.

THREE FRUIT MARMALADE
See Index.

LEMONADE
See variation for Fresh Limeade (see Index).

ALOHA PUNCH
See Index.

MANOA FRUIT PUNCH
See Index.

STRAWBERRY GUAVA PUNCH
See Index.

FRUIT COCKTAIL DRESSING
See Index.

LEMON FLUFF PIE

YIELD: 8-inch pie
(5 servings)

1 baked pie shell (see Index)	1¼ cups sugar
3 tablespoons flour	1 cup water
3 tablespoons cornstarch	4 eggs, separated
⅛ teaspoon salt	¼ cup fresh lemon juice

Combine flour, cornstarch, salt, and ¾ cup sugar in top of double boiler. Gradually stir in the water and cook over direct heat, stirring constantly, until very thick (8 to 10 minutes). Place over boiling water, cover, and cook 10 minutes longer.

Separate eggs, and beat yolks slightly. Gradually add a portion of the hot mixture to the yolks, stirring vigorously, then slowly pour yolk mixture into remaining hot mixture and cook a minute longer. Remove from heat, cool, and stir in the lemon juice.

Beat egg whites until they form soft peaks when beater is lifted (stiff but not dry). Gradually beat in remaining ½ cup of sugar by sprinkling 1½ tablespoons at a time over surface of egg whites, until all is used. Fold about ⅓ of this meringue into the cooked filling; pour into baked shell. Pile remaining meringue around outer edge of the pie filling, being careful to seal meringue to crust. Spread toward center and swirl for decorative top. Bake at 400° F. 8 to 10 minutes, or 325° F. for 15 to 20 minutes.

LEMON SPONGE PUDDING

YIELD: 4 to 6 servings

1¼ cups milk	¼ teaspoon grated lemon rind
2 tablespoons margarine	Juice of 1 large lemon
1 cup sugar	(3 to 4 tablespoons)
3 tablespoons flour	3 eggs
¾ teaspoon salt, if desired	

Heat milk to just below the boiling point and add margarine. Mix flour, sugar, and salt in medium-size bowl.

Separate eggs and mix yolks with flour and sugar mixture. Stir until well blended. Add lemon rind and juice; mix well. Add heated milk gradually but quickly. Beat egg whites until stiff but not dry and fold into mixture.

Pour into unoiled custard cups or baking dish. Set in a pan of hot water and bake in a slow oven (350° F.) for 45 minutes.

LIME

Description. The acid lime (*Citrus aurantifolia*) is a small citrus fruit of characteristic flavor. Several varieties are grown successfully in Hawaii. The common type is a small round or oval fruit about $1\frac{1}{2}$ to $2\frac{1}{4}$ inches in diameter. Its thin skin varies in color from light yellow to green. The flesh, yellow-green and very juicy, contains large quantities of citric acid.

The Bearss lime is a variety of moderate size, with an unusually fragrant rind which gives an exotic flavor to products in which it is used.

History. Like the lemon, the acid lime is a native of southern Asia and has spread to many tropical and subtropical sections of the world. The lime has flourished in Hawaii since its introduction during the early part of the nineteenth century. It seems the most adaptable of the citrus fruits to Island conditions.

Nutritive Value. The nutritive value of the lime is the same as that given for lemon (see above).

Supply. Limes are nearly always in season, the heaviest crop coming in late summer and fall. The supply usually equals the demand.

Use. Lime juice is refreshing and makes a pleasing addition to punch or other iced drinks. It may be substituted for lemon in any recipe, but only $\frac{2}{3}$ to $\frac{3}{4}$ as much should be used because of its higher acidity. Lime sirup may be prepared and kept for future use.

FRESH LIMEADE   YIELD: 4 cups

**1 cup lime juice (16 medium $\frac{1}{2}$ cup sugar
    limes)**

Roll limes on hard surface, cut into halves, squeeze, and strain. Stir lime juice and sugar together until sugar is dissolved. Taste and add more sugar if desired. For each serving, fill glass with cracked ice, add $\frac{1}{4}$ cup of the lime juice and sugar mixture, and fill glass with water. Stir well, garnish with thin slice of lime and a cherry if desired.

Variation. Lemonade may be made by substituting lemon juice for lime juice. Add 1 tablespoon grated lemon rind if desired.

LIME SIRUP

YIELD: 2$\frac{1}{2}$ cups

1 cup lime juice (16 medium limes)	2 cups sugar
	$\frac{1}{4}$ cup water

Wash, dry, and squeeze limes. Boil sugar and water for 10 minutes. Add lime juice, pour into hot sterilized jars, and seal immediately.

To dilute for limeade, use 2 tablespoons of sirup to 1 cup of water. Pour over cracked ice.

LIME SAUCE FOR PUDDINGS

YIELD: 1 cup

1 tablespoon cornstarch	$\frac{3}{4}$ cup boiling water
$\frac{1}{2}$ cup sugar	2 tablespoons margarine
$\frac{1}{4}$ cup cold water	2$\frac{1}{2}$ tablespoons lime juice

Combine sugar and cornstarch and make a smooth paste with cold water. Gradually stir into boiling water. Continue stirring until mixture thickens. Remove from heat and add margarine and lime juice. Serve hot over cottage or steamed pudding.

LIME FLUFF PIE

Substitute lime juice for lemon juice in Lemon Fluff Pie recipe.

LOQUAT

Description. The loquat (*Eriobotrya japonica* Lindl.) has yellow, downy fruit, from 1½ to 2½ inches long. It is egg-shaped or round, and the white or yellow flesh encloses a few large seeds. When half ripe the fruit is very acid, but when fully ripe it is sweet.

History. The native home of the loquat was probably central-eastern China, but the fruit was early introduced into Japan, where it has been greatly developed horticulturally.

The exact date of its introduction into Hawaii is unknown, but Wilder, in 1911, stated that "the loquat has been for many years a familiar fruit in our gardens."

Nutritive Value. Loquats are an excellent source of provitamin A but a poor source of the other vitamins and of calcium, phosphorus, and iron. Two samples showed only traces of ascorbic acid, which finding is confirmed by published values.

Supply. The loquat makes an attractive, evergreen, home-garden shade tree which grows to a height of about 20 feet even at sea level; good quality fruit, however, develops only at higher elevations.

At the time of writing (1963), loquats are grown commercially on the island of Maui at elevations of 2500 to 3000 feet. Clusters of ripe fruit may be found on some Honolulu markets in March, April, and as late as May.

Use. The fruits may be eaten fresh, combined with other fruits in a salad or fruit cup, or made into jam or jelly.

LOQUAT JAM   YIELD: 1 pint

1 pound loquats	1 cup water
1½ cups sugar	¼ cup lemon juice

Wash, scald, and peel the fruit, removing seeds. Put the fruit through a food chopper or chop fine. Mix sugar and water. Add fruit and lemon juice and cook to about 220° F. or until it gives a jelly test (see Appendix III). Pour into hot sterilized glasses and seal.

Fruit and foliage of the loquat *(Eriobotrya japonica)*.

LYCHEE

Description. The lychee (*Litchi chinensis* Sonn.) is a small oval or ovate fruit about 1½ inches in diameter. In most varieties the outer shell-like covering is red and the flesh surrounding the single brown seed is white. The seeds vary considerably in size. Seedless fruits have been grown. Lychees are produced and marketed in clusters of three to twenty or more. The sweet and slightly acid flavor of the fresh lychee reminds many people of that of the Muscat grape. (The dried fruit, known as lychee nuts, are very different from the fresh, bearing somewhat the same relation to the fresh fruit as raisins do to grapes.)

History. The lychee, a native of South China, has been cultivated there for centuries. From China it spread gradually to many other tropical and subtropical countries. The first lychee tree brought into Hawaii is believed to have been planted on the property of C. Afong in 1873. This tree has usually borne abundantly. Within recent years, many other trees in the Islands have come into bearing.

Horticulturists of the Hawaii Agricultural Experiment Station have introduced a number of new varieties from China and elsewhere which are being tested in the station orchards. The Brewster has proved to be a good variety which bears heavily, its only drawback being a relatively large seed. The Groff, a new variety developed by the Horticulture Department of the Hawaii Station, has many desirable characteristics, one being its unusually small seed.

Nutritive Value. Of the two varieties of fresh lychees analyzed, the Kwai Mi has almost twice the sugar content (20.6 percent) of the Hak Ip variety (11.8 percent). The Kwai Mi, though a smaller fruit with a larger percentage of refuse, is considered superior in flavor and quality.

Both varieties were found to be poor sources of calcium and iron but fair sources of phosphorus.

The lychee has no yellow pigment and therefore no provitamin A. The Brewster variety was found to be a poor source of thiamine and a fair source of riboflavin and niacin. Both the Kwai Mi and the Brewster varieties are excellent sources of ascorbic acid.

109

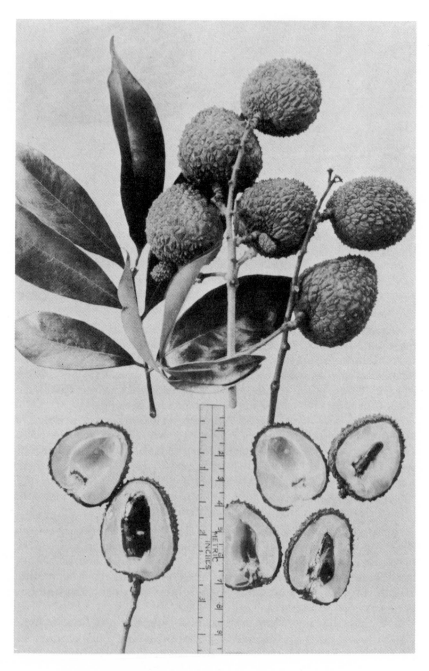

Fruit, foliage, and cross section of the lychee *(Litchi chinensis).*

Supply. The season for the lychee is short, usually part of June and the early part of July. Small quantities of lychees reach Chinese stores, fancy grocers, and other Honolulu stores. The retail supply never meets the demand; consequently lychees command a high price. Because the lychee is highly prized by the Orientals, canned as well as dried lychees are imported from China.

Use. Lychees are most frequently served fresh and eaten out of the shell, but shelled fresh lychees make a pleasing addition to fruit cocktail or fruit salad.

The number of lychees needed to yield a definite measure of the edible portion varies with the size of the seeds as well as the size of the fruit. Twenty to twenty-five large lychees or thirty to thirty-five medium to small lychees are needed to yield a cup of peeled and seeded fruit.

When shelling and removing seeds from lychees, loosen fruit from the seed at the stem end and cut lengthwise; this procedure leaves the fruit as nearly whole as possible.

The fruit may be successfully canned at home in a medium sirup (see Appendix II). Canned lychees may be served alone or in combination with other fruits for dessert, fruit cocktail, or salad, or may be used in a sauce served with fried fish or shellfish in Chinese style.

Lychees may be frozen either in their shells or without them, although the flesh becomes somewhat tough after freezing and storing (see Appendix I).

CANNED LYCHEES
See recipe, Appendix II.

LYCHEE, PINEAPPLE, AND
ORANGE COCKTAIL

YIELD: 8 servings

2 cups seeded fresh lychees cut into halves or quarters	2 cups diced orange sections
	2 tablespoons sugar
2 cups diced fresh pineapple	1 tablespoon lemon juice

Cut fruit into pieces of uniform size and save the juice. Add sugar and lemon juice to the other fruit juice. Pour over diced fruit and chill for 1 hour before serving.

This fruit mixture may be used for a salad if the drained fruit is chilled and combined with sugar and lemon juice just before salad is to be served. Serve with ¼ cup mayonnaise, French, or other dressing (see Index).

LYCHEE, MANGO, AND PAPAYA FRUIT CUP   YIELD: 6 servings

¼ cup sugar
¼ cup water
1 teaspoon grated fresh
   ginger root
1 tablespoon lemon juice

1 cup seeded fresh lychees
   cut into halves
1 cup diced papaya
   (½ medium)
2 medium mangoes cut into
   finger slices (2 cups)

In a small saucepan, bring sugar, water, and ginger root to a boil, and boil 5 minutes. Strain, cool, and add lemon juice. Marinate fruit in the sirup 30 to 60 minutes. Serve as dessert or appetizer.

FIG-LYCHEE COCKTAIL
See Index.

PINEAPPLE FRUIT MOLD
See Index.

ROSELLE FRUIT MOLD
See Index.

LYCHEE, PAPAYA, AND PINEAPPLE SALAD   YIELD: 6 servings

2 cups seeded fresh lychees,
   cut into halves
2 cups diced papaya

2 cups diced fresh pineapple
2 teaspoons lemon juice
⅓ to ½ cup mayonnaise

Combine fruit and add lemon juice. Chill thoroughly. Add mayonnaise, mix, and serve on lettuce leaves.

LYCHEE AND COTTAGE CHEESE SALAD   YIELD: 6 servings

36 large seeded lychees
¾ cup cottage cheese

¼ to ½ cup mayonnaise
¼ cup shelled pecans

Stuff cavities of seeded lychees with cottage cheese. Chill and place on lettuce leaves. Garnish with mayonnaise and pecans.

LYCHEE SHERBET   YIELD: 1 quart

1 cup lychee juice (20 to
   24 lychees)
1 tablespoon gelatin
¼ cup cold water

¾ cup milk
¼ to ½ cup sugar
1 cup thin cream
1 teaspoon lemon juice

Peel lychees and remove seeds. Squeeze in two thicknesses of cheesecloth to obtain juice. Sprinkle gelatin on cold water and let stand 5 minutes. Scald ⅓ cup of the milk, add soaked gelatin and stir until thoroughly dissolved; add sugar, mix well and cool. Add remainder of the milk and the cream; stir in lychee juice and lemon juice.

Freeze in an ice-cream freezer using 8 parts of ice to one of salt.

MANGO

Description. Many recognized varieties of mangoes (*Mangifera indica*), as well as unnamed hybrids, are grown in Hawaii. In general, the mango can be described as a medium-size fruit from 2 to 4 inches in width and from 3 to 7 inches in length. The skin, which is smooth and thick, is strong enough to be pulled from the flesh when the fruit is ripe or nearly so. In most varieties, as the fruit matures the green skin changes to more brilliant colors—purplish red shading to green, deep crimson, or even yellow with red spots.

The flesh varies in color from light lemon to deep apricot. In the most prized varieties, it is juicy, smooth, and free from fiber. The flavor, which varies greatly, may be insipid and sweet or reminiscent of turpentine. In the better varieties, the flavor and texture are excellent. Though sometimes compared with good peaches, mangoes have a characteristic, delicious flavor of their own.

History. Indigenous to southern Asia, the mango is now grown in many subtropical sections of the world. T. G. Thrum stated in the *Hawaiian Annual for 1909* that the first mango trees were brought to Hawaii from Manila in 1824 by Captain John Meek of the brig *Kamehameha*. The small trees were divided between the Reverend Joseph Goodrich and Don Marin. These trees were the source of those mangoes known as the Hawaiian race.

Joseph Marsden in 1885 imported from Jamaica several seedling mango trees, including the famous No. 9, grafts and seedlings from which are still growing in Hawaii gardens. G. P. Wilder and S. M. Damon also brought in several good varieties; and the Hawaii Agricultural Experiment Station, through the United States Department of Agriculture, Bureau of Plant Industry, introduced a number of varieties from foreign countries.

Nutritive Value. Mangoes have a high sugar content, but they are a poor source of calcium, phosphorus, and iron.

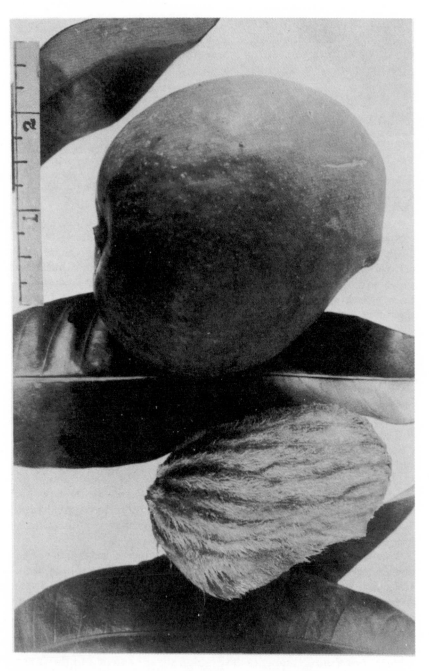

Fruit, foliage, and seed of the Pirie mango *(Mangifera indica)*.

Mangoes have sufficient yellow pigment to make them good to excellent sources of provitamin A. The mangoes tested have been found to be fair to poor sources of all three B vitamins—thiamine, riboflavin, and niacin.

Different varieties of mangoes vary greatly in ascorbic acid content. For example two favorites, the Pirie and the Haden, are only fair sources, whereas others, including some of the common types, are excellent sources of ascorbic acid. All varieties tested contained more ascorbic acid in the green stage than in the half-ripe stage, and more in the half-ripe stage than in the ripe stage. For detailed information regarding ascorbic acid content of various varieties of mangoes grown in Hawaii, the reader should consult Hawaii Agricultural Experiment Station Technical Bulletin 26.

Mango sauce made from half-ripe mangoes, especially common types, is a good to excellent source of ascorbic acid. The ascorbic acid was not destroyed as a result of cooking mangoes with or without sugar and was well retained in the cooked product stored for a week in the refrigerator. This was true even when the product was sieved and a good deal of air was thus incorporated. A longer period of storage without canning is not recommended.

Supply. Mangoes may be found in some Honolulu stores through many months of the year, but because the supply of the superior varieties never equals the demand, they command a high price. The season for mangoes in Hawaii varies with climatic conditions from year to year, but usually they begin ripening in April and are available until September or October.

Use. The mango is used fresh as a dessert fruit or in combination with citrus fruits, pineapple, or papaya. It is delicious in fruit cocktails, salads, shortcake, and frozen desserts. Many people like the flavor of green or half-ripe mangoes, which may be used in pies, or cooked and served as a sauce. Many children eat mangoes when they are green, hard, and very sour. Mango slices and mango sauce may be canned for future use. Mango chutney is a favorite method of preserving, although mangoes also make delicious jams and marmalades.

Different varieties of mangoes vary in their water content and consequently the amount of liquid in the recipes may require some adjustment. Some green or half-ripe mangoes have much more starch than others. The starchy ones make a less desirable sauce even if additional water is used.

Fresh, ripe mangoes of good quality, when peeled and removed from the seed, as well as cooked green mango sauce, make excellent frozen products. For varieties best adapted to freezing, consult Hawaii Agricultural Experiment Station Bulletin 26. For directions on methods of freezing mangoes, see Appendix I.

CANNED MANGO SLICES, AND SAUCE
See recipe, Appendix II.

MANGO SAUCE
YIELD: 1 quart

6 cups green or half-ripe mango slices	**1 to 1½ cups water**
	1 to 2 cups sugar

Cook mangoes in water until soft. Add sugar and cook 5 minutes longer. Serve with meat or as dessert. Mango sauce may be used for shortcake filling or in sherbets, ice creams, or mousses.

If a smooth purée is desired or if stringy mangoes have been used, put sauce through a food mill (p. 1) or sieve while the sauce is hot.

Note. For canned Mango Sauce recipe, see Appendix II. For frozen Mango Sauce, see Mango Purée, Appendix I.

MANGO BUTTER
YIELD: 2 quarts

12 cups peeled half-ripe mango slices	**¼ teaspoon ground cloves**
	¼ teaspoon ground allspice
2 to 3 cups water	**1 teaspoon ground cinnamon**
6 cups sugar	**1 teaspoon ground nutmeg**

Add water to mangoes and cook until soft enough to mash. Press through sieve if mangoes are stringy. Add sugar and spices. Cook slowly until thick (45 minutes). Stir frequently to prevent burning. Pour into hot sterilized glasses and seal with paraffin.

MANGO JAM
YIELD: 1 quart

12 cups half-ripe or ripe mango slices	**2 to 4 cups water**
	6 cups sugar

Add water to mango slices and cook until tender (about 15 minutes). Add sugar, and boil until thick and of proper consistency for jam. Pour into hot sterilized jars and seal with paraffin.

MANGO CHUTNEY I
YIELD: 4 quarts

2 cups vinegar	**4 chili peppers (with seeds removed), finely chopped**
6½ cups sugar	
12 cups green mango slices (about 25 mangoes)	**1 clove of garlic**
	1 box (3 cups) seedless raisins
¼ cup finely chopped fresh ginger root	**¾ cup sliced onion**
	1 teaspoon salt

Boil vinegar and sugar 5 minutes. Add mangoes and other ingredients and cook slowly about 1½ hours or until thick and of the desired consistency. Pour into hot sterilized glasses and seal immediately.

MANGO CHUTNEY II

YIELD: 8 quarts

10 pounds peeled, sliced green mangoes (about 50 fruit)
¾ cup salt
5 pounds sugar
3 to 4 cups vinegar (depending on acidity of mangoes)
3 to 4 cups water
1½ pounds almonds, blanched and cut in thin strips
1 pound finely sliced candied orange peel
1 pound finely sliced candied lemon peel

2 large onions, grated
2 pounds seedless raisins
1 pound finely sliced citron
¾ cup fresh ginger root, cooked and chopped fine (6 ounces)
1 cup finely chopped preserved ginger
2 cloves of garlic, finely chopped
8 small red peppers (with seeds removed), finely chopped

Prepare the mangoes, sprinkle layers of sliced fruit with salt, and allow to stand overnight. Drain well. The total quantity of vinegar and water should equal 7 cups. Bring sugar, water, and vinegar to a boil. Add drained mangoes and cook until tender. Add other ingredients and cook slowly for ½ to 1 hour or until the desired consistency is obtained. Pour into hot sterilized jars and seal immediately. Serve with meat or curried dishes.

SPICED MANGO PICKLE*

YIELD: 3 pints

1½ cups white vinegar
1½ cups water
3 cups sugar
5 sticks cinnamon, or ½ teaspoon ground cinnamon
1 tablespoon whole cloves
¼ teaspoon mace

1 teaspoon chopped fresh ginger root
¼ teaspoon nutmeg
3 pounds peeled, sliced green mangoes (2 large slices from each of 17 mangoes)

Combine all ingredients except mangoes, and boil sirup for 5 minutes. Add mango slices and cook until tender and clear (30 to 45 minutes). Pack mangoes into hot sterilized jars. Add sirup and seal.

If mangoes are sour, add ¼ to ½ cup more sugar to the sirup.

MANGO NECTAR

YIELD: 6 cups

¼ cup sugar
3 cups water
¼ cup lemon juice

1½ cups ripe mango purée
1 cup fresh orange juice

---

* Contributed by the Home Service Department of The Hawaiian Electric Company, Honolulu.

Combine sugar and water, and stir until dissolved. Add mango purée and fruit juice and chill. Pour the mixture over cracked ice before serving. Frozen mango purée may be used (see Appendix I).

LYCHEE, MANGO, AND PAPAYA FRUIT CUP
See Index.

AVOCADO FRUIT SALAD
See Index.

MANGO FRUIT MOLD
YIELD: 6 to 8 servings

2 tablespoons unflavored gelatin
¼ cup water
⅔ cup boiling water
Pinch of salt
1 teaspoon finely chopped fresh ginger root

1 cup sweetened half-ripe Mango Sauce
1½ tablespoons lemon OR 1 tablespoon lime juice
¼ cup pineapple juice
1 cup ripe papaya cubes
1 cup canned crushed pineapple, drained

Sprinkle gelatin over cold water and let stand for 5 minutes; add boiling water, and stir until dissolved. Add salt, ginger, then cool. Combine with mango sauce and fruit juices. Chill until mixture begins to congeal. Stir in papaya and pineapple. Pour into mold and chill until firm. Serve as dessert or with lettuce and mayonnaise as salad.

PINEAPPLE FRUIT MOLD
See Index.

ROSELLE FRUIT MOLD
See Index.

MANGO UPSIDE-DOWN CAKE
YIELD: 6 servings

2 cups sliced ripe mangoes
2 tablespoons lemon juice
1 tablespoon margarine
¼ cup brown sugar
¼ cup fat
⅔ cup sugar

1 egg
½ cup milk
1¼ cups flour
2 teaspoons baking powder
¼ teaspoon salt

Pour lemon juice over mangoes and let stand 15 minutes. Melt margarine in 8-inch cake pan or casserole. Add brown sugar and cover with layer of mango slices.

To prepare cake batter, cream fat, add sugar, and cream together;

then add beaten egg. Sift dry ingredients and add alternately with milk. Pour over mangoes and bake 50 to 60 minutes at 375° F. When cake is done, turn upside down and serve while still warm, with whipped cream or a lemon or lime sauce (see Index).

Note. Do not use iron skillet as mangoes will become discolored.

MANGO PIE

YIELD: 4 to 6 servings

1 recipe Plain Pastry
3½ cups sliced half-ripe mangoes
1 cup sugar
½ teaspoon ground cinnamon
¼ teaspoon ground nutmeg
1 tablespoon lemon juice
2 to 3 tablespoons flour, if desired

Line pie pan with pastry. Mix sugar, spices, and flour. Put in layer of mango slices, sprinkle with sugar mixture, and repeat until all are used. Sprinkle with lemon juice, cover with pastry, and bake in hot oven (425° F.) for 10 minutes. Then bake in moderate oven (350° F.) until mango slices are soft (30 to 40 minutes).

Variation. Substitute 1 cup ripe papaya slices for 1 cup mangoes, and double the quantity of lemon juice.

MANGO CHIFFON PIE*

YIELD: 5 to 6 servings

1 baked 9-inch pie shell (see Index)
1 cup sweetened green Mango Sauce
4 eggs, separated
¾ cup sugar
1⅓ tablespoons unflavored gelatin
¼ cup cold water
1 teaspoon lemon juice
½ teaspoon salt
½ cup sweetened whipped cream

Soak gelatin in ¼ cup water 5 minutes. Press mango sauce through sieve. Beat egg yolks slightly, add mango sauce and ¼ cup sugar. Cook mixture over hot water until it thickens. Add gelatin and stir until dissolved. Remove from heat, add lemon juice, and cool. Add salt to egg whites, beat until stiff, then beat in ½ cup sugar. When gelatin mixture begins to thicken, fold in egg whites, and pour into pie shell. Place pie in refrigerator to chill. Before serving spread top with sweetened whipped cream.

MANGO BROWN BETTY

YIELD: 6 servings

2 cups half-ripe mango slices, firmly packed in cup
3 tablespoons margarine
¾ cup bread crumbs
¾ cup brown sugar
1 teaspoon cinnamon
3 tablespoons water, unless mangoes are very watery

* Bazore, Katherine, *Hawaiian and Pacific Foods*, New York. 1940.

Melt fat and add bread crumbs. Place layer of bread crumbs in oiled baking dish and add layer of mangoes. Sprinkle fruit with sugar and cinnamon and add another layer of crumbs, then of mangoes. Add water and place crumbs on top. Bake in moderate oven (350° F.) until mangoes are soft (about 1 hour). Serve with lemon sauce or cream.

MANGO SHERBET

YIELD: 1½ quarts

2¼ cups sugar
¾ cup water
2 cups thick, unsweetened
   green Mango Sauce

¼ to ½ cup lemon or
   lime juice
3 cups milk
1 egg white

Dissolve sugar in water by bringing to the boiling point. Cool sirup and add to fruit and milk. Add unbeaten egg white. Pour into freezing container and freeze, using 8 parts ice to 1 part salt. Mixture may curdle, but this does not affect the finished product.

To freeze in mechanical refrigerator, dissolve 2 cups sugar in water and combine with fruit and milk. Pour into freezing tray and freeze. When partially frozen, beat egg white until stiff, add ½ cup sugar and beat until sugar is dissolved. Fold into mango mixture and continue stirring every half hour until frozen. See Note under Avocado Milk Sherbet.

MANGO FREEZE

YIELD: 1 quart

3¼ cups unsweetened Mango
   Sauce
¼ cup orange juice
1 tablespoon lemon juice

1¼ cups sugar
¾ cup sweetened whipped
   cream

Combine all ingredients except cream and mix well. Taste, and add more sugar, if desired. Freeze in an ice-cream freezer using 8 parts ice to 1 part salt.

Serve in sherbet glasses and top each with a heaping tablespoon of whipped cream.

MANGO MOUSSE

YIELD: 6 to 8 servings

½ tablespoon unflavored
   gelatin
¼ cup cold water
¾ cup sugar
½ cup hot water
Pinch of salt

1 cup unsweetened Mango
   Sauce (use half-ripe
   fruit)
1 tablespoon lime juice or
   1¼ tablespoons lemon juice
1½ cups whipping cream

Sprinkle gelatin on cold water and let stand for 5 minutes. Combine sugar and hot water, bring to boiling point, add softened gelatin and stir until dissolved. Cool, add mango, salt, and fruit juice. Freeze in refrigerator tray to consistency of mush, then fold in cream which has been whipped until stiff. Return to tray and freeze 4 to 6 hours.

Note. If sweetened mango pulp is used, reduce the sugar to 3 tablespoons.

MOUNTAIN APPLE

Description. The mountain apple (*Eugenia malaccensis*), called *ohia ai* by the Hawaiians, is an oval fruit from 2 to 3 inches long. It has a very thin crimson skin shading to pink or white. The crisp white flesh is juicy and of pleasant, though not distinctive, flavor. Each fruit contains one or two large brown seeds. The fruit is easily bruised and stains the hands deep purple.

History. This fruit, native to the Malayan Archipelago, was brought to Hawaii by the early Hawaiians. It flourishes in the deep mountain valleys of all the islands.

Nutritive Value. Mountain apples are a poor source of calcium, phosphorus, and iron. This fruit has no provitamin A and is a poor source of the B vitamins, thiamine, riboflavin, and niacin. It is a fair source of ascorbic acid.

Supply. The season ranges from June to December. The fruit is brought down from the mountains and sold along the roadside. Only small quantities reach city stores.

Use. Because of its juiciness and delicate flavor, the mountain apple is very refreshing. Most frequently eaten out of the hand, it may be used in salads and fruit cocktails. The fruit does not contain enough pectin or flavor to make it desirable for jelly or preserves, but it makes a delicious sweet pickle.

Mountain apples may be fresh-frozen in combination with acid fruits in fruit cocktails. See Appendix I for directions on freezing.

Fruit, foliage, and cross section of the mountain apple *(Eugenia malaccensis).*

SWEET PICKLED MOUNTAIN APPLES
YIELD: 1½ pints

2¼ pounds ripe mountain apples
2¼ cups sugar
1 cup cider vinegar
1 cup water
1 teaspoon whole cloves

1½ sticks cinnamon broken into ½-inch lengths
1-inch piece fresh ginger root, crushed

Wash apples but do not peel. Cut into halves or quarters, core, remove blossom ends and blemishes. Tie spices loosely in a piece of cheesecloth. Add to sugar, vinegar, and water, and boil 5 minutes. Add apples and cook until apples are tender. Let stand in sirup overnight. Next morning drain off sirup and bring to a boil. Pour the sirup over apples and repeat for three consecutive mornings. Retain spices until desired flavor is obtained.

On the third morning, drain sirup from apples and remove spice bag. Pack apples in hot sterilized jars. Bring sirup to boiling point; pour over apples, making sure to completely fill jars, and seal.

For a less highly spiced product, use less spice and add only at the last cooking period. Pickles may be finished in one cooking period by continuing cooking until apples are translucent.

The flavor is improved if the pickles are allowed to stand for a month or two before using.

BLACK MULBERRY

Description. The black mulberry (*Morus nigra*), a native of Persia and the Caucasus, is a small fruit that varies greatly in size but rarely exceeds 1¼ inches in length and ½ inch in diameter. Perhaps due to lack of cross pollination, it often appears in Hawaii in a seedless form, which may become a permanent variety. The seedless type is an excellent, well-flavored, subacid fruit that should be more widely cultivated.

Mulberry trees will grow to a height of 20 to 30 feet in Hawaii, but for fruit production they may be trimmed to the size of a small tree or even a shrub and used as a hedge. The best quality fruit is produced when the tree is well-trimmed and well-watered.

History. W. Hillebrand states that the first mulberry trees were brought to the Islands for silk culture. This was probably many years

Fruit and foliage of the black seedless mulberry *(Morus nigra).*

before 1870, because in his *Flora of the Hawaiian Islands* he stated that the trees had become naturalized in various parts of the Islands. There have been introductions from the Mainland and the Orient from time to time. In recent years many of the old trees have been cut down.

Nutritive Value. Analyses made elsewhere show that mulberries contain approximately 10 percent sugar. No data are available on the mineral content of mulberries grown in Hawaii. The local black seedless variety has been found to be a poor source of provitamin A and thiamine, a fair source of riboflavin and niacin, and a good source of ascorbic acid.

Supply. Mulberries are not marketed commercially, probably because they are a delicate fruit easily bruised and difficult to handle. However, they are a good home garden fruit; this is especially true of the seedless variety.

Use. Mulberries may be eaten fresh with sugar and cream. They make excellent pie, cobbler, and sherbets. Even those with seeds make a good fruit juice for spiced drinks. Mulberries are best combined with other fruits for jam.

Mulberries make a good frozen product. See Appendix I for methods of freezing and storage.

SPICED MULBERRY JUICE
YIELD: 1 quart

4 cups mulberries

4 cups water

2 whole allspice

2 whole cloves

1 3-inch stick cinnamon

Wash berries and crush. Add water and spices and bring to a boil. Simmer 10 minutes. Strain. Add sugar and boil 5 minutes. Serve hot.

MULBERRY PRESERVES
YIELD: 1½ pints

2 cups crushed mulberries

1 cup crushed pineapple

2 cups crushed papaya

Sugar (⅔ cup to each cup cooked fruit)

Boil the fruits together until soft (10 minutes). Measure fruit and add ⅔ cup sugar for each cup of fruit. Bring to the boiling point and cook, stirring to prevent burning, until jam is thick (about 35 minutes). Pour into sterilized glasses and seal with paraffin.

MULBERRY JAM
YIELD: 3 cups

2 pounds mulberries (8 cups)

Sugar (⅔ cup for each cup cooked berries)

3 to 4 tablespoons lemon juice

Grated rind of ½ lemon

Wash berries and partially crush in large kettle. Heat slowly until juice flows freely, then boil rapidly until about half of the juice is evaporated. Measure cooked berries and add ¾ cup sugar for each cup of berries. Boil rapidly to jelly-like consistency (see Appendix III). Stir frequently to prevent scorching. Add lemon juice and rind. Pour into sterilized glasses and seal with paraffin.

MULBERRY COBBLER

YIELD: 6 servings

¼ recipe Shortcake Dough (see Index)	1 tablespoon quick-cooking tapioca
3 to 4 cups mulberries	1 tablespoon lemon juice
1 cup sugar	2 tablespoons margarine

Wash mulberries. Mix sugar and tapioca together and combine with berries. Pour into greased 8-inch-square cake pan. Sprinkle with lemon juice and dot with margarine. Roll out shortcake dough to ¼-inch thickness and cut with doughnut or biscuit cutter. Place close together on top of the berries. Bake at 450° F. for 10 minutes; reduce heat and bake 25 minutes longer. Serve lukewarm with cream, if desired.

MULBERRY PIE

YIELD: 5 to 6 servings

1 recipe Plain Pastry (see Index)	4 tablespoons flour
	¼ teaspoon salt
3 cups mulberries	1 tablespoon lemon juice,
¾ to 1 cup sugar	if desired

Line pie tin with pastry. Combine sugar, flour, and salt. Place about ¼ mixture in bottom of unbaked shell. Add berries, sprinkle with remaining sugar and flour mixture. Add lemon juice, if used. Cover with top crust. Bake in hot oven, 450° F. for 10 minutes. Reduce heat to 350° F. and continue baking until brown (about 30 minutes longer).

MULBERRY SHERBET

YIELD: 1 pint

20 marshmallows	2 tablespoons lemon juice
1 cup mulberry juice	2 egg whites
¼ cup orange juice	2 tablespoons sugar

Place marshmallows and mulberry juice in double boiler and cook, stirring frequently, until thoroughly melted. Remove, cool, and add orange and lemon juices. Pour into refrigerator tray and chill until partly jellied (about 1 hour). Place large mixer bowl and beater in refrigerator to chill.

Beat egg whites until stiff, gradually add sugar and beat until glossy.

Scrape frozen mulberry mixture into chilled bowl, add beaten egg whites, and beat quickly with rotary beater until smooth and fluffy. Return to freezing tray, moisten bottom of tray and finish freezing (about 3 hours). Cover with foil or wax paper, reset control to slightly colder than normal until ready to serve.

See Note under Avocado Milk Sherbet.

MULBERRY ICE

YIELD: 8 to 10 servings

2 cups fresh mulberries	1 to 2 tablespoons lemon juice
¾ cup sugar	4 tablespoons orange juice
¼ cup water	2 egg whites, if desired
Pinch of salt	

Wash berries and crush in bottom of kettle. Add sugar and cook slowly for 5 minutes. Add water and press through a sieve. Cool, add salt, egg whites, lemon and orange juices, and freeze in ice-cream freezer. Allow 1 part salt to 8 parts ice. Mulberry ice is excellent with meat courses.

OHELO BERRY

Description. The ohelo (*Vaccinium reticulatum* Smith) belongs to the cranberry family. Its fruit is globose, red or yellow in color, may or may not be covered with bloom, and contains a large number of tiny flattened seeds similar to those found in a blueberry. The size varies from ¼ to ½ inch in diameter.

History. The ohelo is one of the few truly native fruits of Hawaii. According to Degener, the "ohelo is found only on the island of Hawaii and on East Maui, where it thrives on the less weathered lava flows and beds of volcanic ash and cinders." Because it grows well near the Kilauea Crater on Hawaii, it was considered especially sacred to Pele, the goddess of the volcano, and it was customary in the olden days to offer some of the berries to her before eating any of them.

Nutritive Value. Ohelo berries are a poor source of the three minerals—calcium, phosphorus, and iron. They are a fair source of provitamin A and a poor source of the other vitamins tested—thiamine, riboflavin, niacin, and ascorbic acid.

Supply. Ohelo berries are not cultivated, but in a few areas on Hawaii and Maui the berries may be picked from the low bushes, which still grow wild.

Use. Since the supply is always limited, the ohelo are commonly eaten raw, but they may also be made into pie, sauce, or jam. The berries have sufficient acid to make good jelly and jam, but because of the weak pectin the products have a tendency to "weep."

OHELO BERRY JAM NO. 1 YIELD: 6 to 7 cups

8 cups ohelo berries (2 quarts) 4 cups sugar
1 cup water

Pick over berries, discarding those that seem very dry, as they will not soften on cooking. Add water and cook, stirring frequently, until berries are tender (20 to 30 minutes). Add sugar, bring quickly to a boil, and cook for 5 to 10 more minutes, until the product gives a jelly test (see Appendix III).

OHELO BERRY JAM NO. 2 YIELD: 4 cups

8 cups ohelo berries   3 tablespoons lemon juice
3 cups sugar

Pick over berries, measure, wash, and drain. Add sugar and stir until most of the sugar is dissolved. Heat slowly, stirring frequently, until juice is drawn out. Add lemon juice and boil rapidly until the mixture gives a jelly test (see Appendix III).

This product is slightly more tart than Jam No. 1, and the skins of the berries are slightly tougher. It can be used as a relish with meat or poultry, or as a jam.

HAWAII ORANGE

Description. Although several varieties of oranges (*Citrus sinensis*) have been introduced into Hawaii, at the present time only the seedling known as the Hawaii is grown commercially. The Hawaii orange is a medium-size round variety. The yellow skin is thin and rather tough. The flesh is commonly yellow orange and very juicy. It varies from acid to sweet but is usually rather mild in flavor.

History. The Hawaii variety of orange has been developed by a long period of cultivation. One of the original orange trees left in Hawaii by Captain George Vancouver in 1792 still lives. He gave the natives a number of small orange seedlings, some of which were planted on land belonging to a prominent Hawaiian at Kealakekua in the district of Kona on the island of Hawaii. In time, the land, which had come into the possession of the famous high chiefess Kapiolani, was obtained by an early missionary, the Reverend J. D. Paris, who began his residence there about 1852. At that time his daughter, Ella Paris, was four years old. In 1936 she still occupied a part of the old Paris home and clearly recalled that the tree was one of several which in her youth were very old. In 1954, relatives of Miss Paris reported that a vigorous young tree from the original root stock was still bearing fruit.

At one time the orange, one of the first fruits to be cultivated commercially in Hawaii, was the leading export from the Kona district. The districts of Waialua on Oahu, and Waimea on Kauai, were also well known for their oranges. Kona, Waialua, and Waimea oranges are named for these districts, but all are of the same variety.

In 1961, the Horticulture Department of the University of Hawaii initiated a twofold program of research on oranges and other citrus fruits. One purpose of the program is to introduce both rootstocks and seeds or scions of the highest quality fruits from other tropical and subtropical countries for testing in Hawaii. The other purpose is to test the standard Valencia and navel oranges on the most widely used virus-tolerant rootstocks at several ecological locations.

Nutritive Value. The nutritive value of oranges has been extolled by so many scientists in recent years that little need be added here.

Though acid to the taste, oranges leave an alkaline ash residue in the body and tend, like most other fruits, to make the urine more alkaline.

Analyses of Hawaii oranges show them to have a chemical composition similar to that of oranges grown on the Mainland. Average analyses show oranges to be superior to most fruits as sources of calcium and equal to or better than other fruits as sources of phosphorus and iron.

It was found that the calcium content of the orange with membrane surrounding the sections is almost twice that of the orange with the membrane removed, but the phosphorus and iron content is about the same in each case. Juice of Hawaii oranges was found to contain 0.010 to 0.013 percent calcium and the juice of California navel oranges prepared in the same manner was found to contain 0.015 percent calcium. The juice for analysis was passed through a copper sieve of 10 meshes to the inch, a size comparable to household orange juice strainers on the market.

It is highly probable that the calcium content of oranges and orange juice may be affected by a number of factors such as variety, soil, and fertilizer.

Analyses done at the University of Hawaii and reports in the literature indicate that the quantity of membranous material included with the orange or in the orange juice markedly affects the quantity of calcium found.

Hawaii-grown oranges have vitamin values similar to those grown elsewhere. Orange juice from locally produced oranges was found to be a good source of provitamin A and thiamine, a fair source of riboflavin, a poor source of niacin, and a good to excellent source of ascorbic acid.

If allowed to stand, juice made from Hawaii oranges, like that made from oranges grown elsewhere, develops a bitter taste. However, fresh juice of local oranges is delicious and a rich source of vitamin C.

Supply. Hawaii oranges are grown principally in the Kona region on Hawaii. The demand for them has not been great because of their quality and appearance and because very little grading has been done for the market. Hawaii oranges are usually in season during October, November, and December.

Use. The well-ripened and mature Hawaii orange may be used in the same ways as Mainland oranges. Marmalade made from some Hawaii oranges is more bitter than that made from California oranges. If the membranes and inner pulp of the peel have a bitter flavor, soak the peel in water, discard water, and then cook the peel in fresh water. This will remove the bitterness and make a more palatable marmalade.

TART ORANGE MARMALADE

2 Hawaii oranges
2 Hawaii lemons
3 cups water to 1 cup fruit

1 cup sugar to 1 cup fruit
pulp and water

Remove rind and soak it overnight. Discard water next morning and cook rind in a large quantity of water 30 minutes. Cool and scrape out white pulp. Cut peeling into very fine strips. Cut fruit into fine pieces. Measure fruit pulp and add three times as much water. Let stand overnight.

Next morning measure fruit pulp and water and add the same amount of sugar. Then add cooked peelings. Cook the mixture until it gives a slight jelly test (see Appendix III). Pour into hot sterilized glasses and seal with paraffin.

ORANGE MARMALADE
YIELD: 3½ cups

2 small oranges (2¼ inches
    in diameter)
1 lemon

5 cups water
5 cups sugar

Wash fruit and cut into quarters or eighths, and slice paper thin. Cook in 5 cups of water until rind is tender (45 minutes to 1 hour), adding more water during cooking period if necessary. Drain off liquid, measure, and add enough water to make 5 cups. Return to kettle, add sugar, and boil until it begins to thicken. Cook to temperature just under jelly stage, 218° to 220° F. (see Appendix III). Pour into hot sterilized glasses and seal with paraffin.

THREE FRUIT MARMALADE
YIELD: 10 to 14 pints
or 14 to 19 pounds*

1 medium-size grapefruit
3 medium-size oranges
3 lemons

Sugar as required
Water as required

Wash fruit thoroughly, cut into halves crosswise, and cut in paper-thin slices about 1 inch long, using a plate to conserve the juice. Press cut pulp and juice firmly into cup or quart measure. To each cup of pulp and juice, add 3 cups cold water. Let stand 12 to 24 hours in covered preserving kettle.

Bring mixture to a full boil and cook until rind is tender (30 minutes).

Mixture may stand for 12 to 24 hours more, or it may be used at once.

---

* Yield depends upon size of fruit used.

Measure, and to each cup (or quart) of cooked juice and pulp add an equal measure of sugar. Stir, bring quickly to full boil, and cook as for jelly or until it gives a jelly test, 218° F. or 221° F. (see Appendix III). For full recipe it is better to cook in two lots. Pour into hot sterilized glasses and cover with paraffin (see Appendix III).

PINEAPPLE CONSERVE
See Index.

PINEAPPLE-HONEY PRESERVE
See Index.

ALOHA PUNCH
See Index.

MANGO NECTAR
See Index.

MANOA FRUIT PUNCH
See Index.

STRAWBERRY GUAVA PUNCH
See Index.

FIG COCKTAIL
See Index.

LYCHEE, PINEAPPLE, AND ORANGE COCKTAIL
See Index.

BANANA CASSEROLE
See Index.

AVOCADO FRUIT SALAD
See Index.

MANGO FRUIT MOLD
See Index.

ROYAL HAWAIIAN DELIGHT
See Index.

PAPAYA

Description. The papaya (*Carica papaya*) is a melonlike fruit which varies greatly in size and shape. The Solo variety is a small fruit from 3 to 5 inches in diameter, but other types, 20 inches or more in length and weighing 10 pounds, may sometimes be seen in home gardens.

The skin is smooth and thin, shading from deep orange to green. The flesh varies in thickness from 1 to 2 inches and from light yellow to deep salmon pink in color. Numerous round, black, wrinkled seeds, each enclosed in a gelatinous membrane, cling to the inner wall. The flavor and odor of the fruit are distinctive. The white latex that exudes from the leaves, stems, and unripe fruit is very irritating to the eye.

History. The date of the introduction of the papaya into Hawaii is uncertain. Because it has a distinctly Hawaiian name, *he-i,* some people believe it grew in Hawaii before the first European voyagers arrived. However, Dr. F. J. F. Meyen, who visited Hawaii in 1831, stated that while visiting Don Marin's possessions he learned of the many kinds of plants introduced by Marin, and among them was the papaya from the Marquesas Islands. This introduction must have been prior to 1823, as William Ellis noted "pawpaw apples" growing in Kona gardens that year.

The Solo papaya was introduced by the Hawaii Agricultural Experiment Station as a new variety in 1919. Since that time, it has been greatly improved through selection and propagation, especially by Dr. William B. Storey in recent years; and the hermaphrodite form of Inbred Line 5 is now practically the only type grown and marketed in Hawaii.

"Pawpaw" is the word commonly used in England for the papaya, but in the southern United States, the name is likely to be confused with "pawpaw" as applied to the *Asimina triloba,* a very different fruit. Most countries now use either the name papaya or some variation of it, as "papaia," "apaeya," or "papaja," which are all believed to be derived from the Carib word *ababai.*

Nutritive Value. The quantity of papain, a protein-splitting enzyme, consumed when even large quantities of papaya are eaten is probably not of any great nutritional significance, but it may be the reason that a few people experience some digestive distress after eating papaya. Ripe papaya contains little or no papain.

Papaya is a fair source of calcium and a poor source of phosphorus and iron. The Solo variety has been found to be an excellent source of provitamin A, a poor source of thiamine and niacin, a fair source of riboflavin, and an excellent source of ascorbic acid.

Weekly tests were made for a year to determine the vitamin C content of Solo papayas from two localities on the island of Oahu—Poamoho Experimental Farm, and Kailua. The ascorbic acid content ranged from 60 to 122 milligrams per 100 grams and averaged 84 milligrams per 100 grams for 85 fruit.

Stewing or baking papaya was found to destroy 7 to 12 percent of the ascorbic acid originally present. The use of lemon or lime juice, called for in most recipes, increases the acidity and probably improves the retention of ascorbic acid in the cooked papaya.

In papaya, ascorbic acid increases as the fruit ripens. When the skin is dark green and the flesh a light yellow, the fruit contains only 60 to 70 percent as much ascorbic acid as when ripe.

As an economical and important source of vitamin A and ascorbic acid, papaya should be more widely used in Hawaii.

Supply. The supply and quality of papayas on the market vary greatly. The quality and flavor of the fruit depend partially on the season and the amount of rainfall. Fruit yields are usually greatest in May and June with another lesser peak of production in October and November.

Use. The papaya is used preferably in the ripe stage. However, green papaya may be boiled and served as a vegetable. Ripe papaya is best used fresh. It makes an excellent breakfast or dessert fruit served with lemon or lime. In fruit cocktails or salads, it is usually combined with pineapple or citrus fruits. Fresh papaya pulp with milk or cream makes a delicious frozen dessert. Papaya alone or combined with other fruits makes excellent jams and marmalades.

One medium papaya ($1\frac{1}{4}$ pounds) yields a little more than 1 cup pulp or $1\frac{1}{2}$ to 2 cups of cubes, according to size of cubes.

Papayas tend to soften when frozen and, therefore, are not recommended for freezing because of the resulting poor flavor and texture.

Fruit, foliage, and cross section of the Solo papaya *(Carica papaya)*.

PAPAYA MARMALADE

10 cups sliced firm-ripe papaya
1 cup fresh shredded pineapple
Grated rind of 1 orange and
2 lemons
½ cup orange juice

½ cup lemon juice
3 tablespoons grated fresh
ginger root
1 cup sugar to each cup
cooked fruit
½ teaspoon salt

Combine all ingredients except sugar. Boil 30 minutes. Measure cooked fruit and add an equal amount of sugar. Cook together 30 minutes, stirring frequently to prevent burning. When done, pour mixture into hot sterilized jars and seal with paraffin. This product does not keep longer than 6 months.

GUAVA-PAPAYA BUTTER
See Index.

KETAMBILLA-PAPAYA JAM
See Index.

PAPAYA-COCONUT JAM

YIELD: 1 quart

4 cups papaya purée
2 cups finely grated fresh coconut
4 cups sugar

¼ cup lemon juice
2 tsp. ginger juice,
if desired

Combine papaya purée, sugar, and coconut in a large kettle. Bring to the boiling point and cook with constant slow stirring for 15 minutes. Add lemon juice and ginger juice, and cook for 5 minutes longer, or until very thick and glossy. Pour into sterilized jars and cover with paraffin.

To prepare the ginger juice, place a thoroughly scrubbed piece of fresh ginger root in a small piece of strong coarse cloth, crush the root by pounding with a hammer or wooden mallet, and squeeze out the desired amount of juice.

Note. As the mixture tends to bubble and splash badly, it is necessary to stir constantly with a long-handled wooden spoon. It is wise to protect the hands with cotton gloves.

PAPAYA CATSUP

YIELD: 2 quarts

14 cups strained papaya pulp
4 tablespoons whole allspice
3 tablespoons whole cloves
3 tablespoons mustard seed
1 stick cinnamon
1 medium-size piece ginger
root, chopped

1 large onion, sliced
¼ teaspoon red pepper
6 tablespoons sugar
2 tablespoons salt
1¼ cups vinegar
¼ teaspoon tartaric acid

Tie spices and onion in a cheesecloth bag, add to papaya pulp, and cook slowly for 40 minutes. Add sugar, salt, vinegar, and tartaric acid crystals. Cook until thick (1 hour). Remove bag of spices. Pour catsup into hot sterilized jars and seal.

PAPAYA-PINEAPPLE MARMALADE

YIELD: $1\frac{1}{2}$ pints

2 cups finely diced ripe pineapple (2 pounds)
2 cups diced ripe papaya
4 cups sugar
$1\frac{1}{2}$ teaspoons grated lemon rind ($\frac{1}{2}$ lemon)
$\frac{1}{4}$ cup lemon juice
1 to 2 tablespoons fresh grated ginger, if desired

Combine pineapple and sugar in large shallow saucepan and let stand while preparing the papaya. Add grated lemon rind and juice. Bring slowly to boiling point and boil about 30 minutes until mixture sheets from spoon, or until temperature reaches 224° F. (see Appendix III). Pour into sterilized half-pint jars and seal. This marmalade does not keep longer than 6 months.

MULBERRY PRESERVES

See Index.

PAPAYA SHAKE

YIELD: 5 servings

2 cups mashed ripe papaya pulp
$\frac{1}{3}$ cup lemon or $\frac{1}{4}$ cup lime juice
$\frac{3}{4}$ cup sugar
3 cups milk
1 teaspoon nutmeg

Combine mashed fruit and sugar; add other ingredients. Chill. Just before serving, shake with cracked ice in jar with tight-fitting lid.

PAPAYA-PINEAPPLE NECTAR

YIELD: 5 cups

2 cups diced ripe papaya
$2\frac{1}{2}$ cups pineapple juice (No. 2 can)
$\frac{1}{4}$ cup lemon juice OR $2\frac{2}{3}$ tablespoons lime juice
$\frac{1}{4}$ cup passion fruit juice OR 3 tablespoons passion fruit pulp, if desired
$\frac{1}{2}$ cup sugar OR $\frac{1}{4}$ cup sugar and $\frac{1}{4}$ cup honey

Peel papaya, cut into pieces, and force through a coarse sieve or ricer. Combine with other ingredients; mix until sugar is dissolved, chill, and pour over cracked ice.

PAPAYA-BANANA NECTAR

YIELD: 3¾ cups

1 cup mashed papaya	¼ cup sugar
½ cup mashed ripe banana	⅔ cup water
1 cup guava juice, unsweetened	2 tablespoons lemon juice

Peel ripe papaya and banana, cut into pieces, and press through a coarse sieve. Combine all ingredients, mix until thoroughly blended, chill, and pour over cracked ice.

If electric food blendor or mixer is used, combine all ingredients and blend for 2 minutes.

PAPAYA ONO-ONO

YIELD: 12 cups

4 cups ripe papaya pulp	¼ cup orange juice
1 cup passion fruit juice	4 cups pineapple juice
¼ cup lemon or lime juice	1 cup sugar
2½ cups guava juice	½ cup water

Peel papaya, cut into small pieces, and force through a coarse sieve. Add fruit juices, sugar, and water. Mix well, chill, and pour over cracked ice.

If electric food blendor is used, combine all ingredients and blend for 2 minutes.

Variation. Omit sugar and use ¾ cup Passion Fruit Sirup instead of the fresh fruit juice.

LYCHEE, MANGO, AND PAPAYA FRUIT CUP
See Index.

PINEAPPLE-PAPAYA CUP
See Index.

PAPAYA AND PINEAPPLE COCKTAIL

YIELD: 6 servings

2 cups diced ripe papaya	6 tablespoons lemon juice
2 cups diced pineapple	2 tablespoons sugar

Mix ingredients and chill for ½ hour before serving.

BAKED PAPAYA

YIELD: 6 servings

2 or 3 firm-ripe Solo papayas	2 tablespoons margarine
2 tablespoons lemon or lime juice	¾ teaspoon salt

Pare and cut papayas lengthwise into halves or thirds. Remove seeds. Sprinkle with salt and lemon juice, and add margarine. Place in baking pan and add enough water to cover bottom of pan. Bake in moderate oven (350° F.) for 35 minutes. Serve immediately. Baked Papaya may be used in place of a vegetable.

Half-ripe papaya may be used if preferred.

LYCHEE, PAPAYA, AND PINEAPPLE SALAD
See Index.

PINEAPPLE FRUIT MOLD
See Index.

ROSELLE FRUIT MOLD
See Index.

MANGO FRUIT MOLD
See Index.

ROYAL HAWAIIAN DELIGHT
YIELD: 6 servings

1 cup whipping cream	1½ cups ripe papaya cubes
¼ cup powdered sugar	½ cup diced orange
8 marshmallows	2 teaspoons lemon juice
¼ cup shredded coconut	¼ teaspoon salt

Chill cream, and whip. Add sugar, then marshmallows cut into quarters. Fold in papaya, lemon juice, orange, and coconut. Pour into serving dish or individual glass dishes. Chill before serving.

PAPAYA UPSIDE-DOWN CAKE
YIELD: 6 servings

2 cups sliced papaya	1 egg
2 tablespoons lemon juice	1¼ cups flour
¼ cup brown sugar	2 teaspoons baking powder
1 tablespoon margarine	¼ teaspoon salt
¼ cup fat	½ cup milk
¾ cup sugar	

Pour lemon juice over papaya and let stand 15 minutes. Melt margarine and brown sugar in shallow pyrex dish. Place a layer of papaya slices on top of sugar mixture. To prepare cake mixture, cream fat, add ¾ cup sugar and, when well mixed, add beaten egg. Sift salt, baking powder, and flour together and add to egg mixture alternately with milk.

Pour batter over papaya slices and bake in a moderate oven (350° F.) from 50 to 60 minutes. When cake is done, turn it upside down on a large plate. Serve hot with whipped cream, lime or lemon sauce (see Index).

HAWAIIAN AMBROSIA
See Index.

PAPAYA-COCONUT PUDDING
See Index.

PAPAYA MILK SHERBET
YIELD: 1 quart

1¼ cups ripe papaya pulp   1¼ cups milk
3 tablespoons lemon juice   1 cup sugar
¼ cup orange juice

Press papaya pulp through a coarse sieve and add fruit juice. Dissolve sugar in milk and add the fruit mixture gradually to the milk. Pour into freezing pan of mechanical refrigerator and freeze quickly, stirring every half hour during process.

A superior product may be obtained by freezing in an ice-cream freezer, using 8 parts ice to 1 part salt.

PAPAYA ICE CREAM
YIELD: 6 servings

Use the above recipe for Papaya Milk Sherbet, substituting thin cream, or 1 cup thin cream and ½ cup whipping cream, for the milk. If ice cream is frozen in mechanical refrigerator trays, stir several times during freezing process.

PASSION FRUIT

Description. The passion fruit (*Passiflora edulis*) is a medium-size oval fruit from 2 to 3 inches long. There are two varieties common in Hawaii, the purple passion fruit (*Passiflora edulis*) and the yellow passion fruit (*Passiflora edulis* forma *flavicarpa*). *Passiflora ligularis,* also called sweet granadilla or waterlemon, which has an orange-colored shell, is seen only occasionally.

The brittle shell encloses a juicy yellow pulp and many small seeds. Although the shell dries up and becomes wrinkled after the fruit has matured, the pulp remains in good condition for several weeks.

History. The passion fruit, native of Brazil, has been carried to all parts of the world. In many places it is grown only as a hothouse plant. Its unusual flowers inspired the Spaniards to name it the passion plant. In Australia, where the purple passion fruit is very popular, it is cultivated on a large scale.

In Hawaii the purple variety is commonly called *Lilikoi* because the first seeds of this variety, which were brought from Australia by Eugene Delemar in about 1880, were planted in the district of Lilikoi on East Maui. The large yellow passion fruit, which was introduced by the Hawaii Agricultural Experiment Station in 1923, is now assuming commercial importance. Although both purple and yellow varieties of the *Passiflora edulis* are locally called "waterlemons," that term is correct only for the *Passiflora ligularis,* which is grown to a limited extent in Hawaii.

Nutritive Value. Analyses of the juice of the purple passion fruit showed it to be high in sugar content and low in calcium, phosphorus, and iron.

The passion fruit juice keeps well because of its natural high acidity reported to be due largely to citric acid. The yellow passion fruit is more acid than the purple variety. The acidity of the purple passion fruit juice was found to be 2.3 percent calculated as citric acid, whereas the acidity of the yellow passion fruit juice was 3.9 percent.

The juice of the yellow passion fruit, prepared by squeezing the pulp through two thicknesses of cheesecloth, was found to be an excellent

141

Fruit, foliage, and cross section of the yellow passion fruit
(*Passiflora edulis* forma *flavicarpa*).

source of provitamin A and niacin, a good source of riboflavin, a fair source of ascorbic acid, but it contains little or no thiamine.

The purple passion fruit juice was found to be a good source of provitamin A, riboflavin, niacin, and ascorbic acid, and a poor source of thiamine.

Supply. Passion fruit ripens during the summer and fall. Some ripen as late as January. The fruit is occasionally found in Honolulu markets.

Use. The fruit is prepared for use by cutting it in two and removing the pulp with a spoon. It may be eaten fresh out of the shell or it may be used to flavor candy, cake icing, or frozen desserts. Some like the pulp with the seeds from one or two fruit used as a topping on fruit salad.

All recipes given in this book have been tested with the yellow passion fruit. If the purple fruit is used, less sugar will be required since it is less acid.

The distinctive flavor of the fruit juice makes it a pleasant addition to iced drinks. Canned passion fruit may be prepared by adding the fresh passion fruit pulp to a boiling hot sirup. If bottled and sealed at once the canned fruit will keep for some months. The sirup loses flavor and changes color if stored more than six to eight months.

The yellow passion fruit has ample acid but insufficient pectin to make a good jelly. Jelly may be made, however, using commercial pectin. The product is an opaque jelly, which tends to weep or exude a thin liquid from the gel when allowed to stand (syneresis).

Passion fruit juice can be readily frozen and used in place of the fresh juice in all the recipes given in this book. For directions on freezing, see Appendix I.

PASSION FRUIT JUICE

YIELD: 1⅓ cups

12 lemon-size passion fruit

Cut fruit into halves and remove pulp with a spoon. Place pulp in a poi cloth or two thicknesses of cheesecloth, squeezing out as much juice as possible. Store in refrigerator until ready to use.

PASSION FRUIT JELLY

YIELD: 10 to 12 6-ounce glasses

3 cups fresh passion fruit juice   **7½ cups sugar**
1 cup water   **1 bottle liquid pectin (1 cup)**

Prepare juice as directed above. Measure sugar into large saucepan; add juice and water and stir well. Place over high heat and bring to a boil, stirring constantly. Immediately add pectin. Bring to a full rolling boil, then boil rapidly for 1 minute, stirring constantly. Remove from the range, skim and pour into sterilized glasses.

This product sets very slowly and results in a soft jelly, which becomes firmer after standing several weeks.

PASSION FRUIT SIRUP
YIELD: 2 quarts

4 cups water	2⅔ cups passion fruit pulp OR
6 cups sugar	2 cups passion fruit juice (24 fruit)

Add sugar to water and heat to the boiling point. Press passion fruit pulp through a sieve or squeeze in poi cloth or cheesecloth to remove seeds. Add pulp to the sirup. Pour into hot sterilized bottles and seal at once. This sirup keeps well 6 to 8 months. It may be used for iced drinks, cake icings, and frozen desserts.

For a thinner sirup use 4 instead of 6 cups of sugar.

PASSION FRUITADE
YIELD: 6 cups

2 cups passion fruit sirup	4 cups cold water

Mix, chill, and pour over cracked ice.

FRESH PASSION FRUIT NECTAR
YIELD: 4 cups

1¼ cups fresh passion fruit juice	½ to 1 cup sugar
1¼ cups pineapple juice	1⅓ tablespoons lemon juice
1¼ cups water	

Press passion fruit pulp through a coarse sieve or squeeze in poi cloth or cheesecloth to obtain juice. Add ½ cup of sugar, stir until dissolved. Taste and add more sugar if a sweeter punch is desired. Chill and pour over cracked ice.

HOT SPICED PASSION FRUIT JUICE
YIELD: 5 cups

3¾ cups water	18 whole allspice
⅞ cup sugar	3 pieces stick cinnamon
6 strips lemon peel (¼ inch wide)	(2 inches long)
18 whole cloves	¾ cup passion fruit juice
	1½ teaspoons lemon juice

Combine all ingredients except fruit juices. Boil 10 minutes in a covered container, stirring occasionally. Add passion fruit and lemon juice and heat to simmering point. Strain and serve hot with a strip of lemon peel in each cup.

FRESH PASSION FRUIT PUNCH

YIELD: 90 servings (⅓ cup each)

4 to 4¼ cups fresh passion fruit
juice (about 36 large fruit)
2 quarts pineapple juice

4 quarts water
2 to 3 cups sugar
¼ cup lemon juice, if desired

Prepare passion fruit juice as described above. Combine with pineapple juice and water and add 2 cups sugar. Stir until sugar is dissolved. Taste and add more sugar if a sweeter punch is desired. Pour over a 1- to 2-pound block of ice in a punch bowl.

PASSION FRUIT PUNCH

YIELD: 6 cups

¼ cup lemon juice
1¼ cups Passion Fruit Sirup

⅔ cup orange juice
2⅔ tablespoons sugar
3¼ cups water

Mix ingredients. Chill, and pour over cracked ice.

PAPAYA ONO-ONO
See recipe p. 116.

PASSION FRUIT CAKE ICING*

YIELD: 1⅛ cups

3 tablespoons margarine
2¼ cups confectioners' sugar

¼ cup fresh passion fruit pulp
OR 3 tablespoons passion
fruit sirup

Press passion fruit pulp through a sieve to remove seeds. Cream margarine, adding ⅓ cup sugar gradually. Add fruit pulp and remaining sugar. Beat until the mixture is smooth and stiff enough to spread on cake.

PASSION FRUIT MERINGUE PIE

YIELD: 8- or 9-inch pie

1 baked pie shell (see Index)
5 tablespoons cornstarch
¼ teaspoon salt
¾ to 1 cup sugar
1¼ cups water
3 eggs, separated
2 tablespoons margarine

¼ cup fresh or frozen passion
fruit juice
6. tablespoons sugar
¼ teaspoon lemon flavoring,
if desired
Pinch of salt

Combine cornstarch, salt, and ¾ cup sugar in top of double boiler. Add about ¼ cup of water and stir until well blended. Add remaining

* Adapted from recipe booklet from Kremer Plantations, Cardiff-By-The-Sea, California.

145

water and cook over direct heat, stirring constantly until very thick and transparent (8 to 10 minutes).

Separate eggs and beat yolks slightly. Add a portion of the hot cornstarch mixture gradually, while stirring vigorously; then slowly pour egg mixture into the remaining hot cornstarch mixture. Stir constantly. Place over boiling water and cook 5 to 10 minutes longer until thick. Add margarine, cool, and add fruit juice. Pour into baked pie shell.

Beat egg whites until they form soft peaks when beater is lifted (stiff but not dry). Gradually beat in the remaining 6 tablespoons sugar by sprinkling about 1½ tablespoons at a time over surface of the egg whites until all is used. Add a pinch of salt and lemon flavoring, if desired. Pile meringue around outer edge of pie filling, being careful to seal meringue to the crust. Spread toward the center and swirl for decorative top. Bake at 400° F. for 8 to 10 minutes; or 325° F. for 15 to 20 minutes or until delicately browned.

PASSION FRUIT CHIFFON PIE
YIELD: 9-inch pie

1 9-inch baked pie shell
  (see Index)
1¼ tablespoons unflavored
  gelatin
¼ cup cold water
3 eggs, separated

½ teaspoon salt
1 cup sugar
½ to ⅔ cup passion fruit juice
½ cup whipping cream,
  if desired

Sprinkle gelatin over cold water and let stand for 5 minutes. Separate eggs, placing whites in medium bowl and yolks in top of double boiler. Add salt and ½ cup sugar to yolks; mix well. Stir in passion fruit juice and cook over hot water until thick and foamy, beating constantly with rotary egg beater (about 3 minutes). Remove from hot water, add softened gelatin and beat until dissolved. Chill until slightly thickened.

Beat egg whites until stiff but not dry; then gradually but quickly beat in ½ cup sugar, sprinkling by tablespoons over the surface of egg whites until all is used. Fold into the gelatin mixture until well blended. Pour into baked shell and chill in refrigerator until firm. Garnish top with whipped cream if desired.

PASSION FRUIT FLUFF PIE
YIELD: 8-inch pie (5 servings).

1 baked pie shell (see Index)
3 tablespoons flour
3 tablespoons cornstarch
¼ teaspoon salt

1¼ cups sugar
1 cup water
4 eggs, separated
¼ cup fresh passion fruit juice

Combine flour, cornstarch, salt, and ¾ cup sugar in the top of a double boiler. Gradually stir in the water and cook over direct heat, stirring constantly, until very thick (8 to 10 minutes). Place over boiling water, cover and cook 10 minutes.

Separate eggs and beat yolks slightly. Gradually add a portion of the hot mixture to the yolks, stirring vigorously, then slowly pour yolk mixture into remaining hot mixture and cook a minute longer. Remove from heat, cool, and stir in passion fruit juice.

Beat egg whites until they form soft peaks when beater is lifted (stiff but not dry). Gradually beat in remaining ½ cup sugar by sprinkling 1½ tablespoons at a time over surface of the egg whites, until all is used. Fold about ⅓ of this meringue into cooked filling and pour into baked shell. Pile meringue around outer edge of the pie filling, being careful to seal meringue to the crust. Spread toward the center and swirl for decorative top. Bake at 400° F. for 8 to 10 minutes, or at 325° F. for 15 to 20 minutes or until delicately browned.

PASSION FRUIT SHERBET
YIELD: 6 to 8 servings

1 cup passion fruit juice (9 lemon-size fruit)	1 teaspoon unflavored gelatin
	2 cups water
⅓ cup white corn sirup	½ to ¾ cup sugar
2 egg whites	Pinch of salt

Prepare passion fruit juice as directed above. Chill corn sirup and egg whites in medium bowl. Sprinkle gelatin over ½ cup of the water (use small saucepan) and let stand 5 minutes. Add sugar and salt and heat until dissolved. Add remaining 1½ cups water and fruit juice. Pour into freezing tray and freeze to a mush.

Beat egg white sirup mixture until very stiff (about 7 to 10 minutes). Add frozen passion fruit mixture and beat until just blended. Pour into 2 freezing trays; moisten bottoms of trays and place on coldest shelf in freezing compartment. Wash bowl and beater and place in refrigerator to chill.

When mixture is frozen stiff (about 1 hour), scrape into chilled bowl; break up with spoon if necessary. Beat until well blended and fluffy. Quickly pile sherbet into trays, moisten bottoms of trays and return to freezing compartment. Freeze to serving consistency, stirring with a fork once or twice. See Note under Avocado Milk Sherbet.

PASSION FRUIT MILK SHERBET
YIELD: 6 servings

2 eggs, separated	¾ cup fresh passion fruit juice
½ cup sugar	1 tablespoon lemon juice
1 cup milk	2 tablespoons sugar
Pinch of salt	

Make a soft custard by combining egg yolks, sugar, milk, and salt in the top of double boiler. Cook over hot water, stirring constantly until the mixture coats a spoon. Cool and add fruit juice. Pour into freezing tray and freeze to a mush in coldest part of the refrigerator.

Beat egg whites until stiff but not dry. Gradually add 2 tablespoons sugar, beating until stiff and glossy. Remove freezing pan and fold meringue into the partially frozen mixture. Moisten bottom of the tray and return to freezing compartment. Stir with a fork once or twice until frozen to serving consistency. See Note under Avocado Milk Sherbet.

PASSION FRUIT ICE CREAM
YIELD: 6 servings

¼ cup Passion Fruit Sirup	2 cups thin cream
¼ cup sugar	¼ teaspoon vanilla

Mix all ingredients and stir until sugar is dissolved. Freeze in ice-cream freezer using 8 parts ice to 1 part salt.

Variation. Fresh passion fruit juice may be used in place of passion fruit sirup if the sugar is increased to ½ cup.

PASSION FRUIT MOUSSE
YIELD: 6 servings

¼ tablespoon unflavored gelatin	3 tablespoons boiling water
2 tablespoons cold water	1¼ cups Passion Fruit Sirup
	1 cup whipping cream

Sprinkle gelatin on cold water and let stand for 5 minutes. Add boiling water and heat mixture over hot water until gelatin is thoroughly dissolved. Chill cream, and whip. Fold in sirup and gelatin. Freeze 4 to 5 hours in a mechanical refrigerator pan.

PINEAPPLE

Description. The pineapple (*Ananas comosus*) is really a collection of small fruits and is called a multiple fruit. In the flower stage the corollas are separate but the ovaries are fused, giving the appearance of a cluster of flowers on a single stalk.

The mature pineapple, a large fruit shaped like a pine cone or pyramid, is about 6 to 10 inches in height and weighs 5 to 8 pounds. It grows on a stalk or peduncle that is a continuation of the plant stem of the low cactus-like pineapple plant. The tough and horny rind is composed of small hexagonal sections, fitted together like pieces of tile. Each of these sections marks a botanically individual fruit.

The skin of a ripe pineapple may be deep yellow, chocolate-green, or mottled green and brown. The flesh is very juicy and has a somewhat fibrous texture. It varies in color from white to deep yellow. The edible portion surrounds a tough central core which was originally the flower stalk.

History. The pineapple, a native of South America, early became a favorite luxury of wealthy Europeans. The history of the introduction of the pineapple into Hawaii is not known, but it is generally believed that the fruit was brought in by some Spaniard who had previously touched the coast of South America. Although Don Marin records in his diary in 1813 that he had pineapples growing in his garden, they were probably first planted on the island of Hawaii, where they now grow wild. A pineapple similar to the Wild Kailua pineapple also grows in Guam, Formosa, and the Philippine Islands. Some of this half-wild fruit was shipped in the fresh state to San Francisco before 1880, but the fruit spoiled easily and was of poor quality.

The pineapple industry was of minor importance in Hawaii until 1886, when the Smooth Cayenne variety was introduced. The first pineapple was canned commercially in 1892. From that time on the industry developed until today it is the second largest industry in the Islands.

Nutritive Value. The pineapple has long been valued for its distinctive flavor and refreshing qualities.

Fresh ripe pineapple is a good source of sugar and a fair source of calcium. Pineapple juice has more calcium than guava juice or juice from Hawaii oranges. The phosphorus and iron contents of fresh pineapple and fresh pineapple juice are low in comparison with those of many other fruits in this series.

Pineapple of the Smooth Cayenne variety is a poor source of provitamin A, a good source of thiamine, a poor source of riboflavin, niacin, and ascorbic acid. The Pineapple Research Institute of Hawaii is developing new varieties that contain larger quantities of ascorbic acid than the Smooth Cayenne.

Pineapple juice, even when consumed in large quantities, tends to make the urine more alkaline. E. K. Nelson has shown that of the nonvolatile acids in pineapple juice, about 87 percent is citric and about 13 percent is *l*-malic.

Some people find that eating large quantities of fresh pineapple causes a soreness of the mouth and the esophagus. It has been suggested that this irritation may result from the combined action of the acid, the protein-splitting enzyme (bromelin), and the calcium oxalate crystals.

Pineapple does not increase in sweetness after it is harvested because there is no starch stored in the fruit that will change to sugar. The sugars are formed in the leaves of the pineapple plant and transferred

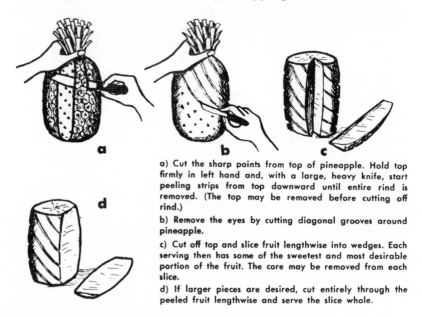

a) Cut the sharp points from top of pineapple. Hold top firmly in left hand and, with a large, heavy knife, start peeling strips from top downward until entire rind is removed. (The top may be removed before cutting off rind.)

b) Remove the eyes by cutting diagonal grooves around pineapple.

c) Cut off top and slice fruit lengthwise into wedges. Each serving then has some of the sweetest and most desirable portion of the fruit. The core may be removed from each slice.

d) If larger pieces are desired, cut entirely through the peeled fruit lengthwise and serve the slice whole.

Fig. 5.—Methods of preparing fresh pineapple family style.

to the fruit. Pineapple is usually sweeter in the summer months when the days are longer and the sunshine more abundant.

Supply. Though the greater portion of the crop is used for canning, excellent pineapples are to be found in the Honolulu markets during the entire year. The fruit is most plentiful during June, July, and August, but a second and smaller crop ripens during December and January.

Selection. Several factors should be considered in the selection of a pineapple. Color and size alone are not always dependable guides.

A yellow rind is not necessarily an indication of a good ripe pineapple. Many pineapples reach the market having what dealers call a chocolate-green color, or mottled green and brown. These fruits may be in prime condition.

If the crown is small and compact, the fruit is likely to be well developed, while a pineapple with the crown as long or longer than the fruit is not likely to be of first quality.

Pulling leaves from the crown is not a dependable test. The best one is to snap the side of the fruit with the thumb and finger. If the result is a hollow thud, the fruit is sour, not well matured, and lacking in juice. If a dull, solid sound results from the snap, it indicates a well-ripened, sound fruit, full of juice. Some experience may be necessary to distinguish between good and inferior fruit by this method, but the sound test is the most dependable guide for choosing a good pineapple.

a) Cut 1½-inch slices from top and bottom of an unpeeled pineapple. Save these pieces. With a long slender knife cut around the fruit ½ inch inside the rind.

b) Loosen fruit at top and bottom and then push it out of rind in one piece. Cut peeled fruit into six or eight wedge-shaped pieces. Refill shell with spears and replace top and bottom. Serve by removing pineapple top and taking out sections with fork or fingers.

Fig. 6.—Preparing pineapple luau style.

Use. Pineapples are frequently used fresh, served alone or combined with avocado, banana, citrus fruits, mango, and papaya. Pineapple and such vegetables as carrots and cabbage make good salad combinations. Finger-length slices of pineapple are delicious served in iced tea. The juice makes an excellent iced drink or may be combined with other fruit juices for punch.

Pineapple may be preserved in the form of jams or pickles, but home canning is not practical in most localities. There is not enough pectin present to make jelly from the juice.

Before being added to a gelatin solution, pineapple must be cooked

151

because bromelin, the enzyme present in uncooked pineapple, prevents gelatin from congealing.

Fruits of the summer season, when the quality is superior, yield an excellent frozen product. Directions for freezing pineapple and pine-apple juice may be found in Appendix I.

FRESH PINEAPPLE JUICE

YIELD: 2½ to 3½ cups

Cut a peeled ripe pineapple into 8 pieces lengthwise and then into cubes of 1 inch or 1½ inches. Squeeze through poi cloth or sugar sack. Chill the juice and serve.

PINEAPPLE JAM

YIELD: 2¼ quarts

12 cups grated or chopped fresh pineapple (2 large fruit)
6 cups sugar
6 tablespoons lemon juice

Rind of 3 lemons, sliced in very narrow strips ¼ inch long

Combine pineapple and sugar and allow to stand overnight. Add lemon juice and rind, then cook slowly for about 2 hours. Pour into hot sterilized jars and seal with paraffin.

PINEAPPLE CONSERVE

YIELD: 3½ pints

¼ cup finely sliced orange peel
2 cups orange sections
6 cups diced pineapple
   (1 medium-size fruit)
¾ cup water

1 cup seedless raisins
6 tablespoons lemon juice
1 cup broken English walnut meats
¾ cup sugar for each cup of cooked mixture

Remove rind from oranges and scrape out inner white pulp with a spoon or dull knife. Cut rind into narrow strips. Remove membrane from the orange sections.

Combine diced pineapple and water and cook until pineapple begins to soften. Add all the remaining ingredients except the sugar. Measure this fruit mixture and for each cup add ¾ cup of sugar. Cook over slow heat until mixture thickens, stirring frequently. Pour into hot sterilized jars and seal at once.

PINEAPPLE-HONEY PRESERVE

YIELD: 2 quarts

10 cups pineapple sections
   (2 medium fruit)
2 cups orange peel, sliced fine
   (6 medium-size oranges)

¼ to ½ cup finely chopped fresh ginger root
3 cups strained honey
2 cups orange sections

Peel fresh pineapple and cut crosswise into slices about $\frac{3}{4}$ inch thick. Remove core and cut into sections $\frac{3}{4}$ inch wide. Remove rind from 6 oranges; soak rind in water for $\frac{1}{2}$ hour. Drain and cook until tender, changing the water three times during the cooking process. Drain, wash with cold water, and remove white pulp from inside of rind by scraping with a spoon. Cut rind into narrow strips. Remove membrane from orange sections.

Combine pineapple, orange rind, ginger, and honey. Cook over slow heat until pineapple is partially tender. Add orange sections and continue cooking until pineapple is tender. Drain honey into separate pan and evaporate to thicker consistency over very low heat. Pack pineapple mixture in hot sterilized jars, fill with hot honey sirup, and seal immediately.

GUAVA-PINEAPPLE MARMALADE
See Index.

PAPAYA-PINEAPPLE MARMALADE
See Index.

PAPAYA MARMALADE
See Index.

MULBERRY PRESERVES
See Index.

PINEAPPLE CHUTNEY
YIELD: 2 quarts

- 1 medium-size pineapple
- 1¼ cups vinegar
- 1½ pounds brown sugar
- 2 cups seedless raisins
- 1 tablespoon salt
- 2 tablespoons finely chopped fresh or candied ginger root
- 1 medium-size bulb of garlic, chopped fine
- 2 or 3 finely chopped small fresh or pickled red peppers (with seeds removed)
- ¼ pound finely chopped blanched almonds or macadamia nuts

Peel pineapple, remove core, and cut into small pieces. Add all ingredients except nuts. Cook slowly until pineapple is tender. Add nuts and cook until mixture thickens to the desired consistency. Stir frequently to prevent scorching. Pour boiling hot chutney into hot sterilized jars and seal at once. Serve with meats or curried dishes. Quality and flavor improve after two to three months' storage.

153

PINEAPPLE PICKLE

YIELD: 1½ pints

12 cups pineapple sections
    (2 medium-size fruit)
2¼ cups white vinegar
4 cups sugar

2 cups water
2 tablespoons whole cloves
2 sticks cinnamon

Peel pineapple and cut crosswise into slices 1 inch thick. Remove core and cut into sections about 1 inch wide. Combine with vinegar, sugar, and water. Tie spices in cheesecloth, add to mixture, and boil slowly 15 minutes. Add pineapple and boil gently in covered container for ½ hour or until tender. Pour into hot sterilized jars and seal immediately.

If pineapple is sour, add ½ cup more sugar to sirup.

PINEAPPLE PUNCH

YIELD: 6 servings

¾ cup sugar
¾ cup water
4 cups fresh pineapple juice
¾ cup orange juice

¼ cup lemon juice
1 teaspoon finely chopped
    mint leaves

Dissolve sugar in water. Combine with fruit juice and mint. Pour over cracked ice before serving.

ALOHA PUNCH
See Index.

MANOA FRUIT PUNCH
See Index.

PAPAYA-PINEAPPLE NECTAR
See Index.

PAPAYA ONO-ONO
See Index.

FRESH PASSION FRUIT PUNCH
See Index.

PINEAPPLE-PAPAYA CUP

YIELD: 6 servings

3 cups pineapple cubes
    (¼ medium-size fruit)
48 to 60 papaya balls

¼ cup Fruit Cocktail Dressing
    or ginger ale
Mint sprigs, if desired

Cube and chill pineapple. Prepare papaya balls using French ball cutter or a half measuring teaspoon. Place pineapple in sherbet glasses and circle edges with papaya balls. Pour about a tablespoon of dressing or ginger ale over the fruit. Garnish with sprigs of mint if desired. Serve as a first course or dessert.

PINEAPPLE PLUME

YIELD: 4 to 6 servings

1 ripe pineapple   Mint leaves

Do not remove top or peel pineapple. Wash and cut lengthwise into quarters or sixths. With a sharp knife or grapefruit knife, cut fruit from rind leaving it in place in one piece. Remove core by slicing lengthwise, starting 1 inch from top. Slice pineapple wedge lengthwise through the center parallel to rind, and then crosswise into $\frac{3}{4}$- to 1-inch pieces. Leave fruit in place on rind to look as if it had not been cut. Sprinkle with powdered sugar and chopped mint leaves if desired. Serve as an appetizer or dessert.

Fig. 7.—Pineapple Plume.

PINEAPPLE WEDGES

YIELD: 8 servings,
8 to 10 wedges each

1 pineapple (4 pounds)   Mint leaves, if desired
1 to 2 tablespoons powdered
   sugar per serving

Wash and dry pineapple. Discard crown. Do not peel. With sharp paring knife, cut around each eye toward core, making a pointed piece that may be pulled away from core (fork may also be used). Remove wedges lengthwise of pineapple so that there will be an even distribution of sweet and sour wedges for each serving. Arrange in a circle on 6- or 7-inch plate.

Just before serving, place sugar in the center and top with finely chopped mint leaves, if desired. Pick up with the fingers, dip into the sugar and bite fruit from the rind. Usually served as an appetizer.

LYCHEE, PINEAPPLE, AND ORANGE COCKTAIL
See Index.

155

Fig. 8.—Pineapple Wedges.

PAPAYA AND PINEAPPLE COCKTAIL
See Index.

POHA FRUIT CUP
See Index.

POHA-PINEAPPLE COCKTAIL
See Index.

MALIHINI DINNER
See Index.

PINEAPPLE-CABBAGE SALAD
YIELD: 6 to 8 servings

4 cups shredded cabbage
2 cups shredded fresh
    pineapple
    ($\frac{1}{4}$ medium-size fruit)

$\frac{1}{4}$ to $\frac{1}{2}$ cup salad dressing
$\frac{1}{4}$ teaspoon salt

Combine cabbage and pineapple; chill. Drain off juice; add salt. Serve on lettuce leaves with French dressing or mayonnaise. Chopped peanuts or chopped green pepper may be added for color.

PINEAPPLE-CRAB SALAD
YIELD: 6 servings

2$\frac{1}{4}$ cups diced fresh pineapple
    ($\frac{1}{4}$ medium-size fruit)
1$\frac{1}{2}$ cups shredded crab meat
1 tablespoon tomato catsup

1 teaspoon Worcestershire
    sauce, if desired
$\frac{1}{4}$ cup mayonnaise

Mix chilled pineapple and crab meat. Serve on lettuce leaves. Add catsup and Worcestershire sauce to mayonnaise and pour over salad.

SALAD IN PINEAPPLE HALF SHELL YIELD: 6 servings

3 small pineapples (3 to 4 pounds including tops)

Select ripe pineapples; do not remove tops or peel. Wash and cut lengthwise into halves. Scoop out the fruit from each half, leaving rind about $\frac{1}{2}$ inch thick; chill until needed. Fill with any desired chilled fruit salad:

> Banana Waldorf
> Hawaiian Ambrosia
> Lychee, Papaya, and Pineapple Salad
> Pineapple Chicken Salad

Top each salad with about $\frac{1}{4}$ cup of any desired sherbet, such as:

> Avocado Milk Sherbet
> Guava Sherbet
> Papaya Milk Sherbet
> Mango Sherbet
> Passion Fruit Sherbet
> Soursop Sherbet

Garnish with sprig of mint.

Note. If Pineapple Chicken Salad is used, omit the sherbet and garnish with pimiento strips and parsley sprigs.

PINEAPPLE-CHICKEN SALAD YIELD: 4 to 5 servings

1¼ cups pineapple cubes	**¼ cup slivered toasted**
(¼ medium-size fruit)	**almonds, if desired**
2 cups cut-up cooked chicken	**¼ to ½ cup mayonnaise**
1 cup diced celery	**¼ to ½ teaspoon salt**
(½-inch pieces)	

Combine all ingredients, using $\frac{1}{4}$ cup of the mayonnaise. Toss lightly together with two forks. Taste and add salt and more mayonnaise if necessary. Serve in lettuce cups, garnished with a dash of paprika or ripe olives.

PINEAPPLE-CARROT SALAD YIELD: 6 servings

2 cups grated raw carrots	**¼ to ½ cup salad dressing**
(½ pound)	
3 cups cubed fresh pineapple	
(½ medium-size fruit)	

157

Toss carrot and pineapple together. Place about ⅔ cup of the mixture on a bed of lettuce.

Serve with French Dressing or Sesame Seed Fruit Dressing. Garnish each serving with 1 tablespoon chopped peanuts, raisins, or grated coconut.

AVOCADO-PINEAPPLE SALAD
See Index.

BANANA WALDORF SALAD
See variation under Banana Waldorf Salad (see Index).

LYCHEE, PAPAYA, AND PINEAPPLE SALAD
See Index.

HAWAIIAN DRESSING FOR FRUIT SALAD
See Index.

PINEAPPLE PIE*

YIELD: 9-inch pie
(5 to 6 servings)

1 recipe Plain Pastry	1 tablespoon lemon juice
¼ cup flour	2 cups finely chopped fresh
½ to 1 cup sugar	pineapple
¼ teaspoon salt	2 tablespoons margarine
2 eggs	

Prepare pastry. Mix together flour, ½ cup sugar, and salt. (The amount of sugar used depends upon tartness of the pineapple.) Beat eggs slightly and combine with the flour and sugar mixture. Stir in lemon juice and pineapple; taste and add more sugar as needed. Pour into 9-inch unbaked shell, dot with margarine, and moisten edge with water. Cover with top crust as described on page 24. Bake 10 minutes at 450° F.; reduce heat to 350° F. and bake 35 minutes longer.

POHA SAUCE
See Index.

PINEAPPLE FRUIT MOLD

YIELD: 6 serving

1 tablespoon unflavored	1½ cups hot pineapple juice
gelatin	¼ cup sugar
¼ cup cold cooked pineapple	Pinch of salt
juice.	1½ cups fresh Hawaii fruits

---

* Contributed by Elsie M. Boatman, Professor of Home Economics, University of Hawaii.

Sprinkle gelatin over cold juice and let soften for 5 minutes. Dissolve sugar, salt, and softened gelatin in the hot juice. Taste and add more sugar if desired. Cool, and when mixture begins to thicken, fold in any desired combination of the following fruits, sliced or diced: banana, papaya, mango, lychee, and cooked pineapple (see Use, above).

Pour into molds that have been slightly oiled or rinsed in cold water. Chill in refrigerator until firm. Unmold and serve with whipped cream as a dessert. Or unmold on bed of greens, garnish with mayonnaise, and serve as a salad.

HAWAIIAN AMBROSIA
YIELD: 6 servings

2 cups pineapple cubes
 (¼ small)
1 cup diced papaya
 (¼ medium)
¼ cup maraschino cherries

8 to 10 marshmallows,
 if desired
1 large banana, sliced
¾ to 1 cup fresh grated
 coconut

Combine pineapple, papaya, cherries, and marshmallows cut into quarters. Chill. Just before serving, add bananas and coconut. Toss lightly and serve as a dessert in sherbet glass or pineapple shell (see above, Salad in Pineapple Half Shell).

Note. Different proportions of fruit may be used. Surinam cherries may be substituted for maraschino cherries.

MANGO FRUIT MOLD
See Index.

FRESH PINEAPPLE ICE
YIELD: 1 quart

3¼ cups pineapple juice

¼ cup sugar

Use only ripe, sweet pineapple. (See Fresh Pineapple Juice for preparation.) Add sugar. If a sweeter ice is desired, add more sugar to taste. Freeze in an ice-cream freezer, using 8 parts of ice to 1 part of salt. Serve with or without sprigs of fresh mint.

PINEAPPLE MINT SHERBET
YIELD: ½ quart
(4 to 6 servings)

¼ cup milk
¼ cup crushed mint leaves
¼ cup crushed pineapple
 (fresh or canned)
¼ to ½ cup sugar
 Pinch of salt

2 tablespoons white corn sirup
¼ cup coffee cream or
 top milk
A few drops of green coloring

Scald ½ cup milk until bubbles form around the edge; add mint leaves, sugar, salt, and sirup. Stir until sweetening is dissolved and let stand 30 to 40 minutes. Strain out the mint leaves; add all other ingredients, using only enough coloring to tint a delicate green. Pour into freezer trays; moisten bottoms of trays and place on coldest shelf in freezing compartment.

When mixture is frozen stiff (1 to 1½ hours), turn into a chilled bowl; break up with a spoon if necessary. Beat until fluffy but not melted. Quickly pile back into trays. Moisten bottoms of trays and return to freezing compartment. Freeze to serving consistency. See Note under Avocado Milk Sherbet.

AVOCADO PINEAPPLE SHERBET
See Index.

SOURSOP AND PINEAPPLE SHERBET
See Index.

METHLEY PLUM

Description. The only variety of plum grown extensively at higher elevations in Hawaii is the Methley (*Prunus Salicina* X *Cerasifera Myrobalana*). The fruit vary in shape; some are round and squat and others tend to be slightly oval with a distinct point at the blossom end. The size also varies, but good plums are 1½ to 2 inches in diameter.

The dark-red skin has a light bloom, and the flesh, which is a rich red color, adheres rather tightly to the seed. When picked prematurely the plums may be very sour, but when fully ripe the flesh is sweet, though tart, and of good flavor. The skin, like that of many other plums, is bitter.

History. The Methley plum was received in 1926 by the Experiment Station of the Hawaiian Sugar Planters' Association, along with other plants from the U. S. Department of Agriculture, Bureau of Plant Industry, Division of Foreign Seed and Plant Introduction. The first plantings were made at Nauhi Gulch on the windward slopes of

Mauna Kea at an elevation of 5,100 feet. Since that time they have been planted extensively on Hawaii, Maui, and Kauai. E. W. Bryan reported in 1945 that they grow and produce from 2,600 feet to 8,000 feet elevation, but that 5,000 feet appears to be ideal.

Nutritive Value. The Methley plum is a fair source of provitamin A, a poor source of thiamine, riboflavin, niacin, and ascorbic acid.

Supply. For the past several years the supply has been greater than the demand owing to the fact that they must compete with plums shipped from the Mainland during the summer season.

Use. When fully ripe the Methley plum is best eaten as a fresh fruit. When cooked with skins and seeds, the plums may develop a bitter flavor which some people do not like but others find desirable. The plums may be used for pie or cobbler and make a satisfactory jam but are not recommended for jelly. The red pigment, probably an anthocyan, changes to a blue, green, or brown when it comes in contact with certain metals, and tends to stain the hands when the fruit is peeled with a steel knife. Because of the changes in color, the use of tin in cooking or canning is not recommended.

Methley plums may be frozen, but this is not recommended since they tend to develop a bitter flavor. Directions for freezing may be found in Appendix I.

PLUM JAM*

YIELD: 4 pints

5 pounds ripe plums
(52 to 58 medium)
1¼ cups water

1 cup sugar to each cup of
pulp (see below)

Wash and drain plums. Remove stems and damaged spots. Add water and boil gently for 10 to 15 minutes, stirring occasionally, until fruit is very soft. Strain through a coarse sieve or food mill to remove pits and skins. (The cone-shaped aluminum strainer with wooden pestle shown on page 2 is especially satisfactory.)

Measure pulp and add an equal amount of sugar. Mix well and cook rapidly until it gives a good jelly test, 221° to 222° F. Remove scum during cooking. Put hot jam into sterilized jars (see Appendix III) and seal.

Note. For best color and flavor use fully ripe plums. The jam may be slightly bitter when first made but the bitterness gradually disappears upon storage. For a less sweet jam use ¾ cup sugar to each cup of pulp.

---

* Contributed by the Food Processing Laboratory, Hawaii Agricultural Experiment Station.

Fruit, foliage, and cross section of the Methley plum *(Prunus Salicina* ✕ *Cerasifera Myrobalana).*

PLUM PRESERVES

**5 pounds ripe plums
(52 to 58 medium)**

**¾ cup sugar to each cup of
sliced plums (see below)**

Wash and drain plums. Cut the plums from the seeds in wedge-shaped pieces and measure. (There should be about 2½ quarts.) Use ¾ cup sugar to each cup of sliced plums. Combine plums and sugar. Let stand in preserving kettle until some juice is extracted (about 10 minutes). Place kettle over heat and bring to a boil. Stir occasionally to prevent sticking, and remove scum during cooking. Boil about 15 minutes, or until a good jelly test is obtained (221° F.).

Note. Plums may be peeled if desired; the yield is somewhat less and the product a little lighter red. Some consider it a more delicate product. For a sweeter product, use 1 cup sugar to each cup of fruit.

SPICED PLUMS

**2 pounds ripe plums
(20 to 25 medium)
¼ cup vinegar
4½ cups sugar**

**1 teaspoon ground cinnamon
¼ teaspoon ground allspice
¼ teaspoon ground cloves**

Wash and drain plums. Cut the plums from the seeds in wedge-shaped pieces and measure. (There should be about 4½ cups.) Use an equal measure of sugar and mix thoroughly with the spices. Combine all ingredients; place kettle over heat and bring to the boiling point. Cook, stirring occasionally, for about 15 minutes, or until the mixture gives a good jelly test, 221° to 222° F. (see Appendix III). Pour into sterilized jars; seal or cover with paraffin.

PLUM PIE

**1 recipe Plain Pastry
3 cups sliced plums
1¼ cups sugar**

**2 tablespoons flour
Pinch of salt
2 tablespoons margarine**

Wash and drain plums, but do not peel. Cut the plums from the seeds in wedge-shaped pieces. Mix sugar, flour, and salt. Put about ¼ of the sugar and flour mixture on the bottom crust. Combine the remainder with the sliced plums, put into unbaked shell, and dot with margarine. Cover with top crust and bake at 450° F. for 10 to 15 minutes; reduce temperature to 350° F. and bake about 30 minutes longer.

POHA

Description. The poha (*Physalis peruviana*) is a small yellow-green or orange fruit resembling a cherry in size and shape. It is enclosed in a thin, cream-colored, paper-like husk. The skin of the fruit is thin and waxy and surrounds a juicy pulp which contains many small seeds. The poha, also called Cape gooseberry and husk tomato, is related to the ground cherry.

History. This plant was introduced into the Hawaiian Islands soon after the beginning of travel to the Islands by Europeans. Very likely it was brought here in the early nineteenth century from the Cape of Good Hope. It is a native of Brazil but is now grown in many tropical and subtropical countries. It grows well in Hawaii, especially on the islands of Maui and Hawaii at heights from 1,500 to 4,000 feet.

Nutritive Value. Pohas are a poor source of calcium, a good source of phosphorus, and a fair source of iron. They are an excellent source of provitamin A, a good source of thiamine and niacin, a fair source of riboflavin, and an excellent source of ascorbic acid.

Supply. The pohas in Honolulu stores come from both the cultivated and wild plants, but there seems to be little difference in appearance or flavor. Although the plants bear throughout the year, the period of heaviest production is usually from June through October.

Use. The poha has a pleasing and distinctive flavor. It may be used raw for a dessert or shortcake in much the same ways as the strawberry. Pohas may be used in pie or cooked and served as a sauce on cakes and puddings, but are more favored for use in jam. Because the pectin content is low, pohas are not good for jelly.

Pohas make a good frozen product. For directions on freezing, see Appendix I.

POHA JAM   YIELD: 1½ quarts

    6 pounds pohas before husking   **1 cup sugar to each cup of**
         (4 quarts husked)   **cooked pohas (5 to 6 cups)**

Fruit, foliage, flower, and cross section of the poha *(Physalis peruviana).*

Husk, wash, and cook pohas slowly for 30 minutes. Stir frequently until there is sufficient liquid to prevent fruit from scorching. Let stand overnight. Measure poha pulp and juice and add an equal quantity of sugar. Cook slowly 30 minutes to 1 hour, stirring mixture frequently until juice thickens slightly when cooled. Pour into hot sterilized jars and seal with paraffin.

The quantity of juice resulting from the cooking process varies according to whether pohas are obtained during the dry or the rainy season. When the water content of pohas is unusually high, it is necessary to pour off some of the juice before adding the sugar if more fruit than jelly is desired.

POHA PRESERVES

YIELD: 1 quart

3 pounds pohas before husking (7 cups husked)	¾ cup water
¼ cup water	¼ cup sugar
1 lemon, cut in small paper-thin slices (½ cup)	1½ tablespoons lemon juice
	1 cup sugar to each cup of cooked pohas

Husk and wash pohas; add ¼ cup water and cook over low heat, stirring frequently until there is sufficient liquid to prevent fruit from scorching. Let stand overnight. Combine lemon slices and ¾ cup water and let stand overnight. Cook over low heat until rind is transparent, adding ¼ cup sugar near end of cooking period. Combine with poha mixture. Measure and add an equal quantity of sugar and the lemon juice. (See Poha Jam recipe for amount of liquid used.) Cook slowly for 30 minutes or until fruit is soft and juice sheets from spoon and gives a slight jelly test (219° F.; see Appendix III). Pour into hot sterilized half-pint jars and seal immediately.

POHA-PINEAPPLE COCKTAIL

YIELD: 6 servings

2 cups ripe pohas cut into halves	¼ cup lemon juice
2¾ cups diced fresh pineapple (½ medium fruit)	¼ cup sugar

Mix ingredients and chill thoroughly. Serve in cocktail glasses.

POHA FRUIT CUP

YIELD: 6 servings

1½ cups ripe pohas	¼ cup lemon juice
1½ cups diced bananas	¼ to ¾ cup sugar
½ cup diced orange	2 teaspoons finely chopped mint
1 cup diced fresh pineapple (½ medium fruit)	

Cut pohas into halves, mix with other ingredients, and chill. Serve in cocktail glasses. This also makes a good salad combination if the lemon juice, sugar, and mint are omitted. The fruit is then served on lettuce leaves with mayonnaise or Hawaiian Dressing (see Index).

POHA SAUCE FOR PUDDINGS

YIELD: 6 servings

3 cups ripe pohas
1¾ cups sugar
2 tablespoons cornstarch
Pinch of salt

1¼ cups water or pineapple juice
1 teaspoon vanilla
1 tablespoon margarine

Add ½ cup of sugar to the pohas and let stand 15 minutes. Add water or pineapple juice and bring to the boiling point. Mix thoroughly remaining sugar, salt, and cornstarch, and add to the hot liquid, stirring constantly. Boil 5 minutes. Remove from heat; add margarine and vanilla. Serve hot or cold on cake, rice or bread puddings, or vanilla ice cream.

ROSELLE

Description. The roselle (*Hibiscus sabdariffa*) is an annual plant that commonly grows to a height of 5 to 8 feet in Hawaii. The fleshy, bright-red calyx is the portion of the plant that is used as a fruit (Fig. 9).

History. The plant is reported to have been first introduced into Hawaii from Australia, but in 1904 the Hawaii Agricultural Experiment Station obtained seed from Puerto Rico, made many experimental plantings, and for a number of years fostered its cultivation on a commercial scale. It is reported that at one time more than 200 acres of roselles were under cultivation in Hawaii.

The roselle is commonly propagated by seeds which, if they are planted about March and the plants are transplanted to the garden in May, yield fruit in November and December. The roselle can be readily cultivated in home gardens.

Nutritive Value. The roselle calyx is very acid to taste and has little or no sugar. Roselles are a fair source of provitamin A, a poor source of the B vitamins, and a fair source of ascorbic acid.

Fruit, foliage, and flower of the roselle *(Hibiscus sabdariffa).*

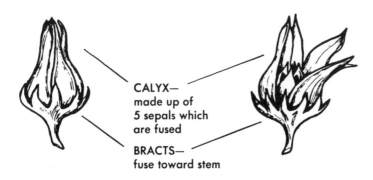

CALYX—
made up of
5 sepals which
are fused

BRACTS—
fuse toward stem

Fig. 9. —Diagram showing parts of edible portion of roselle fruit.

Supply. Roselles are not commonly found in Honolulu stores. The yield in home gardens varies with soil and moisture, but six to eight plants should produce enough for the average family.

Use. When the fruits are young they can easily be pulled off the plant. As the seed pod ripens and the fruit grows more mature it must be cut from the plant with a knife or pruning shears.

John C. Ripperton of the Hawaii Agricultural Experiment Station determined that the calyx of the roselle is the only part of the plant which contains sufficient pectin and acid to produce a satisfactory jelly. From a series of experiments he also concluded that cooking the seed pods with the calyxes does not affect the flavor or consistency of the jelly and that the tedious separation of the calyxes and seed pods is unnecessary.

The roselle makes an excellent jelly of a flavor and color resembling a mixture of currant and raspberry jelly. When a more concentrated juice is used it is similar to red currant jelly. Roselle juice may also be used in flavoring sherbet or gelatin desserts and for punch. Thoroughly cooked and sweetened, the calyxes may be used as a substitute for cranberry sauce.

Roselles may be frozen in the raw or cooked state. For directions on freezing, see Appendix I.

ROSELLE JUICE   YIELD: 4¾ cups of juice

    2 pounds whole fruit   **6 cups water**
    (4 quarts firmly packed)

Wash fruit thoroughly. Do not remove the calyxes from the seeds. Add water; it should about half cover the fruit. Place over heat, cover, bring to boil quickly and boil until calyxes are soft (about 7 minutes). Remove from heat and strain juice through a flannel jelly bag or 2 thicknesses of sugar or flour sack. The juice may be canned for future use (see Appendix II). The juice may be made stronger or milder by altering the amount of water used.

ROSELLE JELLY
YIELD: 3 cups

3 cups Roselle Juice   2¼ cups sugar

Bring juice to a boil and add sugar. Again bring to boiling point and cook until a jelly test is obtained (see Appendix III). Pour into hot sterilized glasses and seal with paraffin.

If juice of a stronger flavor is used, add 1 cup sugar for each cup of juice.

Better jelly is obtained if not more than 3 cups of juice are boiled at a time.

ROSELLE SAUCE
YIELD: 1 pint

6 cups roselle calyxes   1¼ cups sugar
1¼ cups water

Wash the fruit thoroughly; remove the calyxes and measure them. Add water and cook until soft. Add sugar and heat until it is dissolved. Serve hot or warm as a sauce with meat.

ROSELLE MARMALADE
YIELD: 1 pint

6 cups roselle calyxes   1¼ to 1¾ cups sugar
1¼ cups water

Prepare as for Roselle Sauce. Cook mixture slowly until thick, but not until it gives the jelly test (see Appendix III). Pour into hot sterilized glasses and seal with paraffin (see Appendix III).

SPICED ROSELLES
YIELD: 1 pint

Prepare Roselle Marmalade as directed above, adding ¼ to ½ teaspoon ground cinnamon and a pinch each of ground allspice and ground cloves to the sugar.

ROSELLE PUNCH
YIELD: 8 servings (½ cup each)

1 quart Roselle Juice   Juice of ½ lemon
¾ cup sugar   Pinch of salt
¼ cup orange juice

Prepare Roselle Juice as directed. Combine all ingredients and stir until sugar is dissolved. Pour over cracked ice just before serving.

Note. Juice may be prepared as above, poured into ice cube trays and used in place of cracked ice.

HOT SPICED ROSELLE PUNCH YIELD: 8 servings (½ cup each)

1 quart Roselle Juice	4-inch piece stick cinnamon
¾ cup sugar	¼ cup orange juice
16 allspice	Juice of ¼ lemon
16 cloves	

Prepare Roselle Juice as directed. Add spices, bring to the boiling point and simmer for 10 minutes. Strain. Just before serving, add fruit juices. Serve hot.

ROSELLE FRUIT MOLD YIELD: 6 servings

1½ tablespoons unflavored gelatin	½ to ¾ cup sugar
	Pinch of salt
¼ cup cold water	1½ cups fresh fruit
1½ cups Roselle Juice	

Sprinkle gelatin over cold water and let stand 5 minutes. Bring half of the Roselle Juice to the boiling point. Add sugar, salt, and softened gelatin. Stir until dissolved. Add remaining Roselle Juice. Taste and add more sugar if desired. Cool until mixture begins to thicken; fold in any desired combination of the following fruits, sliced or diced: banana, papaya, mango, lychee, and cooked pineapple.

Pour into molds that have been slightly oiled or rinsed in cold water. Chill in refrigerator until firm. Unmold and serve with whipped cream as a dessert. Or unmold on bed of greens, garnish with mayonnaise and serve as a salad.

Fruit and foliage of the soursop *(Anona muricata)*.

SOURSOP

Description. The soursop (*Anona muricata*) is a large heart-shaped fruit. A single fruit may weigh 5 pounds, and much larger ones have been reported. The thick skin, or rind, is a deep green and covered with numerous short pliable spines. The flesh resembles cotton soaked in a highly aromatic liquid. The pulp contains many shiny brown seeds.

History. The fruit, a native of tropical America, was described as early as 1528 by Gonzalo Fernandez de Oviedo in his *Natural History of the Indies*. At present, it can be found in most tropical countries, although it is probably more popular in Cuba than in any other place. The name "soursop" by which the fruit is known in most English-speaking countries is of West Indian origin. The history of its introduction into Hawaii is unknown.

Nutritive Value. The juicy pulp of soursop is a poor source of calcium and iron and a fair source of phosphorus. The soursop has no yellow pigment and is, therefore, assumed to have no provitamin A value. It is a good source of riboflavin and niacin and a fair source of thiamine and ascorbic acid.

Supply. In Honolulu, the soursop is occasionally found in the stores, but the supply is not equal to the demand. The season ranges from February to September.

Use. The soursop has an acid flavor and a pleasant, refreshing odor. The purée may be extracted by forcing the pulp through a potato ricer or food mill, or by squeezing it through several thicknesses of cheesecloth. The pulp, freed from the seeds and pulled or cut into small pieces, may be chilled, sweetened, and served as a breakfast fruit, or it may be used in a salad. Iced drinks, sherbets, and gelatin dishes may be made from the extracted juice. The soursop blends well with banana, orange, and pineapple.

Soursop freezes well in the form of a thick juicy pulp or purée. For full information, see Appendix I.

SOURSOP PURÉE

YIELD: About 2 cups from a 2-pound fruit

Allow the fruit to become soft. Remove pulp from within the green peel and cut or tear it into small pieces, removing most of the seeds. Force the pulp through a potato ricer or food mill, or squeeze it through several thicknesses of cheesecloth. The product is a thick juicy pulp or purée.

SOURSOPADE

YIELD: 6 servings

3¼ cups soursop purée
2¾ cups water

1 cup sugar
2¾ tablespoons lemon juice

Mix ingredients and stir them until sugar is dissolved. Pour over cracked ice and serve.

SOURSOP AND PINEAPPLE SHERBET

YIELD: 6 to 8 servings

1 cup sugar
1 cup water
1 cup pineapple juice

1½ cups soursop purée
1 egg white

Combine sugar and water, and boil 5 minutes. Cool to lukewarm. Add fruit juice, purée, and unbeaten egg white. Freeze in an ice-cream freezer, using 8 parts ice to 1 part salt.

SOURSOP SHERBET I

YIELD: 1½ quarts

⅞ cup sugar
2 cups water
2 cups soursop purée

1 tablespoon lemon juice
1 egg white

Combine sugar and water, and boil 5 minutes. Cool to lukewarm. Add purée and unbeaten egg white. Freeze in an ice-cream freezer, using 8 parts ice to 1 part salt.

SOURSOP SHERBET II

YIELD: 6 to 8 servings

2 cups soursop purée
(1¾ pounds fruit)
¼ cup white corn sirup
2 egg whites

¼ cup water
1 teaspoon unflavored gelatin
¼ to ¾ cup sugar
Pinch of salt

Prepare Soursop Purée as described above. Chill corn sirup and egg whites in medium bowl. Sprinkle gelatin over ½ cup of water and let stand 5 minutes, then add ½ cup sugar and salt; heat until dissolved. Cool; add 2 cups soursop purée. Taste, and stir in more sugar if desired. Pour into freezing tray and freeze to a mush (1 to 1½ hours).

Beat egg white sirup mixture until very stiff (about 7 to 10 minutes). Add frozen soursop mixture and beat until just blended. Pour into 2 freezing trays; moisten bottoms of trays and place on coldest shelf in freezing compartment. Wash bowl and beater and place in refrigerator to chill.

When mixture is frozen stiff (about 1 hour), scrape into chilled bowl; break up with spoon if necessary. Beat until well blended and fluffy. Quickly pile sherbet into trays, moisten bottoms of trays; return to freezing compartment. Freeze, stirring with a fork once or twice if desired, to serving consistency. See Note under Avocado Milk Sherbet.

SOURSOP MOUSSE I
YIELD: 6 servings

20 marshmallows
¼ cup water
2 tablespoons sugar

1 cup soursop purée
1 cup whipping cream

Add sugar and marshmallows to the water. Place over low heat until marshmallows are softened and a smooth mixture is obtained. When mixture is cool, add soursop purée and let stand in cool place until partially congealed. Add cream which·has been whipped. Pour into mold, seal, and pack in ice, using 3 parts ice to 1 part salt, or freeze in refrigerator.

SOURSOP MOUSSE II
YIELD: 6 servings

½ tablespoon unflavored
    gelatin
2 tablespoons cold water
¼ cup boiling water

1 cup soursop purée
1 cup sugar
1 cup whipping cream

Sprinkle gelatin over cold water and let stand 5 minutes. Pour boiling water over the gelatin and stir until dissolved. Combine gelatin mixture and soursop purée. Add sugar and stir until dissolved. Chill and whip cream, then fold into gelatin mixture. Freeze as directed in recipe for Soursop Mousse I.

STRAWBERRY

Description. The cultivated strawberry (*Fragaria chiloensis*) is a juicy red fruit which grows on a low, herbaceous plant. Structurally, it is an enlarged fleshy receptacle from $\frac{1}{2}$ to $1\frac{1}{4}$ inches in diameter, on the outside of which are imbedded many small seeds. The flavor combines acidity and sweetness in proportions pleasing to most people. Some varieties are more strongly flavored than others.

History. There are numerous varieties of the strawberry native to widely separated sections of the world. These vary considerably in size, shape, color, and flavor. Many varieties have been developed under cultivation. Several commercial varieties imported from the Mainland are now grown successfully in Hawaii.

A white strawberry indigenous to the Hawaiian Islands was at one time fairly abundant on the islands of Kauai and Hawaii. It still thrives in protected areas such as Kipuka Puaulu (Bird Park), Hawaii National Park.

Nutritive Value. In comparison with other fruits strawberries may be considered a fair source of calcium and phosphorus and a good source of iron. The values found for iron were high and may be in error because of contamination with soil, although great care was used in preparing the sample.

Local strawberries of an unknown variety were found to be a poor source of provitamin A, thiamine, riboflavin, and niacin, and an excellent source of ascorbic acid.

Supply. The supply is small, fairly constant, and rarely equal to the demand. The season ranges from December through July.

Use. In Hawaii, strawberries are practically always used fresh because they are too expensive to buy for preserving.

No freezing experiments with strawberry varieties grown in Hawaii have been made. Work elsewhere has shown that not all varieties are suitable for freezing and that berries which are of a good red color on the inside as well as the outside produce the best-looking product.

176

SURINAM CHERRY
(Pitanga)

Description. The Surinam cherry (*Eugenia uniflora*) is a small bright-red fruit about 1 inch in diameter, oblate in form, and conspicuously eight-ribbed. When ripe the color varies from a glistening light red to a very dark red. The flesh surrounding the single large seed is soft and juicy. The fruit from most plants is distinctly acid and slightly bitter, but some plants produce subacid, sweet fruit.

History. The Surinam cherry is known as the Pitanga in Brazil, where it grows wild along the banks of the streams and edges of the forests. It is also an important cultivated fruit of that region. W. Popenoe reports that it is used more extensively by the inhabitants of Brazil than by the people of any other country. The date of its introduction into Hawaii is unknown.

Nutritive Value. The acidity of Surinam cherries is great compared with other fruits in this series; it is exceeded only by tamarinds and the yellow passion fruit. The expressed juice from two different samples showed pH values of 2.7 and 3.0. Due to this high acidity, the fruit does not seem very sweet to taste although it has a large quantity of carbohydrate—22 percent—which must be mainly sugars.

Surinam cherries were found to be a fair source of calcium, and a poor source of phosphorus and iron. They are a good source of pro-vitamin A, a poor source of the B vitamins, and a fair source of ascorbic acid.

Supply. Surinam cherries are not sold in Honolulu markets. The quality and quantity of the fruit obtainable from private gardens vary with the amount of moisture. The season varies with the locality but in many places the shrub bears fruit the year round.

Use. In Hawaii, the Surinam cherry is frequently grown for decorative purposes. One or two raw cherries cut in small pieces and added to each serving of fruit cocktail give piquancy of color and flavor. The cherries may be cooked and used as sauce or for jam, preserves, or jelly. Because of the tart flavor the jelly or sherbet made from the cherry juice may be served with meat or fowl. Combined with apple and raisins, the cherries may be used for pies and puddings.

177

Fruit and foliage of the Surinam cherry *(Eugenia uniflora)*.

The juice, prepared as for jelly making, may be used as a foundation for an iced drink. The juice of the firm-ripe cherries gives a good test for pectin. The fruit and juice are high in acid but seem to develop a bitter taste on standing. For this reason the fruit should be used as soon as it is picked.

Surinam cherries may be used in frozen fruit cocktails. See Appendix I for suggestions on freezing.

SURINAM CHERRY JUICE
YIELD: 7 cups

5 pounds Surinam cherries　　**Water to barely cover fruit**

Wash fruit and remove stems and blossom ends. Add water, mash fruit, and boil gently until soft (about 20 minutes). Pour into jelly bag and hang to drip. For clear juice, do not squeeze bag.

SURINAM CHERRY JELLY
YIELD: 3 cups (6 four-ounce glasses)

4 cups Surinam cherry juice　　**4 cups sugar**

Place juice in a shallow kettle with a capacity of at least 4 quarts. Boil 5 to 10 minutes, add sugar, and bring back to the boiling point. Remove scum which forms. Boil vigorously about 15 minutes. As mixture nears the jelling stage, test frequently with a metal spoon or thermometer (see Appendix III). Pour jelly into hot sterilized glasses and seal with paraffin.

SURINAM CHERRY JAM
YIELD: 1 quart

2 cups water　　　　　**3¾ cups seeded Surinam**
3¾ cups sugar　　　　　**cherries**

Combine the sugar and water and bring to the boiling point. Add cherries. Cook slowly for 20 to 25 minutes or until the juice thickens slightly, but not until it gives the jelly test (see Appendix III). Pour into hot sterilized jars and seal with paraffin.

SURINAM CHERRY SAUCE
YIELD: 1 pint

1 pound (1 pint) Surinam　　**½ cup water**
cherries　　　　　　　　**1¼ to 1½ cups sugar**

Wash cherries and remove blossom ends. Add water and simmer 20 minutes over a low heat. Remove from heat and press cherries through a coarse sieve to remove seeds. Add sugar to fruit pulp and reheat to dissolve sugar. Cool. Serve with meat or fowl. This makes a thin sauce. If a sauce stiff enough to mold is desired, mixture must be cooked a few additional minutes.

SURINAM CHERRY PUNCH

YIELD: 6 servings (1 cup each)

1¼ cups Surinam cherry juice
4½ cups water

3 tablespoons lemon juice
1⅓ cups sugar

Prepare Surinam Cherry Juice as directed. Combine all ingredients and stir until sugar is dissolved. Pour over cracked ice before serving.

SURINAM CHERRY PIE

YIELD: 8-inch pie

1 recipe Plain Pastry
1¼ cups seeded Surinam cherries
¼ cup seedless raisins
¾ cup diced apple (1 medium)

1¼ cups sugar
3 tablespoons flour
1 teaspoon margarine

Line a pie tin with pastry. Mix the fruit and pour into pie shell. Sprinkle with flour and sugar which have been well mixed, and dot with small pieces of margarine. Moisten the edge of the pie crust and cover with a second crust. Place in a hot oven (450° F.) for 10 minutes, then reduce the temperature to 350° F. and bake until fruit is soft (30 to 40 minutes).

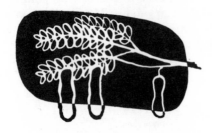

TAMARIND

Description. The fruit of the tamarind tree (*Tamarindus indica*) consists of a brittle brown pod, varying from 2 to 6 inches in length and from ½ to 1 inch in width. This encloses a very sticky acid pulp which surrounds from 1 to 12 shiny brown seeds. In maturity the edible pulp shrinks slightly from the pod.

History. The tamarind is believed to be a native of tropical Africa and perhaps southern Asia, where it has long been popular. It was early introduced into tropical America and from there was probably brought to Hawaii. One of the first tamarind trees in Hawaii was planted in 1797 by Don Marin at Little Greenwich in Pauoa Valley, Honolulu. It was a favorite tree of the early settlers and is found on many of the old homesteads. An avenue of tamarind trees grew in the palace grounds until King Kalakaua, who did not like the fruit, had the trees removed.

Fruit, foliage, and seed of the tamarind *(Tamarindus indica)*.

In more recent years, the fruit has lost its popularity, partly because of the small beetle which infests most of the pods and partly because of the availability of other fruits.

Nutritive Value. Analyses at the University of Hawaii and elsewhere indicate that tamarinds, as compared with all other fruits, have an unusually high acid and high sugar content. The acid is reported to be largely tartaric. The acid of the sample analyzed in the Hawaii Agricultural Experiment Station Foods and Nutrition Department was calculated as 14 percent tartaric acid or as 12 percent citric acid. One investigator reports an invert sugar content of 41.2 percent for tamarinds, and University analyses show a carbohydrate by difference of 45.8 percent.

The calcium and phosphorous contents are also unusually high; the value of 0.113 percent for calcium is the highest reported in the literature for any fruit and is equivalent to that reported for some vegetables. Whether or not the calcium is well utilized by humans is unknown.

Tamarinds contain no provitamin A. The ripe ones are a good source of thiamine and niacin, and an excellent source of riboflavin. Though its high acidity might suggest to some that it should be a good source of ascorbic acid, numerous tests of the fruit in both the ripe and green stages have shown the variety grown in Hawaii to contain little or none of this vitamin.

Supply. In Hawaii, the fruit ripens during the late summer and fall. No attempt is made to market it commercially.

Use. Tamarinds are more widely used in other tropical countries than in Hawaii, although many Island children eat the edible portion as do the East Indians and Arabs, who prize tamarinds as highly as dried dates and figs.

Tamarinds may be preserved indefinitely by pressing the shelled fruit into cakes and keeping these in a cool place, or by packing in jars alternate layers of whole tamarinds and sugar. The shelled fruit may be cooked in a sirup until the fruit is quite soft, and then put through a coarse sieve. As much pulp as possible is pressed through. This sirup may be canned and used diluted in a pleasing, refreshing iced drink. Because of their high acidity, tamarinds may be substituted for lemons or limes.

W. Popenoe states that in the Orient tamarinds are widely used in chutneys and curries and for pickling fish.

TAMARIND SIRUP
YIELD: 2 quarts

2 cups shelled tamarinds pressed down in cup	6 cups water
	5½ cups sugar

Pour water over tamarinds and let stand overnight. Add sugar and boil 15 minutes. Strain through coarse sieve, rubbing through as much pulp as possible. Heat sirup to the boiling point. Pour into hot sterilized jars and seal.

FRESH TAMARINDADE
YIELD: 6 servings

21 shelled tamarinds
6 cups water

¾ cup sugar

Add tamarinds to water and let stand 10 minutes. Stir well, strain, add sugar, and chill. Serve with cracked ice.

TAMARINDADE
YIELD: 6 servings

1 cup tamarind sirup
4¾ cups water

6 sprigs of mint

Mix sirup and water. Chill and serve with cracked ice. Place a sprig of mint in each glass.

TANGERINE

Description. The tangerine (*Citrus reticulata* Blanco) is shaped like a flattened globe, sometimes depressed at the apex. The fruit is 2 to 3 inches in diameter and has a loose skin. This has led some people to call it the "kid glove" orange.

The tangerine is one of two groups of mandarin oranges. The other is the Satsuma mandarin, the principal variety of Japan, which fruits poorly in Hawaii.

Most Hawaii tangerines are of the Dancy variety. Unlike those grown elsewhere, they rarely develop a deep orange color in Hawaii but are likely to have a decidedly green tinge at maturity. The flesh is orange in color, sweet, and usually contains numerous seeds.

History. The tangerine is thought to have originated in China. According to the *Encyclopaedia Britannica,* the mandarin orange is so called because of its resemblance in color, shape, and size to the large button worn on the hat of high officials (mandarins) during the Ch'ing dynasty. It has also been suggested that the fruit may have been given this name because of its similarity in color to the brilliant yellow or orange of the silk robes these officials wore.

The Satsuma variety was taken from Japan to the United States in 1876. According to Pope (who refers to them as mandarins) the Hawaii Agricultural Experiment Station first introduced budded plants of four varieties of tangerines from California in 1906.

Nutritive Value. The tangerine is a poor source of calcium, phosphorus, and iron. It is a good source of provitamin A, thiamine, and ascorbic acid, and a poor source of riboflavin and niacin.

Supply. Tangerines are grown on all the Islands, from sea level to 2000 feet elevation, especially in the cooler valleys. They are grown in home gardens but only to a small extent commercially (about 50 acres). The season extends over several months, from October through January, when they are often found on the Honolulu markets along with tangerines from the mainland. They come especially from Pahoa and other parts of Hawaii, while some come from Maui.

Use. Tangerines are commonly eaten as a fresh fruit out of hand. They may be used in fruit salad and fruit cup. They make a satisfactory marmalade and excellent juice, especially if a little lime or lemon is added.

TANGERINE MARMALADE

YIELD: 6 to 7 cups

1 pound tangerines (5 or 6 medium to large fruit)

¼ cup lime or lemon juice
Sugar as required

Wash fruit thoroughly and remove peel in 4 large sections from each tangerine. Cover peels with boiling water and cook until they are tender and their white portions are clear (about 30 minutes). Drain and cut peel in very fine strips with a knife on a cutting board.

Remove membranes and seeds from sections, add cut peel, and measure by pressing gently but firmly into cup. To each cup of pulp and peel, add 2 cups water and stir. Measure again, and for each cup of the mixture, add ¾ to 1 cup sugar.

Combine all ingredients, including lime or lemon juice. Stir well, bring quickly to a full boil, and cook as for jelly to a temperature of 218° to 220° F., until it gives a jelly test (see Appendix III). Pour into hot sterilized glasses and cover with paraffin, or put in sealed glasses or jars.

Note. Tangerines with some white inner peel are best for marmalade as they furnish more pectin.

To facilitate removal of membrane from sections, cut off inner edge with a kitchen shears.

WATERMELON

Description. The watermelon (*Citrullus vulgaris*), a large smooth green melon, is cultivated in many sections of the world. The rind varies from ⅜ to 1½ inches in thickness and, from the outside in, shades from green to white to pink. The crisp, juicy, pink flesh contains many flat, slippery black or white seeds. In good melons, the flavor is delicate, sweet, and refreshing. The watermelons grown in Hawaii average from 10 to 20 pounds and usually have thin rinds, ⅜ to ½ inch thick. Few really large melons are seen on the market.

History. The watermelon is a native of Africa but has spread throughout the world. David Livingston in 1857 wrote that in Africa when watermelons were plentiful they were a favorite food of the wild animals as well as the natives. Although in Hawaii a large supply of melons has been grown only during the last few years, some have been grown here continuously since the first seeds were left by Captain James Cook in 1779.

Nutritive Value. Watermelons, like strawberries and mountain apples, contain 90 percent or more of water and 7 to 8 percent of carbohydrate in the form of sugar.

Watermelons are a poor source of calcium, phosphorus, and iron. The thin-rind types grown in Hawaii are a fair source of provitamin A and a poor source of the three B vitamins and of ascorbic acid.

Supply. The season varies from year to year in Hawaii but watermelons are likely to be most abundant from May through September.

Use. The watermelon grown in Hawaii provides a delicious and refreshing dessert. It may be used for fruit cocktail with the addition of lemon or grape juice, or in combination with other fruits. Fruit salad is made more attractive by the addition of watermelon cubes or balls. The rind may be prepared as a preserve or pickle.

WATERMELON PICKLE

3 pounds or 2½ quarts watermelon rind (rind of 1 melon)
6 to 7 cups salt water (1 tablespoon salt to 1 cup water)
4 to 5 cups weak vinegar
solution (1 cup vinegar
to 2 cups water)

1½ cups vinegar
1½ cups sugar
2¼ cups water
1 tablespoon whole allspice
2 tablespoons stick cinnamon
¼ teaspoon salt
1 tablespoon whole cloves

Choose a watermelon with a thick rind. Pare, removing all outside green rind and practically all the pink meat. Cut into pieces about 3 inches long and ¾ inch wide. Soak 24 hours in salt water sufficient to cover rind. Drain and soak 24 hours in weak vinegar solution sufficient to cover rind. Drain and cook in clear water 1½ hours, or until tender; then drain off water.

Make a sirup by heating vinegar, sugar, water, and salt. Tie spices loosely in a piece of cheesecloth and add to the mixture. Cover and allow to stand 1 hour to absorb spice flavor.

Add rind and boil gently for 1½ hours in a covered kettle. Pour into hot sterilized jars and seal at once. Exposure to air darkens the pickle.

WATERMELON COCKTAIL

2 tablespoons sugar
Pinch of salt

4 tablespoons lemon juice
4 cups ripe watermelon cubes

Add salt and sugar to the lemon juice and pour the mixture over watermelon cubes. Let cubes stand 1 hour or more in refrigerator before serving them in cocktail glasses. A sprig of fresh mint may be used as a garnish for each serving.

Amounts of sugar and lemon juice may be varied with the sweetness of the watermelon and the taste of the individual.

WATERMELON AND
GRAPE JUICE COCKTAIL

Pinch of salt
4½ tablespoons lemon juice

¼ cup grape juice
4 cups ripe watermelon cubes

Mix salt, lemon juice, and grape juice; pour the mixture over watermelon cubes. Let cubes stand in the juice for 1 hour or more in a refrigerator. Serve in cocktail glasses.

APPENDIX

I. FREEZING HAWAII FRUITS

KATHRYN J. ORR* AND CAREY D. MILLER

Fruits and vegetables contain enzymes that must be destroyed or inactivated prior to or during the freezing process if good results are to be obtained. Vegetables are always blanched in hot water to destroy the enzymes and cooled in cold water before freezing. Because blanching impairs the flavor of fruits and tends to give them a cooked taste, some other methods must be used. To date, the best method known for retarding enzyme action and yet retaining the fresh flavor of the fruit is to use sufficient sugar, either dry or in the form of sirup.

QUALITY CONTROL OF FROZEN FRUITS

Fruits are the most difficult food to freeze properly. The frozen product will be no better than the fresh fruit from which it is prepared. Best results will be obtained if the following recommendations are observed:

Variety. All varieties of fruit may not produce equally good frozen products. While the choice of fruit variety may depend on such general factors as freedom from disease and insect pests, ease of culture, and size of yield, of greater importance to the housewife are uniformity of color, firmness of texture when mature, palatability, and vitamin content.

Maturity. Fruits should be frozen at the peak of their perfection when they are firm-ripe but not mushy, preferably tree- or vine-ripened. Uniformity of ripeness is also important.

Overripe fruit should not be used, even for purées; enzymatic and bacterial changes that cause "off flavors" are more likely to occur with bruised or overripe fruit.

Speed from Harvest to Freezer. Berries, pineapple, and Surinam cherries are best when harvested fully ripe. They should be prepared and frozen immediately. If it is necessary to hold foods under refrigeration, they should not be kept in the hydrator of refrigerator longer than 24 hours.

---

* Foods and Nutrition Specialist, University of Hawaii Cooperative Extension Service.

Fruits to which sugar or sirup has been added require sturdy packages for freezing, above. Fruits which tend to float can be kept below the surface of the sirup with crushed waxed paper, below. The surface of purées can be protected with cellophane or pliofilm cut to fit.—Photos from University of Hawaii Agricultural Experiment Station Circular 27, *Home Freezers and Packaging Materials*, by Faith Fenton.

Packaging. Any style of heavily waxed, rigid container is suitable providing it has a tight-fitting cover. Containers requiring liners of moisture-vapor-proof cellophane or polyethylene bags are favored by some. Glass containers may be reused. Aluminum containers, specially designed for freezing, are usually expensive, but they are highly recommended, since with care they can be used many times. Aluminum freezer foil is excellent for odd-shaped fruits, such as bananas.

Space for expansion of liquid products when frozen should always be left, especially in glass.

Packing is often the weak link in the freezing and storing of foods. Whatever the type of package used, it should be moisture-vapor-proof to prevent not only the loss of moisture, aroma, and flavor, but the entrance of air, odors, and flavors.*

Freezing and Storage. Place packages of fruit on freezing shelves as soon as possible after they are prepared. Fruit should be frozen and stored at 0° F. The space in an ordinary refrigerator for ice cubes is not satisfactory for freezing or for holding frozen fruits. A separate freezer compartment or a "deepfreeze" cabinet is required.

A storage period of not longer than six to nine months is recommended for most Hawaii fruits; after that they begin to lose flavor.

Thawing. The most troublesome changes occur in texture on freezing and thawing. *Holding* after thawing is equivalent to long storage. Fruits have a tendency to collapse and shrivel as the result of moisture loss.

Fruits should be packed in containers small enough to permit rapid thawing. They should be thawed in the original container, which should not be opened until the fruit is ready to serve. Serve fruit with a few ice crystals still present.

Refreezing fruit after it has been thawed is not recommended.

Never thaw fruits in hot water. The recommended method is in the refrigerator. Approximate thawing temperatures and time required for 1 pint of fruit are:

> Food-storage area of refrigerator—5 hours
> Room temperature—2 to 3 hours
> Room temperature with electric fan—about 1 hour
> Watertight packages in cold running water—about 45 minutes

Sugar Sirups for Use in Freezing Fruits. To make sirup for freezing fruits, dissolve sugar in boiling water and bring to a full rolling boil. Let sirup cool in the refrigerator before using. The following

---

* For further details on packaging materials and techniques see University of Hawaii Experiment Station Circular No. 27, *Home Freezers and Packaging Materials.*

table shows the concentration obtained by mixing a given amount of sugar with boiling water:

Sugar per 2 cups water	Concentration
½ cup	20%
⅔ cup	25%
1 cup	30%
1⅛ cups	35%
1⅔ cups	40%
2½ cups	50%

DIRECTIONS FOR FREEZING SOME HAWAII FRUITS*

FRUIT	PREPARATION

AVOCADO

Wash fruit, cut into halves, remove large seed and membrane. Scoop out pulp. Mash or purée. To 1 cup purée, add 1½ tablespoons sugar and 2 teaspoons lemon juice. Make a smooth paste; place in cartons and freeze. Purée may be used in ice cream, sherbets, cocktail dip, or gelatin salad.

BANANA
eating varieties

Satisfactory as purée only. Two to 3 bananas yield 1 cup purée. Add ½ teaspoon ascorbic acid powder to 1 pint of 20 percent sirup. Use 1 to 2 tablespoons sirup for each banana frozen.

cooking varieties

Excellent precooked and then frozen.
Prebaked.—Bake in skins for 30 minutes at 350° F. Let cool to room temperature. Wrap peeled or unpeeled in cellophane or aluminum foil, or pack in waxed or aluminum containers. To reheat: place frozen banana in oven, loosen foil or cellophane wrapper, heat through. Serve as a vegetable.
Preboiled.—Boil in skins for 10 to 20 minutes. Remove from water, let cool, and wrap for freezing as described above. To reheat: place in a steamer over boiling water until heated through. Loosen packaging around fruit but leave in aluminum foil to retain juices. Serve as a vegetable or a fruit.

COCONUT

Grate meat from halves on Hawaiian grater, or peel off brown skin and grate on hand grater, or put through food chopper (see chapter on Coconut). One coconut yields about 3 cups grated meat. Pack either plain or mixed with sugar in proportion of 1 part sugar to 10 parts coconut.
For convenience, grated coconut may be wrapped in waxed paper in small quantities of ¼ or ½ cup and placed in moisture-vapor-proof packages. Coconut may be pressed tightly into packages, because it contains so little water that it does not expand in freezing as do fruits.

---

* For more detailed information regarding the freezing of Hawaii fruits, consult Hawaii Agricultural Experiment Station publications.

DIRECTIONS FOR FREEZING SOME HAWAII FRUITS(Con't.)

FRUIT	PREPARATION
GUAVA (common)	May be frozen as purée, juice, or shells. *Purée.*—Use whole guava or inner pulp; put through strainer or sieve to remove seeds. Add 1 part sugar to 4 to 5 parts purée, according to sweetness desired. Purée from the pulp and seeds has a smoother texture and better color than that made from whole guavas or from the shells. *Juice.*—Prepare Guava Juice (see Index) as for jelly. Freeze either sweetened or unsweetened, but sweetened is preferred. Use 1 part sugar to 8 parts juice. *Shells.*—Use only large, ripe, tender guavas. Freeze for salads and desserts. Combine 1 part sugar to 4 parts shells, or use 35 percent sugar sirup to cover; package, and freeze.
LYCHEE	Freeze whole, either in shell or peeled. Cover whole unshelled fruit with 35 to 50 percent sugar sirup. Discard sirup on thawing and peel fruit. Peeled and seeded halves for cocktails may be frozen in 35 percent sugar sirup. A dry sugar pack is not recommended.
MANGO	The more tart varieties are preferred for freezing, and may be frozen as cheeks, finger slices, purée, or green mango sauce. *Cheeks and finger slices.*—Use firm-ripe fruit. Peel, cut cheeks from seed. Cut into finger slices if desired. Pack in 20 to 35 percent sugar sirup for dessert and in 1 part sugar to 8 parts fruit for pie or cobbler use. Sirup pack is preferred for best product. *Purée.*—Put flesh through strainer or sieve to remove fiber. Add 1 part sugar to 8 parts purée plus ½ teaspoon ascorbic acid to protect flavor. Excellent for ice cream, sherbet, sauces. *Cocktail.*—Combine finger slices or chunks with pineapple chunks, lychee halves, and Surinam cherry for a tropical fruit cocktail. *Green mango sauce.*—Cook 4 cups green mango slices with 1½ cups water until tender; stir in ½ cup sugar. Purée mixture, chill quickly, package, and freeze. Serve with meat dishes or as a dessert.
MOUNTAIN APPLE	Freeze unpeeled cubes or chunks in a tropical fruit cocktail with mangoes, pineapple, and lychees for texture and color accent.
MULBERRY	Freeze for use in pies or cobblers. Wash, discarding inferior or unripe fruit. Pack with 1 part dry sugar to 5 parts fruit by weight.
PAPAYA	Not recommended for freezing. Texture and flavor are only fair.

DIRECTIONS FOR FREEZING SOME HAWAII FRUITS(Con't.)

FRUIT	PREPARATION
PASSION FRUIT	Freeze as juicy pulp with or without sugar. Press juice through poi cloth or colander to remove seeds. Add 1 part sugar to 2 to 3 parts sieved pulp. Passion fruit juice makes an excellent beverage and sherbet base.
PINEAPPLE	Smooth Cayenne variety freezes well. It may be prepared in the following forms: wedges, cubes, sticks, crushed, or juice. *Wedges, cubes, sticks.*—Ripe fruit of summer season is preferred. Pare, remove eyes and core, cut as desired, cover with 30 to 35 percent sugar sirup, and freeze. *Crushed.*—Utilize odd and broken pieces by crushing. Pack 8 parts of crushed fruit to 1 part sugar. It is best served with a few ice crystals present. *Juice.*—Cut ripe fruit into 8 or more pieces and squeeze through 1 thickness of poi cloth or sugar sack. If fruit is sweet, freeze without added sugar. If it is not sweet enough, use 1 cup sugar to 10 cups juice.
PLUM, METHLEY	Use firm, but fully ripe fruit. Plums may be frozen with skins, but for a less bitter product, remove skins and seeds. Use 3 to 5 parts plums to 1 part sugar for pie or cobbler.
POHA	Berries, either whole or crushed, may be frozen plain or with sugar added in the proportion of 1 part sugar to 4 parts fruit. Pohas are excellent for jams, preserves, or sauces for puddings.
ROSELLE	Excellent as juice or ground with citrus fruit as relish. Juice may be used for jellies and fruit drinks or as a punch base; relish may be served with meat courses as substitute for cranberries.
SOURSOP	Freeze as purée for ice cream, sherbet, and beverage base. Select soft ripe fruit, peel, and cut lengthwise through center. Discard core and seeds; purée pulp and add 1 part sugar to 6 parts purée. Add ¼ teaspoon ascorbic acid to retain better flavor and color.
SURINAM CHERRY	Best used as a garnish or color accent for tropical fruit cocktail. Its very tart, almost acrid, flavor is not pleasant to many. Select ripe, freshly picked fruit; wash cherries, and discard green or damaged fruit. Remove stems, blossom ends, and seeds. Pack whole or in halves in 50 percent sugar sirup.

When frozen fruits, either home or commercially prepared, are used in recipes that call for sugar, allowance must be made for the sugar in the frozen product.

II. CANNING AND BOTTLING FRUIT AND FRUIT JUICE

In addition to preserving fruits by freezing, the older methods of preservation with heat and sugar are highly recommended. Use Hawaii-grown fruits as follows:

For canning—fig (see Preserved Figs), guava, lychee, and mango. mango.

For bottled juices—grape, guava, mulberry, passion fruit (see Passion Fruit Sirup), and roselle.

For jelly—grape, guava, Java plum, ketambilla, passion fruit, roselle, and Surinam cherry (see Appendix III and recipes under individual fruits).

For preserves, jams, marmalades, and butters—fig, grape, guava, kumquat, mango, pineapple, mulberry, orange, papaya, poha, plum, and Surinam cherry (see recipes under each fruit).

CONTAINERS

Selection. Jars suitable for canning must form an airtight seal if the product is to keep indefinitely. Do not attempt to reuse old lids having rubber sealing compound. With Mason jars and covers, use new rubber rings whenever possible.

Inspect carefully all glass jars and covers to be used. Discard any with cracks, chips, dents, or any other defects that would prevent airtight sealing.

Clean beverage bottles may be used for fruit juice and for juicy fruit pulp if they can be made airtight. Use clean, new, crown caps and a hand-operated capping device.

Preparation. Wash containers with warm, soapy water. A bottle brush is convenient for jars and is essential for thorough cleaning of bottles.

Place a towel or rack in the bottom of a kettle to keep the containers from breaking, and add cold water to a depth of 1 to 2 inches. Rinse the containers and place them upside down in the kettle. Place the kettle on the range, bring the water to a boil, and continue boiling

20 minutes. Keep the containers hot until the boiling fruit or juice is ready. Then remove containers from the kettle, drain but do not wipe dry, and fill immediately.

Wash rubbers with soap and water, then rinse. Plunge bottle caps or self-seal lids into boiling water for 1 minute—if left longer the seal will be destroyed. Jar covers, rubbers, or corks should be put into boiling water for 2 or 3 minutes just before being used.

Jars and bottles used for the "open kettle" method should always be thoroughly sterilized as recommended. If the jars are to be processed by means of the "water bath" or in a pressure cooker, they should be clean and thoroughly heated but do not need the 20-minute boiling period prior to using. The processing that sterilizes the food will also sterilize the jar.

METHODS OF COOKING FRUIT

It is desirable to precook practically all fruits before canning. Drawing out the juices shrinks the fruit and makes it possible to pack the jars more firmly. Precooking also shortens the time necessary for sterilizing the fruit in the jar. Fruits may be cooked in their own juice, in water, or in sirup. Directions for making canning sirups are given in the chart below.

Open kettle. This method may be used for fruit packed in a sugar sirup or for fruit and fruit juices high in acid content. If directions are followed carefully, the open kettle method is satisfactory for guavas and mangoes but not for fruits such as lychees. Although this is the simplest method of canning, it is not the safest, since the fruit may come in contact with bacteria when the jars are being filled and sealed.

All fruit products canned by the open kettle method should be thoroughly cooked and should be boiling hot at the time they are poured into hot sterilized bottles or jars. The containers should be sealed immediately. If a number of jars are to be filled at one time the fruit remaining in the kettle should be reheated to boiling several times during the process.

Hot pack. When fruit is to be canned by this method, blanch* or precook it as directed in the specific recipe being used. Then pack hot fruit quickly into hot, clean jars. Pack well, but do not force in so much fruit that there is no room for liquid—it is difficult for heat to penetrate to the center of a too solidly packed jar, and such penetration is necessary to insure complete sterilization. Add boiling juice or sirup to within $\frac{1}{2}$ inch of the top of the jar. Insert sterilized knife blade or spoon handle into filled jars to allow air bubbles to escape. Wipe excess food from top of jar.

---

* To blanch fruit, cover it with boiling water for 1 to 2 minutes to facilitate the removal of skins.

Place sterilized rubbers and covers on jars at once. If food has been precooked or completely cooked, covers may be screwed on tightly or clamps fastened securely before processing. If fruit has been packed in hot sirup without cooking, loosen top slightly—about one-quarter turn with screw-type jar, or with only one wire clamped tight on the other type of jar.

The fruit is then ready to be processed* in either boiling-water bath or pressure cooker.

PROCESSING

Boiling-water bath. The "boiling-water bath" may be used successfully for acid fruits canned in water or sugar sirup, for sweetened or unsweetened fruit juice, fruit sauce, and thin fruit pulp. A large tightly covered container deep enough to allow covering tops of jars with at least 2 inches of water is needed. There should be a wooden or wire rack that will fit into the canner to hold the jars upright at least ½ inch apart and keep them from touching the bottom of the canner. A canner may easily be made by fitting a rack in a deep-well cooker of an electric stove, or other large deep kettle or can with tight-fitting lid. If possible, a handle or a bail should be fastened to the rack to make lifting jars in and out of the hot water easier.

When the canner has been prepared, fill it with hot water to a depth slightly less than the height of the jars to be put in it. To avoid breakage lower the filled jars into the container while they are still hot. Add enough hot water to cover the tops of the jars to a depth of 2 inches. Cover the canner, bring the water bath to a boil, and keep it at the boiling point during the entire time of processing.

The time required for processing varies with each product and with the size of the jar. (See chart, below.) Processing time is counted only from the time the water begins to boil after the jars have been placed in it. Hot water should be added as needed to keep the level of water in the canner 2 inches above the tops of the jars.

When the fruit has been processed the required time, remove jars with tongs or dip out sufficient water so that the covers of the jars may be grasped. Remove one jar at a time. If the jar was sealed before processing, do not tighten screw top again. If it was not sealed before processing, it should be sealed completely at this time.

Change in processing time for increased altitude. The Bureau of Human Nutrition and Home Economics recommends that for each 1,000 feet above sea level, 1 minute should be added to the processing time if the time called for is 20 minutes or less. If the processing called

---

* Processing fruit requires heating or cooking in jars or cans to insure sterilization.

for is more than 20 minutes, add 2 minutes for each 1,000 feet.

Pressure cooker. The "pressure cooker" need not be used for acid fruits or other fruits canned in a sugar sirup, but it must be used for non-acid foods. Since it may be used for any kind of fruit, some prefer it to the boiling-water bath. Because steam is enclosed in the cooker, a temperature above boiling is obtained and the temperature inside the jar becomes higher than that reached when the boiling-water bath is used.

Prepare the jars of fruit as for the boiling-water bath method, place the filled jars in the pressure cooker or pressure cooker saucepan, and attach the cover of the cooker. Steam should be allowed to escape from the vent for 7 minutes before closing the petcock on pressure cookers of the size commonly used in home canning. Thus all air in the cooker is driven out and the temperature within is the same as that shown on the dial. For further directions regarding the use of a pressure cooker for processing fruit, follow the instructions issued by the manufacturer.

Change in pressure for increased altitude. The Bureau of Human Nutrition and Home Economics recommends that for each 2,000 feet altitude above sea level, the pressure should be increased by one pound. For example, if the directions call for 10 pounds pressure at sea level, increase to 11.5 pounds at 3,000 feet.

CARE AFTER CANNING

Never open a jar to replace liquid which has been lost in processing. Place jars right side up to cool. Do not set them on a cold surface or in a draft while they are still hot.

When jars have cooled overnight, test for leaks around the lids by carefully tilting each jar. If a leak is found, or if rubber ring bulges out from a lid, open the jar, pour the contents into a kettle and heat to boiling. Then pack fruit in hot sterilized jar with new rubber ring, and process again. If the self-seal type of cover is being used always use a new inner lid when resealing.

When all jars have been tested and are ready to store, wipe them clean with a damp cloth. Label each jar as to contents and the date of canning. Store in a cool, dark, dry place. Inspect the jars frequently thereafter for the first few days for signs of leakage. If any leaks appear, empty fruit into kettle and repeat the whole canning process.

Storage of any canned fruit for longer than one year is not recommended because it tends to lose flavor, color, and nutritive value.

If there is any sign of spoilage, discard the contents of the jar, wash the jar thoroughly, and boil it for at least 20 minutes before using again.

CHART FOR MAKING SIRUPS USED IN CANNING

SIRUP	SUGAR	WATER OR JUICE
	cups	cups
Thin	⅓	1
Moderately thin	½	1
Medium (for sour fruit)	1	1
Thick (for fruit to be preserved)	1⅓ to 2	1

Method: Combine ingredients and heat. Stir until sugar is dissolved and sirup begins to boil.

PREPARATION AND TIME CHART FOR CANNING FRUIT*

FRUIT	PREPARATION	PROCESSING TIME, PINTS OR QUARTS
FRUIT JUICES: Blackberry Isabella grape Java plum Roselle Surinam cherry Mulberry	Select ripe fruit for juice to be used as a beverage and half-ripe fruit for juice intended for jelly. Wash fruit and remove blemishes. Place in a kettle and add water to partially cover the fruit. Mash fruit and simmer until it is soft. Pour into thick cloth bag and allow juice to drain. Add sugar to juice according to taste. *Open kettle.*—Heat juice to a boil and continue boiling for only 3 minutes. Pour into hot sterilized bottles and seal at once. *Water bath.*—Heat juice to simmering, pour into hot sterilized jars or bottles, seal and process.	5 to 10 minutes
GUAVA JUICE	*Open kettle.*—Prepare Guava Juice as directed (see Index). Add ⅓ cup sugar to each cup of juice if desired. Bring to a boil, stirring until sugar is dissolved. Continue boiling vigorously for 3 minutes. Pour into hot sterilized bottles or jars and seal at once. *Water bath.*—Prepare juice as directed in open kettle method, heating only to the simmering point. Pour into hot sterilized jars or bottles, seal and process.	5 to 10 minutes
GUAVA SLICES	*Open kettle.*—Prepare as directed in recipe for Guava Sauce (see Index). Heat until boiling vigorously. Pour imme-	

* For more detailed information about methods of canning, see circulars and bulletins from the Agricultural Research Service, United States Department of Agriculture. These may be obtained free or for a nominal sum from the Superintendent of Documents, United States Government Printing Office, Washington, D. C.

FRUIT	PREPARATION	PROCESSING TIME, PINTS OR QUARTS

diately into hot sterilized jars. Seal at once.

Water bath.—Cook slices or shells 2 to 3 minutes in medium sirup. Pack and process.

20 minutes

LYCHEE

Water bath. — Wash and peel lychees. Loosen fruit from seed at stem and cut lengthwise. Remove seed, leaving fruit in one piece. Add enough thin or moderately thin sirup (see chart, above) to half cover the fruit. Heat to boiling and boil gently for 2 minutes. Fill hot sterilized jars to within $\frac{1}{2}$ inch of the top with boiling hot fruit, add 1 teaspoon lemon or lime juice to each pint, cover with boiling juice. Seal and process in water bath.

15 minutes

Pressure cooker. — Prepare fruit as directed for water-bath method. Prepare moderately thin sirup (see chart, above), add fruit, and boil 2 minutes.

5 minutes at 10 lbs. pressure

Pack fruit in hot sterilized jars, and cover with sirup to within $\frac{1}{2}$ inch of top of the jar.

For additional flavor, add 1 teaspoon lemon or lime juice to each jar before processing.

MANGO SAUCE

Prepare green or half-ripe mangoes as directed for Mango Sauce (see Index). Press pulp through a sieve if mangoes are stringy. Sweeten if desired. Sauce should be fairly thin; add boiling water if necessary.

Only distinctly acid mangoes should be used for open kettle or water bath. If sauce is made from mild or ripe mangoes the pressure cooker must be used for processing.

Open kettle.—Heat green or half-ripe mango sauce to a boil, and continue boiling vigorously 5 to 8 minutes. Pour into hot sterilized jars. Sauce should be fairly thin; add boiling water if necessary.

Water bath.—Pour boiling sauce, prepared as for open kettle canning, into hot sterilized jars to within $\frac{1}{2}$ inch of

FRUIT	PREPARATION	PROCESSING TIME, PINTS OR QUARTS
	the top. Insert sterilized knife and allow air bubbles to escape. Seal and process in water bath.	10 to 15 minutes
	Pressure cooker.—Prepare sauce as directed for water bath. Process in pressure cooker.	5 minutes at 10 lbs. pressure
MANGO SLICES	Select firm-ripe or half-ripe mangoes that are not fibrous. Peel and slice lengthwise in large slices. Use remaining pulp for sauce. Prepare sufficient medium or heavy sirup to half cover fruit (see chart, above).	
	Open kettle.—Add mango slices to hot sirup and cook 10 to 15 minutes or until edges become transparent. One tablespoon lemon juice may be added for each pint if desired. Pack slices in hot sterilized jars, cover with boiling sirup, and seal at once.	
	Water bath.—Add mango slices to hot sirup. Cook ripe fruit 5 minutes, half-ripe fruit 10 minutes. Pack in hot sterilized jars and cover with boiling sirup to within ½ inch of the top. Seal and process.	15 to 20 minutes
	Pressure cooker.—Pack partially cooked mango slices, prepared as directed in water-bath method, in hot sterilized jars. Seal and process.	5 minutes at 10 lbs. pressure
	Uncooked slices may be packed in hot sterilized jars and covered with boiling sirup to within ½ inch of the top. Partially seal and process.	10 minutes at 10 lbs. pressure

III. HOW TO MAKE JELLY

SELECTION OF FRUIT

Firm-ripe or underripe fruit should be used for jelly. Pectin and acid content decrease as the fruit ripens. Overripe fruit may be used for butter, jam, or marmalade, but not for jelly.

EXTRACTION OF JUICE

Wash, remove blossom and stem ends, and cut fruit into slices. Small fruits, such as berries, cherries, or grapes should be cooked whole. Place fruit in a kettle and add enough water to almost cover so that water can be seen around the edge of kettle. For berries and grapes, add only enough water to prevent scorching. Cook slowly until fruit is soft, stirring frequently.

Further instructions may be found under recipes for the individual fruits.

To drain juice. Pour cooked fruit into a triangular-shaped jelly bag made of flannel or two thicknesses of a flour or sugar sack. Allow to drain; do not squeeze the bag if a clear jelly is desired.

The fruit pulp remaining in the bag may be used in making fruit butter, jam, or catsup. Press through a sieve to remove seeds and skins.

When ample supplies of fruit are available, fresh, whole fruit is preferred for jams and butters.

PECTIN TEST

Some fruits contain more pectin than others. Juice which contains little or no pectin will not jell. It is necessary to combine it with fruit high in pectin, such as guavas, or with commercial pectin. It is desirable to test juice for pectin in order to judge the amount of sugar to be used. Juice containing a large amount of pectin needs more sugar than juice low in pectin.

Jelmeter. The proportion of sugar required for each cup of juice may be determined by a glass tubular device called a Jelmeter.* It is

---

* The Jelmeter Co., P.O. Box 300, Milford, Delaware 19963.

shown in the illustration on p. 2. Directions given by the manufacturer should be carefully followed.

Alcohol test. A test for pectin is made by combining in a glass 1 tablespoon of juice with 1 tablespoon of grain alcohol or wood alcohol. Shake the mixture gently but do not stir. Examine after a few seconds, and if the mixture slips from the glass in one large mass, there is considerable pectin present. In that case 1 cup of sugar should be used to each cup of juice. Because guavas usually contain more pectin than other fruits, 1 to $1\frac{1}{4}$ cups sugar may be used with the juice of sour guavas. If juice and alcohol mixture thickens slightly, $\frac{2}{3}$ to $\frac{3}{4}$ cup sugar for each cup of juice should be used. Strawberry guavas, grapes, and roselles may be used with the latter proportions.

COOKING JELLY

Jelly should not be made in quantities larger than 3 to 4 cups at one time. A strong flavored, dark, gummy jelly results from long cooking in large quantities. Use a shallow kettle which will hold four times the amount of juice to be cooked. Rapid evaporation and a short cooking period are desirable for good jelly.

Bring the juice to the boiling point and, if more than 2 cups are used, boil vigorously 5 to 10 minutes. Add sugar and stir until it is dissolved. Remove scum which forms on top. Boil rapidly, testing frequently, until a jelly test is obtained.

JELLY TESTS

After boiling jelly mixture 5 to 10 minutes, test it by one of the following methods:

Sheet test. Allow juice to cool slightly in a large metal spoon, then return it to the kettle a drop at a time. When three or four large drops run together and "sheet" off in one large drop the juice has reached the jelly stage. In order to avoid overcooking, it is well to remove the kettle from the fire during testing.

Fig. 10.—Jelly test (sheet test). Top, too thin. Bottom, proper jelly stage.

Thermometer test. Place a thermometer in the boiling jelly mixture (juice and sugar), making sure it does not touch the bottom or sides of the pan and is held upright at the time of reading.

To obtain a good jelly at sea level

203

cook the juice and sugar mixture to one of the following temperatures: 221° F. or 105° C. on a clear day, and 222° F. or 106° C. on a damp rainy day. Marmalades may be cooked to a temperature of 218° to 221° F.

Decrease the temperature 1° on the Fahrenheit scale and 0.6° on the Centigrade scale for each 500 feet of elevation above sea level. For example, if the recipe calls for cooking a jelly to 221° F. or 105° C. at sea level, at 1,000 feet elevation the temperature should be 219° F. or 103.8° C., and at 3,500 feet elevation the temperature should be 214° F. or 100.8° C. The temperatures given in all recipes in this book are for sea level.

CONTAINERS

Jelly glasses holding 6 to 8 ounces with metal covers (either those which screw or slip on) are recommended. However, other glass containers of suitable size may be used for jellies and jams if they are sealed with a layer of hot melted paraffin and then covered.

STERILIZING GLASSES

Wash glasses and covers thoroughly with warm soapy water and rinse well in clear water.

Glass containers should be sterilized by one of the following methods:

1. Place clean glasses upside down in hot water. Bring water to a boil and continue boiling 10 to 15 minutes.

2. Place glasses in a pressure cooker or pressure saucepan, exhaust air, and bring to 5 pounds pressure. Turn off heat and wait until pointer returns to zero before opening.

After either method of sterilization, hot glasses should be drained but not wiped.

Sterilize covers by placing them in boiling water 2 to 3 minutes.

SEALING AND STORING

As soon as the jelly test is obtained, remove the kettle from the heat and skim if necessary. Pour jelly into hot sterilized glasses, filling them to within $\frac{1}{2}$ inch of the top. Cover immediately with a thin layer of paraffin. When jelly is cold, seal by adding another layer of melted paraffin (about $\frac{1}{8}$ inch thick); tip glass and allow paraffin to run around the edges in order to insure a perfect seal.

A piece of clean string may be cut about 1 inch longer than the diameter of the jar and placed on top of the first paraffin layer before the second layer is poured onto it. This aids in removal of the paraffin.

When paraffin is firmly set, wipe glasses with a damp cloth and cover with lids or pieces of heavy paper or metal foil. Label and store in a cool, dry, dark place.

Caution. Since paraffin is highly inflammable, great care should be taken in melting it. Heat it slowly and remove it from the burner when melted. The best method is to melt the paraffin over hot water as recommended by the manufacturer.

CAUSES OF UNSATISFACTORY JELLY

Inexperienced jelly-makers sometimes obtain unsatisfactory products without knowing why. Characteristics of poor jellies and the cause for them follow:

CHARACTERISTICS	CAUSES
Sirupy	Too much sugar; undercooking
	Too long cooking of a very acid juice and sugar
Tough	Too little sugar; overcooking
Dark	Too slow cooking; cooking in too large quantities
Cloudy	Improper straining of juice
Fermented	Improper sterilization; delayed or improper sealing of glasses

IV. HAWAII FRUITS AS SOURCES OF VITAMINS

EXCELLENT	GOOD	FAIR	POOR
VITAMIN A*			
Loquat	Orange	Acerola	Breadfruit
Mango	Passion fruit,	Avocado	Carambola
Papaya	purple	Banana, cooking	Carissa
Passion fruit,	Surinam cherry	Banana, eating	Fig
yellow	Tangerine	Ketambilla	Grape, Isabella
Poha		Ohelo berry	Guava, Cattley
		Plum, Methley	Guava, common
		Roselle	Mulberry
		Watermelon	Pineapple
			Strawberry
THIAMINE			
	Breadfruit, ripe	Avocado	Acerola
	Orange	Grape, Isabella	Banana, cooking
	Pineapple	Grapefruit	Banana, eating
	Poha	Soursop	Carambola
	Tamarind		Carissa
	Tangerine		Coconut
			Coconut milk
			Fig
			Guava, Cattley
			Guava, common
			Java plum
			Ketambilla
			Lime juice
			Loquat
			Lychee
			Mango
			Mountain apple
			Mulberry
			Ohelo berry
			Papaya
			Passion fruit
			Plum, Methley
			Roselle
			Strawberry
			Surinam cherry
			Watermelon
RIBOFLAVIN			
Java plum	Avocado	Acerola	Carambola
Tamarind	Passion fruit	Banana, cooking	Coconut
	Plum, Methley	Banana, eating	Coconut milk
	Soursop	Breadfruit	Fig
		Carissa	Grape, Isabella
		Ketambilla	Grapefruit

* Vitamin A refers to the yellow pigments or provitamin A (see Appendix VI).

EXCELLENT	GOOD	FAIR	POOR

RIBOFLAVIN (Cont.)

EXCELLENT	GOOD	FAIR	POOR
		Lychee	Guava, Cattley
		Mango, common	Guava, common
		Mango, Haden	Lime juice
		Mulberry	Loquat
		Orange	Mango, Pirie
		Papaya	Mountain Apple
		Poha	Ohelo berry
			Pineapple
			Roselle
			Strawberry
			Surinam cherry
			Tangerine
			Watermelon

NIACIN

EXCELLENT	GOOD	FAIR	POOR
Passion fruit, yellow	Avocado	Banana, cooking	Acerola
	Breadfruit, ripe	Banana, eating	Carissa
	Passion fruit, purple	Breadfruit, green	Fig
	Poha	Carambola	Grape, Isabella
	Soursop	Coconut	Grapefruit
	Tamarind	Coconut milk	Java plum
		Guava, Cattley	Ketambilla
		Guava, common	Lime juice
		Lychee	Loquat
		Mango, common	Mango, Haden
		Mulberry	Mango, Pirie
			Mountain apple
			Ohelo berry
			Orange
			Papaya
			Pineapple
			Plum, Methley
			Roselle
			Strawberry
			Surinam cherry
			Tangerine
			Watermelon

ASCORBIC ACID

EXCELLENT	GOOD	FAIR	POOR
Acerola	Carambola	Banana, cooking	Avocado
Carissa	Java plum	Breadfruit	Banana, eating
Grapefruit	Mulberry	Lime juice	Fig
Guava, Cattley	Orange	Mango, Haden	Ohelo berry
Guava, common	Passion fruit, purple	Mango, Pirie	Pineapple
Ketambilla	Tangerine	Mountain apple	Plum, Methley
Lychee		Passion fruit, yellow	Tamarind
Mango, common		Roselle	Watermelon
Papaya		Soursop	
Poha		Surinam cherry	
Strawberry			

V. VITAMIN CONTENT OF HAWAII FRUITS*

NAME	APPROX. AMOUNTS EDIBLE PORTIONS WEIGHING 100 gms.	VITAMIN A† I.U./100 gms.	THIAMINE mg/100 gms.	RIBOFLAVIN mg/100 gms.	NIACIN mg/100 gms.	ASCORBIC ACID mg/100 gms.
ACEROLA	1 cup, scant	408	0.03	0.08	0.3	2330
AVOCADO (range of summer and winter)	⅓ medium; ½ cup, cubed	310 to 2080	.04 to .10	.06 to .17	.8 to 1.9	2 to 10
BANANA, COOKING (average cooked values)	1 medium	420	.04	.06	.6	12
BANANA, EATING (average Bluefields, Brazilian, Chinese)	1 medium	120	.03	.05	.6	9
BREADFRUIT (ripe, cooked)	⅓ cup, scant	30	.12	.07	1.4	11
CARAMBOLA	2 large	20	.04	.04	.7	35
CARISSA	5 medium	20	.04	.06	.2	53
COCONUT, MATURE	¾ cup, grated	0	.03	.01	.8	0
COCONUT "MILK"	½ cup	0	.04	.01	.7	2
FIG	2 medium	60	.08	.04	.3	2
GRAPE, ISABELLA (whole)	⅝ cup, seeded	80	.05	.03	.2	0
GRAPEFRUIT SECTIONS	1 small; ⅓ cup	0	.05	.02	.2	54
GUAVA, CATTLEY (red or light yellow)	10 to 12	90	.03	.03	.5	43
GUAVA, COMMON (seeds removed)	1½ medium	90	.04	.04	.9	95 to 300
GUAVA JUICE AND PULP	⅓ cup, scant					30 to 130
JAVA PLUM (jambolan)	25 medium; ¾ cup, seeded	0	trace	.27	.2	29
KETAMBILLA	16 medium; ⅝ cup, sliced	230	.01	.05	.2	66

* Table prepared by Barbara Branthoover. Figures taken largely from unpublished data in the Foods and Nutrition Department, Hawaii Agricultural Experiment Station.
† One microgram of total carotinoids equivalent to one International Unit.

V. VITAMIN CONTENT OF HAWAII FRUITS (Continued)

NAME	APPROX. AMOUNTS EDIBLE PORTIONS WEIGHING 100 gms.	VITAMIN A† I.U./100 gms.	THIAMINE mg/100 gms.	RIBOFLAVIN mg/100 gms.	NIACIN mg/100 gms.	ASCORBIC ACID mg/100 gms.
LIME JUICE	½ cup	0	.02	.03	.2	24
LOQUAT	4 medium	1122	.02	.02	.2	trace
LYCHEE	10 to 20	0	.02	.07	.8	83
MANGO, COMMON (ripe)	1 medium	1600	.04	.06	.5	114
MANGO, HADEN	½ medium	2500	.04	.05	.3	10
MANGO, PIRIE	⅔ medium	3000	.05	.04	.3	14
MOUNTAIN APPLE	2 to 3	0	.03	.04	.2	20
MULBERRY, BLACK	1 cup, scant	20	.02	.08	.5	29
OHELO BERRY	¾ cup	498	.02	.04	.3	6
ORANGE	1 medium; ½ cup sections, without membrane	560	.10	.08	.3	40
PAPAYA, SOLO	⅛ to ½	3500	.02	.05	.4	84
PASSION FRUIT JUICE, YELLOW	½ cup, scant	2400	trace	.10	2.2	20
PASSION FRUIT, PURPLE	½ cup, scant	700	trace	.13	1.5	33
PINEAPPLE	½ cup, ½-inch cubes	50	.13	.03	.2	8
PLUM, METHLEY	5 medium fruit	100	.01	.12	.4	<1
POHA	1 cup	1470	.15	.05	1.6	42
ROSELLE	2 cups	170	.01	.08	.3	10
SOURSOP, PULP	½ cup, scant	0	.07	.12	1.5	16
STRAWBERRY	¾ cup	10	.02	.04	.3	62
SURINAM CHERRY	28 large; ⅔ cup, stoned	670	.03	.03	.3	20
TAMARIND (ripe)	⅓ cup pulp	0	.15	.22	1.3	1
TANGERINE SECTIONS	1 medium; ½ cup	830	.10	.02	.2	31
WATERMELON	⅔ cup, ½-inch cubes	450	.03	.04	0.2	6

† One microgram of total carotinoids equivalent to one International Unit.

VI. MINERALS AND VITAMINS

The following criteria have been used as bases for statements regarding the vitamin and mineral values of fruits discussed in this book.

MINERALS

Since fruits on the whole are poor sources of calcium, phosphorus, and iron, they should not be depended upon to contribute significant quantities of these minerals. (There are more base-forming elements than acid-forming elements in fruits so that practically all fruits yield an alkaline ash and make the urine more alkaline.) Nutritionists recommend that the daily diet of the average adult should supply 1.0 gram of calcium, 1.32 grams of phosphorus, and 12 milligrams (0.012 gm.) of iron.

For purposes of comparison of the fruits in this book, the *arbitrary scale* given below has been used for rating them as good, fair, and poor sources of calcium, phosphorus, and iron.

MINERALS	RATING		
	GOOD	FAIR	POOR
CALCIUM (*Mg. per 100 gm. edible fruit*)	More than 30	15 to 30	Less than 15
PHOSPHORUS (*Mg. per 100 gm. edible fruit*)	More than 40	25 to 40	Less than 25
IRON (*Mg. per 100 gm. edible fruit*)	More than 1.0	0.5 to 1.0	Less than 0.5

VITAMINS

Fruits constitute the best source of ascorbic acid (vitamin C) in the diet, but they vary greatly in their content of this vitamin. Fruits are usually poor sources of thiamine, riboflavin, and niacin, furnishing but little of the daily quota for these three B vitamins. Fruits have no vitamin A, but those having yellow or orange color contain carotene or other carotenoid pigments. These pigments are referred to as precursors or provitamin A because they can be changed by the body to vitamin A, which is colorless. The term "provitamin A" has been used throughout this book to indicate the vitamin A value of the fruits.

The Food and Nutrition Board, National Research Council, recommends that the daily diet of an adult should supply 5,000 International Units of vitamin A, 1.5 milligrams thiamine, 1.8 milligrams of riboflavin, 15 milligrams of niacin, and 75 milligrams of ascorbic acid.

For purposes of comparison of the fruits in this book, the *arbitrary scale* given below has been used for rating them as excellent, good, fair, and poor sources of five vitamins.

VITAMINS	RATING			
	EXCELLENT	GOOD	FAIR	POOR
VITAMIN A *(International Units per 100 gm. edible fruit)*	More than 1000	500 to 1000	100 to 500	Less than 100
THIAMINE *(vitamin B$_1$)* *(milligrams per 100 gm. edible fruit)*	More than 0.2	0.1 to 0.2	0.05 to 0.1	Less than 0.05
RIBOFLAVIN *(milligrams per 100 gm. edible fruit)*	More than 0.2	0.1 to 0.2	0.05 to 0.1	Less than 0.05
NIACIN *(milligrams per 100 gm. edible fruit)*	More than 2.0	1.0 to 2.0	0.5 to 1.0	Less than 0.5
ASCORBIC ACID *(milligrams per 100 gm. edible fruit)*	More than 40	25 to 40	10 to 25	Less than 10

VII. AVERAGE WEIGHT AND PERCENTAGE OF REFUSE OF HAWAII FRUITS (AS PURCHASED).

NAME AND VARIETY	SAMPLES BY NUMBER OR WEIGHT	AV. WEIGHT PER FRUIT ounces*	REFUSE percentage	PORTIONS CONSIDERED REFUSE
ACEROLA	4 lbs.	0.1 to 0.4	20	seed and stem end
AVOCADO				
SUMMER	4	24	18	skin and seed
WINTER	6	30	26	skin and seed
BANANA				
CHINESE	5	3.5	33	skin
BLUEFIELDS	12	5	34	skin
BRAZILIAN	10	4.8	34	skin
COOKING (4 varieties)	32	4.5 to 6.5	19	skin
BREADFRUIT, HAWAII	7	38	20	skin, stem, and core
CARAMBOLA	29	1.7	6	stem, blossom end, ribs, seeds, and damaged area
CARAMBOLA JUICE	280	1.7	34	skin, seeds, and pulp
COCONUT, without husk	5	26	50	shell and water
FIG, TURKEY	18	2.6	13	skin
GRAPE, ISABELLA	1 lb.	} 6.0	8	stem and seeds
	3 lbs.	} per bunch	34	stem, skin, and seeds
GRAPEFRUIT	12	8	40	skin, seeds, and membrane
GUAVA				
COMMON	37 lbs.	2 to 3	3	stem and blossom end
			19	stem, blossom end, and seeds
CATTLEY	2½ lbs.	0.3	3	stem and blossom end
KETAMBILLA	2½ lbs.		1.2	blossom end
KUMQUAT	9	<0.5	2	seeds
LIME JUICE	38	1.5	61	skin, seeds, and pulp
LOQUAT	8½ lbs.	1	40	skin, seeds, and stem end
LYCHEE				
BREWSTER	3½ lbs.	0.4	40	leaves, stem, shell, and seed
HEI YEH	3½ lbs.	0.3	27	leaves, stem, shell, and seed
KWAI MI	3½ lbs.	0.2	44	leaves, stem, shell, and seed
MANGO				
COMMON	10	7	46	skin and seed

* Weight is given in ounces unless otherwise indicated.

VII. AVERAGE WEIGHT AND PERCENTAGE OF REFUSE OF HAWAII FRUITS (AS PURCHASED).

NAME AND VARIETY	SAMPLES BY NUMBER OR WEIGHT	AV. WEIGHT PER FRUIT ounces*	REFUSE percentage	PORTIONS CONSIDERED REFUSE
MANGO				
HADEN	30	18	30	skin and seed
PIRIE	10	7	43	skin and seed
MOUNTAIN APPLE	29	2.3	12	stem and seed
OHELO BERRY	6 lbs.	0.1	0	none
ORANGE, HAWAII	12	6	33	skin and seeds
	12	6	57	skin, seeds, and membrane
ORANGE JUICE	12	6	58	skin, seeds, and pulp
PAPAYA, SOLO	11	1¼ lbs.	51	skin, seeds, and membrane
PASSION FRUIT				
PURPLE	86	1.3	51	shell, seeds, and membrane
PURPLE, JUICE	86	1.3	71	shell, seeds, and pulp
YELLOW	10	2.8	42	shell, seeds, and membrane
YELLOW, JUICE	78	2.4	62	shell, seeds, and pulp
PINEAPPLE, SMOOTH CAYENNE with crown	10	4½ lbs.	40	crown, core, and parings
PINEAPPLE JUICE	4	4½ lbs.	55	crown, core, parings, and pulp
PLUM, JAVA	9 lbs.	0.2	20	seeds
PLUM, METHLEY	45	1.4	6	seed
POHA	6 sep. 1-lb. samples	<0.1	8	husk and stem
ROSELLE	6 lbs.	0.18	30	seed pod
SOURSOP	19	1¾ lbs	34	skin and seeds
SOURSOP PULP	19	1¾ lbs.	47	skin, seeds, and pulp
STRAWBERRY	1 lb.		3	stem and cap
SURINAM CHERRY	5 samples, total, ⅓ lbs.	0.14	26	stem, blossom end, and seeds
TAMARIND	1 lb.	0.5	69	pod and seeds
TANGERINE	8½ lbs.	3.5 to 4	32	skin, seeds, and membrane
WATERMELON	2	18¾ lbs.	36	rind and seeds

* Weight is given in ounces unless otherwise indicated.

VIII. APPROXIMATE MEASURE AND CALORIE VALUE OF HAWAII FRUITS PER POUND

As purchased and edible portion

NAME AND VARIETY	MEASURE PER LB. AS PURCHASED	MEASURE PER LB. EDIBLE PORTION*	CALORIES PER LB. EDIBLE PORTION†
AVOCADO			
SUMMER	2 small	3 cups cubes; 1⅓ cups pulp	480
WINTER	1 medium	3½ cups ½-inch cubes; 1⅔ cups pulp	980
BANANA			
CHINESE	4¼ medium	6¼ medium; 1½ cup pulp	......
BLUEFIELDS	2⅔ large	1⅓ cups pulp	500
BRAZILIAN	4¼ medium; 3¾ large	6¼ medium; 1½ cups pulp	580
COOKING	2⅔ medium	4 medium	600
BREADFRUIT, HAWAII	⅔ medium	2 cups pulp	650
CARAMBOLA	17 small	19 small	190
CARAMBOLA JUICE		2 cups	......
COCONUT	½ medium (without husk)	4¼ cups, grated	1900
FIG, TURKEY	6 medium	7 medium; 2⅔ cups, ¼-inch slices (without skin)	250
GRAPE, ISABELLA	4 medium bunches	2 cups (without stems and seeds)	330
		1½ cups (without stems, skins, and seeds)	320
GUAVA			
COMMON	4½ to 6 medium	3½ cups, sliced shells	200
		2½ cups pulp (without seeds)	220
STRAWBERRY	51 fruit; 3 cups	54 fruit; 3⅓ cups, whole	220
LIME	16 to 18 medium	1¾ cups juice	......

* For portions of fruit considered as refuse see Appendix VII.
† Because of the variation in composition of different samples, figures for calories have all been rounded to the nearest 10 units. The factors 4, 9, and 4 were used for calculation of caloric values.

VIII. APPROXIMATE MEASURE AND CALORIE VALUE OF HAWAII FRUITS PER POUND (Con't.)

As purchased and edible portion

NAME AND VARIETY	MEASURE PER LB. AS PURCHASED	MEASURE PER LB. EDIBLE PORTION*	CALORIES PER LB. EDIBLE PORTION†
LYCHEE			
BREWSTER	33 medium	2 cups	......
HEI YEH	30 large	2 cups, 42 large	230
KWAI MI	40 medium	$1\frac{3}{4}$ cups, 72 medium	400
MANGO			
COMMON	$2\frac{1}{4}$ medium	$4\frac{1}{4}$ medium	320
HADEN	1 medium	$1\frac{1}{2}$ medium	.....
PIRIE	$2\frac{1}{3}$ medium	$4\frac{1}{4}$ medium	350
MOUNTAIN APPLE	5 medium	$2\frac{1}{4}$ cups; $\frac{1}{2}$-inch cubes	130
ORANGE, HAWAII	$2\frac{1}{2}$ medium	$3\frac{3}{4}$ medium; $2\frac{3}{4}$ cups pulp (with membrane)	210
		$5\frac{3}{4}$ medium; $2\frac{1}{2}$ cups pulp (without membrane)	190
ORANGE JUICE		2 cups	170
PAPAYA, SOLO	1 medium	$1\frac{3}{4}$ cups pulp; $2\frac{1}{2}$ cups, $\frac{1}{2}$-inch cubes	240
PASSION FRUIT, YELLOW	5 medium; 7 small	$1\frac{3}{4}$ cups pulp (with seeds)	......
PASSION FRUIT JUICE		2 cups	......
PINEAPPLE, SMOOTH CAYENNE	$\frac{1}{4}$ fruit (with crown)	2 cups, $\frac{1}{2}$-inch cubes	250
PINEAPPLE JUICE		$1\frac{3}{4}$ cups	240
POHA	$5\frac{1}{3}$ cups	$2\frac{1}{2}$ cups, whole	260
SOURSOP	$\frac{2}{3}$ medium fruit	2 cups (without seeds)	340
SOURSOP PULP		$1\frac{3}{4}$ cups	......
STRAWBERRY	$4\frac{1}{2}$ cups	$3\frac{1}{3}$ cups, whole	150
SURINAM CHERRY	$3\frac{1}{8}$ cups	$4\frac{1}{3}$ cups	420
TAMARIND	32 fruit	$1\frac{1}{2}$ cups pulp	680
WATERMELON	1 sector {$9\frac{1}{2}$ in. diameter; $1\frac{1}{2}$ in. at circumference}	3 cups, $\frac{1}{2}$-inch cubes	170

BIBLIOGRAPHY

Bailey, Liberty Hyde. *The Standard Cyclopedia of Horticulture.* 2nd ed. New York: The Macmillan Company, 1914–1917. 6 vols., illus.

Bishop, Sereno Edwards. *Reminiscences of Old Hawaii.* Honolulu: Hawaiian Gazette Co., Ltd., 1916. 64 pp.

Deuel, H. J., and A. D. Holmes. "Digestibility of Avocado and Certain Other Oils," *Science,* LI (April, 1920), 397–398.

Fenton, Faith. *Home Freezers and Packaging Materials.* Hawaii Agricultural Experiment Station Circular, No. 27. Honolulu: University of Hawaii, 1949. 26 pp., illus.

Fraser, E. R. "Where Our Bananas Come From," *National Geographic Magazine,* XXIII (July, 1912), 713–730, illus.

Hillebrand, William. *Flora of the Hawaiian Islands.* Heidelberg: Carl Winter, 1888. 673 pp.

Miller, Carey D. *Food Values of Breadfruit, Taro Leaves, Coconut, and Sugar Cane.* Bernice Pauahi Bishop Museum Bulletin, No. 64. Honolulu: Bishop Museum, 1929. 23 pp.

———— and Katherine Bazore. *Some Fruits of Hawaii.* Hawaii Agricultural Experiment Station Bulletin, No. 77. Honolulu: University of Hawaii, 1936. 133 pp., illus.

———— B. Branthoover, N. Sekiguchi, H. Denning, and A. Bauer. *Vitamin Values of Foods in Hawaii.* Hawaii Agricultural Experiment Station Technical Bulletin, No. 30. Honolulu: University of Hawaii, 1956. 94 pp.

———— Lucille Louis, and Kisako Yanazawa. *Vitamin Values of Foods in Hawaii.* Hawaii Agricultural Experiment Station Technical Bulletin, No. 6. Honolulu: University of Hawaii, 1947. 56 pp.

———— Nao S. Wenkam, and Katherine O. Fitting. *Acerola—Nutritive Value and Home Use.* Hawaii Agricultural Experiment Station Circular, No. 59. Honolulu: University of Hawaii, 1961. 18 pp.

Nelson, E. K. "The Non-Volatile Acids of the Strawberry, the Pineapple, the Raspberry, and the Concord Grape," *Journal of the American Chemical Society,* 47 (1925), 1177–1179.

Pope, Willis Thomas. *The Acid Lime Fruit in Hawaii.* Hawaii Agricultural Experiment Station Bulletin, No. 49. Honolulu: University of Hawaii, 1923. 20 pp., illus.

Pope, Willis Thomas. *The Guatemalan Avocado in Hawaii.* Hawaii Agricultural Experiment Station Bulletin, No. 51. Honolulu: University of Hawaii, 1924. 24 pp., illus.

———— *Banana Culture in Hawaii.* Hawaii Agricultural Experiment Station Bulletin, No. 55. Honolulu: University of Hawaii, 1926. 48 pp., illus.

———— *Mango Culture in Hawaii.* Hawaii Agricultural Experiment Station Bulletin, No. 58. Honolulu: University of Hawaii, 1929. 27 pp., illus.

———— *Manual of Wayside Plants of Hawaii.* Honolulu: Advertiser Publishing Co., Ltd., 1929. 289 pp., illus.

———— *Papaya Culture in Hawaii.* Hawaii Agricultural Experiment Station Bulletin, No. 61. Honolulu: University of Hawaii, 1930. 40 pp., illus.

———— *Citrus Culture in Hawaii.* Hawaii Agricultural Experiment Station Bulletin, No. 71. Honolulu: University of Hawaii, 1934. 37 pp., illus.

———— *The Edible Passion Fruit in Hawaii.* Hawaii Agricultural Experiment Station Bulletin, No. 74. Honolulu: University of Hawaii, 1935. 22 pp., illus.

Popenoe, Wilson. *Manual of Tropical and Sub-Tropical Fruits, Excluding the Banana, Coconut, Pineapple, Citrus Fruits, Olive, and Fig.* New York: The Macmillan Company, 1920. 474 pp., illus.

Saywell, L. G. "The Effect of Grapes and Grape Products on Urinary Acidity," *Journal of Nutrition,* V (March, 1932), 103–120.

Schuck, Cecilia. "Urinary Excretion of Citric Acid. I. Effect of Ingesting Large Amounts of Orange Juice and Grape Juice," *Journal of Nutrition,* VII (June, 1934), 679–689.

Thompson, A. "The Composition of Hawaiian Fruits and Nuts." Hawaii Agricultural Experiment Station, *Annual Report,* 1914, 62–75, illus.

Vancouver, George. *A Voyage of Discovery to the North Pacific Ocean, and Round the World.* London: G. G. and J. Robinson [etc.], 1798. 3 vols., illus.

Wilder, Gerrit Parmile. *Fruits of the Hawaiian Islands.* Rev. ed. Honolulu: Hawaiian Gazette Co., Ltd., 1911. 274 pp., illus.

———— *Flora of Rarotonga.* Bernice Pauahi Bishop Museum Bulletin No. 86. Honolulu: Bishop Museum, 1931. 24 pp.

U.S. Department of Agriculture. *Home ·Canning of Fruits and Vegetables.* A1S-64. Washington: 1947. 23 pp., illus.

INDEX

F

Fig
  Description, 68
  History, 68
  Nutritive value, 69, Appendix VIII, see
    also Vitamins
  Supply, 69
  Use, 69
  Vitamins, 69, 206-211
Fig Recipes: Fig
  and Lychee Cocktail, 70
  Cocktail, 70
  Filling for Cake, 70
  Jam, 69
  Pickled, 70
  Preserved, 69
Fillings (see Cake Fillings)
Freezing Fruits
  Directions for freezing: Avocado, 192;
    Banana, 192; Coconut, 192; Guava,
    193; Lychee, 193; Mango, 193; Moun-
    tain Apple, 193; Mulberry, 193; Pa-
    paya, 193; Passion Fruit, 194; Pine-
    apple, 194; Plum, Methley, 194;
    Poha, 194; Roselle, 194; Soursop, 194;
    Surinam Cherry, 194
  Packaging, freezing, thawing, etc., 191
  Quality control of frozen fruits, 189
  Sugar sirups for freezing fruits, 191
Frostings (see also Cake Fillings)
  Fresh Guava Icing, 90
  Guava Jelly Icing, 90
  Passion Fruit Cake Icing, 145
Fruit Cup (see Cocktail)

G

Grape
  Description, 71
  History, 71
  Nutritive value, 71, Appendix VIII, see
    also Vitamins
  Supply, 71
  Use, 71
  Vitamins, 71, 206-211
Grape Recipes: Grape
  Butter, 72
  Conserve, 72
  Jelly, 72
  Juice, 72
  Spiced, 73
Grapefruit
  Description, 73
  History, 74
  Nutritive value, 74, see also Vitamins
  Supply, 74
  Use, 74
  Vitamins, 74, 206-211

Grapefruit Recipes: Grapefruit
    and Avocado Salad Dressing, 66
  Candied Grapefruit Peel, 75
  Halves, 75
  Sections, 75
Guabana, 39
Guava, Cattley (Strawberry)
  Description, 76
  History, 76
  Nutritive value, 76, Appendix VIII, see
    also Vitamins
  Supply, 78
  Use, 78
  Vitamins, 78, 206-211
Guava, Strawberry, Recipes:
  Ade, 78
  Jelly, 78
  Juice, 78
  Punch, 79
Guava, Common
  Description, 79
  Freezing, 82, 193
  History, 79
  Nutritive value, 81, Appendix VIII, see
    also Vitamins
  Supply, 82
  Use, 82
  Vitamins, 81, 206-211
Guava, Common, Recipes: Guava
  and Acerola Jelly, 12
  and Banana Nectar, 31
  and Ketambilla Jelly, 100
  and Papaya Butter, 85
  and Pineapple Marmalade, 86
  and Purple-Fleshed Java Plum Jelly,
    97
  Brown Betty, 92
  Butter, 85
  Catsup, 86
  Delicious, 91
  Dumplings, 89
  Guabana, 39
  Guavalets, 87
  Ice Cream, 93
  Icebox Cake, 92
  Icing, Fresh Guava, 90
  Icing, Jelly, 90
  Jelly, 83
  Juice, 83
  Juice, Hot Spiced, 88
  Marmalade, 84
  Meringue Squares, 89
  Milk Shake, 88
  Mousse, 94
  Papaya Ono-Ono, 138
  Pickle, 86
  Pie, Chiffon, 90
  Punch, Aloha, 87
  Punch, Fresh Guava, 87
  Punch, Manoa Fruit, 88
  Purée, 84